THE EVERYTHING®
GUIDE TO CROWDFUNDING

Dear Reader,

Do you want to create your first professional video, record your first CD, or write the great American novel? Perhaps you have a great idea for a new business that you would like to launch? All of these projects require start-up funding, and this book can help you obtain it via crowdfunding.

Crowdfunding is the newest way to fund projects and start businesses. Instead of hitting up family and friends, using credit cards, or getting second mortgages, you can pitch your idea to perfect strangers who will then help you fund your idea. These are people who have interests similar to yours and, believe it or not, want to see your project come to life, often just so they can have a copy of what you are going to create.

Whatever your dream idea or business, there is no reason that it can't become a reality as soon as you want it to. All it takes is hard work and determination to make it succeed. You can do it!

Thomas Elliott You--

Welcome to the EVERYTHING® Series!

These handy, accessible books give you all you need to tackle a difficult project, gain a new hobby, comprehend a fascinating topic, prepare for an exam, or even brush up on something you learned back in school but have since forgotten.

You can choose to read an Everything® book from cover to cover or just pick out the information you want from our four useful boxes: e-questions, e-facts, e-alerts, and e-ssentials.

We give you everything you need to know on the subject, but throw in a lot of fun stuff along the way, too.

We now have more than 400 Everything® books in print, spanning such wide-ranging categories as weddings, pregnancy, cooking, music instruction, foreign language, crafts, pets, New Age, and so much more. When you're done reading them all, you can finally say you know Everything®!

QUESTION
Answers to common questions

FACT
Important snippets of information

ALERT
Urgent warnings

ESSENTIAL
Quick handy tips

PUBLISHER Karen Cooper
MANAGING EDITOR, EVERYTHING® SERIES Lisa Laing
COPY CHIEF Casey Ebert
ASSOCIATE PRODUCTION EDITOR Mary Beth Dolan
ACQUISITIONS EDITOR Lisa Laing
SENIOR DEVELOPMENT EDITOR Brett Palana-Shanahan
EVERYTHING® SERIES COVER DESIGNER Erin Alexander

Visit the entire Everything® series at www.everything.com

THE EVERYTHING® Guide to Crowdfunding

LEARN HOW TO USE SOCIAL MEDIA FOR SMALL-BUSINESS FUNDING

- Understand crowd psychology
- Gain an online presence
- Create a successful crowdfunding campaign
- Promote your campaign to reach hidden funding sources

THOMAS ELLIOTT YOUNG

Avon, Massachusetts

Copyright © 2013 by F+W Media, Inc. All rights reserved.
This book, or parts thereof, may not be reproduced
in any form without permission from the publisher; exceptions
are made for brief excerpts used in published reviews.

An Everything® Series Book.
Everything® and everything.com® are registered trademarks of F+W Media, Inc.

Published by Adams Media, a division of F+W Media, Inc.
57 Littlefield Street, Avon, MA 02322 U.S.A.
www.adamsmedia.com

ISBN 10: 1-4405-5033-6
ISBN 13: 978-1-4405-5033-1
eISBN 10: 1-4405-5034-4
eISBN 13: 978-1-4405-5034-8

Printed in the United States of America.

10 9 8 7 6 5 4 3 2 1

This publication is designed to provide accurate and authoritative information with regard to the subject matter covered. It is sold with the understanding that the publisher is not engaged in rendering legal, accounting, or other professional advice. If legal advice or other expert assistance is required, the services of a competent professional person should be sought.

—From a *Declaration of Principles* jointly adopted by a Committee of the American Bar Association and a Committee of Publishers and Associations

Many of the designations used by manufacturers and sellers to distinguish their products are claimed as trademarks. Where those designations appear in this book and Adams Media was aware of a trademark claim, the designations have been printed with initial capital letters.

This book is available at quantity discounts for bulk purchases.
For information, please call 1-800-289-0963.

Contents

The Top 10 Things You'll Learn from This Book 10
Introduction 11

01 Crowdfunding Basics / 13
Crowdfunding 14
Crowdfunding Pros 15
Crowdfunding Cons 17
Key Factors of Success 21

02 Crowdsourcing / 23
Crowd + Outsourcing 24
Crowdsourcing Long Ago 24
Crowdsourcing Today 26
Other Ways of Using the Crowd 26
Crowdsourcing Websites 28
When Crowds Don't Think Well 30
Can Crowds Be Made to Think Better? 31
Companies That Do It Right 33

03 Raising Funds / 37
Fundraising Defined 38
Common Fundraising Organizations 38
Professional Fundraisers 40
Five Things to Always Do When Fundraising 40
Five Things to Never Do When Fundraising 42
Using the Internet as a Tool 44
Popular Fundraising Websites 45

04 Crowdfunding 101 / 49
Crowdfunding the Statue of Liberty 50
Types of Crowdfunding 51
The Origins of Crowdfunding on the Internet 55
A Typical Crowdfunding Campaign 56

05 A Crowdfunding Platform Examination / 61
Kickstarter.com 62
The Kickstarter Introductory Page 63
The Discover Tab 63
The Blog Tab 64
The Help Tab 65
Kickstarter School 68
Start Your Project 72

06 Other Crowdfunding Sites / 77
Indiegogo 78
RocketHub 81
Peerbackers 85
Quirky 86

07 The Keys to a Successful Campaign / 91
Choose the Right Crowdfunding Site 92
Craft a Passionate Pitch 93
A Good Campaign Video 95
A Proper Funding Goal 96
An Effective Reward Structure 98
A Comprehensive Outreach Plan 101
Your Campaign's Duration 102
Additional Keys to Success 102

08 Using Social Media for Crowdfunding and Business / 103
What Is Social Media? 104
Your Social Media Strategy 105
Starting a Website 106
Blogs 109
Facebook 110
Twitter 112
LinkedIn 114
Google+ 114
Affiliate Marketing 116
Reddit 117
Managing the Social Media Beast 118

09 Pay Per Click and Crowdfunding / 119
Two Types of Advertising 120
What Search Engines Do 121
Organic and Sponsored Searches 122
How Google Ranks Ads 123
Setting Up a Google AdWords Program 124
Picking the Best Keywords 126
Making Keywords Work for You 127
Writing Magnetic Ads 130
Split Testing 132

10 Using Twitter for Promotion / 135
Introducing the Twitterverse 136
Why People Use Twitter 137
The Anatomy of a Tweet 138
Twitter Third-Party Applications 139
Getting on Twitter 141
Finding People 142
Connecting Websites to Twitter 143
Best Practices for Businesses 144
Final Thoughts for Crowdfunders 147

11 Promoting Your Project on Facebook / 149
The History of Facebook 150
Who Is on Facebook? 150
What Do People Do on Facebook? 151

Nine Reasons Why Your Business
Needs to Be on Facebook **152**

Some Facebook Terminology **154**

A Page or a Profile for Your
Business? **155**

Setting Up a Business Page **156**

How to Promote Your Page **157**

How to Use Facebook Ads **158**

Best Practices for Using Facebook **159**

How to Analyze Your Facebook
Presence **160**

12 Using YouTube / 163

The Beginnings **164**

YouTube Today **164**

YouTube Communities **165**

Channeling **166**

Your Comments Please **167**

Let YouTube Do the Hosting **169**

Search Optimization **170**

Tracking **172**

13 Making Your Campaign Video / 173

First Impressions **174**

Do Your Research **174**

Develop Your Pitch **175**

Your Pitch Checklist **176**

Recording Your Video **177**

Recording Audio **179**

Editing Software **179**

Action! **182**

Storyboarding **183**

Final Checklist **184**

Spread the Word **185**

14 Protecting Your Idea / 187

Intellectual Property **188**

Protecting Your Intellectual Property **189**

Patents **189**

Trademarks **193**

Copyrights **194**

Obtaining Patents and Trademarks **195**

15 The Campaign's Finished / 199

The End of a Campaign **200**

What's Next? **200**

Survey Says! **203**

Keeping Records of Your Campaign **204**

How Do You Get Your Money? **205**

Shipping Your Product **205**

Ongoing Updates **207**

16 Five Successful Campaigns / 209

TikTok+LunaTik Multi-Touch
Watch Kits **210**

Mosquita y Mari **211**

Natural Resources **213**

She and the Sun **215**

Flint and Tinder **216**

17 Local Investing / 219

The Definition of Investing **220**

It Was a Wonderful Life **220**

Korean Kyes **221**

A Shift in Attitudes **221**

Local Crowdfunding Websites **223**

Community Crowdfunding Ventures **226**

The National Crowdfunding Association Gets Local **227**

A Perfect Opportunity **228**

Your Opportunity **229**

18 Crowdfunding for Social Good / 231

The Social Enterprise Movement **232**

Nonprofits **232**

Social Enterprises **234**

Why Are Social Enterprises Necessary? **235**

Social Entrepreneurs **236**

Crowdfunding Social Change **237**

Before You Start Your Social Change Campaign **238**

Fundraising Is Storytelling **240**

The Top Four Lessons **242**

19 Equity-based Crowdfunding / 245

Equity **246**

The Roaring Twenties **246**

The Stock Market Crash of 1929 **248**

The Securities Act of 1933 **249**

State Securities Laws **250**

Rise of Equity Crowdfunding **251**

The House Proposes H.R. 2930 **251**

The Senate Proposes S. 1791 **252**

Single Bill H.R. 3606 Is Formed **253**

20 Interpretations of the JOBS Act / 255

The JOBS Act **256**

Overview of the H.R. 3606 Titles **257**

A Look at Title III: Crowdfunding **260**

Crowdfunding Intermediary Requirements **262**

H.R. 3606—Other Issues **263**

Waiting for Equity Crowdfunding **264**

Appendix A: Glossary **266**

Appendix B: Bill H.R. 3606 **271**

Index **282**

Acknowledgments

First and foremost, I want to thank my wonderful wife Mary who provided me with constant support during this project. I couldn't have completed this Everything® guide without her. Also, to my wonderful children, son, Elliott, and daughter, Madeline, who got a lot less time with Dad while this book was being researched and written.

Special thanks to:

- Lisa Laing, Brett Shanahan, Brendan O'Neill, Kate Petrella, and the others at Adams Media for helping make this book become a reality.
- Jack Mayer, my friend and fellow author who provided great support and feedback during the process of completing this book.
- Paul Druskat, my friend and business associate who was a great sounding board for my crowdfunding content and opinions.
- Ted Green and Richard Frank, business associates and good friends who provided support and guidance.
- Tom Elliott, from The Idea Greenhouse who was actually the first to suggest I write a book on this topic.
- Kathleen Callahan, from the *NH Business Review* who originated the first articles about my successes with crowdfunding.
- Thanks also for permission to use original material from:
- Matt Benson from Cook, Little, Rosenblatt & Manson
- Vanessa Urch Druskat Phd, Associate Professor of Organizational Behavior at the University of New Hampshire
- Brian Meese from RocketHub.com
- Tom Dawkins and Alex Budak of StartSomeGood.com
- Monica Hamburg, author and social media evangelist
- Pierre and Lisa Fiorini, of CF Search Marketing
- Rachel Durfee, public relations at Google
- Amy Cortese, the author of *Locavesting: The Revolution in Local Investing and How to Profit from It*
- David Barach, Executive Director, Good Done Great
- John Jantsch, the author of *Duct Tape Marketing: The World's Most Practical Small Business Marketing Guide*

The Top 10 Things You'll Learn from This Book

1. What crowdfunding is, and the benefits and shortcomings of this new type of funding.

2. How to tap into the power of crowds and crowd psychology.

3. The various facets of a crowdfunding campaign—from the passionate pitch to the catchy video.

4. The different crowdsourcing platforms to choose from and which one best matches your idea or project.

5. How to run a successful campaign—from picking a reasonable goal to setting a time frame.

6. How to select the right rewards to get donors to donate.

7. How to use Facebook, Twitter, YouTube, and other social media sites to promote your crowdfunding campaign.

8. How to protect your idea or product.

9. How to successfully deal with donors after your campaign finishes.

10. What equity crowdfunding is, and how to get ready for it.

Introduction

FUNDING IS THE FUEL that allows ideas to be developed and new businesses to be launched. Without funding, brilliant ideas fermenting away in the minds of entrepreneurs, artists, and other creatives may be destined to remain trapped inside forever. Sometimes this is because a proposed new business simply needs capital for equipment, such as the commercial ovens and mixers necessary to open a new bakery. Sometimes, such as for writers and artists, cashflow is necessary simply to pay for living expenses while one takes the time "to work and create."

Unfortunately, the intertwining of creative ventures and the need for financial fuel has kept untold numbers of ideas and dreams from ever reaching fruition. Not long ago this was acknowledged by entrepreneurs as simply the nature of the beast. With the exception of those who raise money from "family and friends," the likelihood of getting funding from professional investors, such as banks, angel investors, and venture capitalists, was slim. Professional investors such as these are just too risk-averse. They are highly unlikely to engage in any enterprise unless they are virtually guaranteed to make a return on their investment. A "sure thing," so to speak. Today, thankfully, there is a wonderful alternative. Today, entrepreneurs can seek funding for ventures and projects via crowdfunding.

Normally one doesn't think of a crowd of strangers as being a terribly good source of funding, but the connectedness of the Internet has catalyzed this. You will find that there are many people in the crowd who are willing to help you out. Some want to help entrepreneurs, artists, and other creative types simply to obtain a copy of the "thing" that is being created. This could be a movie, a book, a video game, or something else enticing and unique. Others simply want to assist fellow artists or entrepreneurs and "become a part of the process."

If you have been thinking of raising funds via crowdfunding, you have come to the right place. This book is designed to give you the background of raising money directly from the crowd and provides you with a survey of the state of crowdfunding today. Special emphasis is paid to the ins and outs of social media because the success of crowdfunding campaigns is directly tied to the integration of social media into the process. Throughout the book you will also find tips and techniques that are important to know for successful crowdfunding campaigns.

The last two chapters of this book cover the rapidly evolving topic of equity-based crowdfunding. Because of the passage of H.R. 3606 on March 22, 2012, for the first time since the 1930s it is now legal for small businesses to sell ownership in their companies to non-accredited investors. Titled the Jumpstart Our Business Startups Act (JOBS Act), H.R. 3606 promises to change the equity investing landscape in the United States in profound ways.

Finally, some supportive words of advice to those considering crowdfunding: Learn all you can before you jump into the fray (by the way, this book is certainly a nice start!). The process of creating a crowdfunding campaign is relatively easy but, as you will learn in this guide, many crowdfunding campaigns fail and it is generally because of lack of preparation. So do your homework, look at lots of successful campaigns, and if you are up for the adventure—go for it. After all, crowdfunding is more than just a way to raise funds, it is also a way to change your life or the lives of others. Use it well and good luck!

CHAPTER 1

Crowdfunding Basics

Do you want to start your own business or take your existing business to the next level? Do you have a great idea for a documentary film that you would like to create? Perhaps you have an idea for a new invention that you would like to produce? Well, we live in a new era in which the power to develop projects and fund businesses is in *your* hands. That power is called *crowdfunding*. In this chapter you will learn the basics of crowdfunding along with some of the pros and cons involved. At the end of this chapter, you'll see a checklist of some of the key factors of success that you should think about before you leap into the crowdfunding pool.

Crowdfunding

Crowdfunding is the process of soliciting funds from the general public to create projects or fund businesses. It represents a radical change in the way entrepreneurial projects are capitalized today. Thanks to crowdfunding, no longer do entrepreneurs and businesspeople have to rely on the famous "family and friends" loans. No longer do they have to approach banks that require hard assets to secure loans. No longer do they need to pitch concepts to risk-averse venture capital and angel groups. Today anyone can pitch directly to individual investors and often get funding in just a few weeks.

FACT

> The term *crowdfunding* is actually broadly used to cover several different ways that people can provide funding for projects and businesses. Later in this book, the distinctions between the different types of crowdfunding are discussed. Until then, the term is used in this book to mean funding that does *not* involve the sale of ownership, or equity, in the business or project being crowdfunded.

Crowdfunding also provides entrepreneurs with another advantage. In addition to the actual money you can receive, you will also get validation of your idea or concept. The people backing your crowdfunding campaign will provide you with lots of valuable input and, in many ways, you should consider this feedback just as important as the actual funding you receive. What you are doing with your campaign is putting your concept up for the world to see and asking interested people to pledge if they like it. In essence the crowd is voting with their dollars, and this provides you with both funding and valuable concept validation.

Most crowdfunders offer rewards to those who pledge. In many cases, these rewards are directly tied to the project and are often samples of the project itself. This concept is especially powerful for those seeking funding for projects that are artistic and can be replicated. Fiction and nonfiction books, documentary DVDs, comic books, and photographic albums are all excellent projects for crowdfunding because backers usually want to get a copy of the project's output. Perhaps one of the finest examples of this concept is the funding of video game development, where the reward is a copy

Chapter 1: Crowdfunding Basics

of the game. In fact, crowdfunding is already changing the way the video game industry is funding new titles and new companies in very major ways.

> Crowdfunding campaigns can forge relationships between you and some of your backers. Relationships with some of your most committed backers may develop because they feel like they are part of your project's creation. In many cases, they may be some of your strongest advocates during your crowdfunding campaign and may help you immensely afterward, as you start your new business.

One of the more significant benefits of reward-based crowdfunding is that you don't have to give up ownership (equity) in the enterprise being created. Entrepreneurs who start businesses with venture capital and angel investors have a quite different experience. Venture capitalists (VCs) and angels typically take an ownership stake in businesses they fund. They do this in anticipation of return on their investment and the resultant growth in value of their shares. However, as partial owners, these investors typically play an active role in the operations of the business. Sometimes this is advantageous because they may bring operational skills, but it is not unusual for the goals of investors and business owners to clash. Remember, VCs and angels are in it for ROI (return on investment). They may not share the passion for the product and mission nearly as strongly as the founder does, and this may cause friction.

Crowdfunding is becoming a mainstream option for business funding. More and more people are funding projects and building businesses via crowdfunding. In particular, creative ventures, such as filmmaking, music, live performances—which can be nearly impossible to fund in any other way—are being brought to reality by the backing of crowds. Crowdfunding puts control into the hands of those who are doing the creating, and this can benefit everyone involved.

Crowdfunding Pros

Crowdfunding is not a silver bullet to use whenever funding is needed. It should be viewed in context with traditional investment instruments and

15

other sources of money. However, with that caveat in mind, here are some of the pros of funding your enterprise or project via crowdfunding.

Minimal Financial Risk

Most crowdfunding sites charge you nothing to place your campaign on their site. They make their money by charging a percentage of what backers pledge, not upfront charges. This means that if you do all the creative elements yourself—writing the text, taking photos, and crafting the video—then starting a crowdfunding campaign costs you nothing but your time. This is obviously a tremendous advantage because you can essentially risk nothing. If your crowdfunding campaign fails to reach its financial goal, none of your pledgers are charged and the project simply ends.

Testing Demand

One of the best parts of crowdfunding is that you get a built-in focus group that will give you feedback on your project. This is useful because you will quickly find out if the crowd likes what you are doing. Believe it or not, you may find that people like "most" of what you propose in your crowdfunding project, but would like a few minor changes to make it a complete winner. Often this is a suggestion for additional options and other details that you can add during the campaign. And, unlike the focus groups of the old days where you would pay six to eight people several hundred dollars per day to participate, crowdfunding allows you to tap the knowledge and advice of hundreds of people, maybe even thousands, absolutely free.

ALERT

Several of your backers may want to actively help you with your crowdfunding campaign. They may offer to build websites, post on social media sites, contribute to blogs, and even create promotional assets for you. In general this is helpful, but make sure that a unified voice is applied to everything that is broadcast. It might be helpful to make a quick "mission statement" of what your campaign is all about and forward it to your helpful backers.

You Keep Control

With crowdfunding, it's your show. You keep complete control of all decisions. In the film world, they refer to this as the *auteur* theory, which means that an entire film represents one voice: the voice of the director. In the crowdfunding world, as the creator of the project, you are the auteur. You control all facets: the creative vision, the costs, the product delivery, the marketing, all the customer interactions—everything. Yes, it's an awful lot of hats to wear, but the big advantage is that you don't have to compromise on anything. You're the boss and the entire venture represents your vision.

100 Percent Ownership

When you are performing standard crowdfunding, you are technically soliciting donations and in return giving your backers "rewards." This is not to be confused with selling equity or ownership in a business. When you obtain financing from venture capital groups or angels, you usually have to offer them part of your business, which means issuing shares of ownership. In contrast, a crowdfunding campaign means you retain 100 percent ownership in the business. There's only one boss, and you are it. Not only do you get to be in charge, you get to profit entirely from the success of the business.

Brand Evangelists

When you crowdfund, you may rapidly accumulate brand evangelists. You will find many of your backers will want to become part of your virtual team. Because crowdfunding is a collaborative model rather than a retail model, you will attract many backers who not only want to see your product or service succeed; they want to see you personally succeed. This is one of the most gratifying parts of crowdfunding: working with those in the crowd who really want to help you out.

Crowdfunding Cons

Crowdfunding is not a fundraising method that replaces all the funding techniques of the past. It is best to think of it as simply a new way of obtaining funding and should be evaluated in light of the other alternatives that you may have. Let's look at some of the disadvantages of crowdfunding, especially as contrasted to earlier fundraising and investment methods.

It's Continuous Work

When you run a crowdfunding campaign, you are constantly working at it. You will have untold numbers of people viewing your campaign and constantly asking questions. Unlike traditional bank loans and other funding methods, during a crowdfunding campaign you are on call 24/7. Considering all the advantages of crowdfunding this may seem like a small price to pay, but you need to be prepared for all the work involved. If you're working at a day job, the information flow and interactions with the crowd can prove challenging.

FACT

> If your crowdfunding campaign is unsuccessful, most of the major sites will allow you to run it a second time. This may be a good idea if you can identify obvious reasons that your campaign didn't do so well the first time. However, if you can't easily identify issues and make the appropriate changes, it is unlikely that simply running it a second time will bring big success. In fact, the results may be somewhat worse because some visitors may recognize it as a campaign that failed before and may avoid it.

Lack of Guidance

Although it has been around for a few years, crowdfunding is still a relatively new concept. As you plan your crowdfunding campaign, you are certain to have lots of questions and you will find there are few places to get solid information (other than this excellent guide, of course). Most of the major crowdfunding sites do have educational materials on them, but none are terribly intensive. Most, in fact, are written to be nonintimidating and thus are rather fundamental. Be prepared for this dearth of information to be difficult at times. Until crowdfunding has matured a bit more, there will probably continue to be a lack of thorough guidance online.

High Visibility

When you create a crowdfunding campaign, you, as a person, are on display just as prominently as your project is. There is little privacy. In fact, people want to know about you, so you will need to have an extensive bio and picture on your campaign or you will handicap your project. This is where the difference between a retail model and a crowdfunding model really kicks in. For example, someone looking to buy a new book at a bookstore expects to see little more than a catchy title, a peek at a few pages, and a short bio on the author. The author can still retain a modicum of privacy. Someone looking to crowdfund a book, however, needs to be aware that potential funders expect to see a "full pitch video" of the author explaining why the book is so important, along with an impassioned request to participate in the campaign. An extensive bio, including the author's location and contact information, also is the norm. To be a successful crowdfunder, you must be prepared for full personal exposure. If you don't do so, you will not build the trust necessary to convince potential backers to pledge your campaign.

You Need to Be a Social Media Guru

You will find that just a small percentage of the people who back your campaign happened to be surfing around on the crowdfunding platform site and have stopped in. Most backers are alerted to your campaign from other sites on the web, and these are often social media sites. Bottom line: in order to run an effective campaign, you need to be working with social media almost constantly. This means interacting on Facebook, Twitter, and blogs; posting to newsletters; issuing press releases; and generally using every social network and method you can manage. This, of course, means you need to understand these social networks and the best practices to disseminate information. If communicating on these networks isn't your strength, either hold off and become more knowledgeable about them (which isn't difficult), or get someone who is a social network junkie to help you out. However, it's best to do it yourself because you will likely need to post and update constantly throughout your campaign, and communications should come directly from you, the project creator.

ESSENTIAL

Although it's a new area, there are firms starting to spring up that will help you "reach out" to the social media during your campaign. You may want to take a good look at some of these firms and what they offer. In contrast to traditional advertising, a well-crafted outreach program run during your crowdfunding campaign could yield enormous payback, possibly paying for itself many times over.

Funding Is Not Professional

When you get funding from traditional sources, such as banks or other financial institutions, you establish a lender/client business relationship. This generally operates in well-established ways that are orchestrated by contractual obligations outlining the duties and behavior of both parties. It's a fairly well-known paradigm. However, when you crowdfund, you may have hundreds or thousands of backers who have diverse expectations and demands about the process. While there certainly are rules to guide the expectations of those who participate in a crowdfunding campaign, most of the backers will be weakly versed in them. It is difficult to avoid this: You, as the project creator, will be dealing with many backers and explaining how the crowdfunding process works.

Sometimes It Doesn't Work

It's easy to focus on all the successes that you find on the crowdfunding sites on the Internet and assume that the end result of your campaign will be similar. The reality is that over 50 percent of the crowdfunding campaigns that are launched fail to meet their goal. Usually when an unsuccessful campaign is examined, it isn't hard to see why, but in many cases it isn't entirely obvious. This is when the lack of historical data and guidance on crowdfunding can prove frustrating. Sometimes a campaign seems positioned to do well, but it just simply doesn't. This, obviously, can be frustrating.

Chapter 1: Crowdfunding Basics

Key Factors of Success

There is a common business school concept that is often used when analyzing business cases. Students will analyze all the facets of a business enterprise and then boil them down into a list of key factors of success. In a nutshell, these are the characteristics of an enterprise that are direct contributors to the future success of the company.

Are You Comfortable with Digital Media?

If working with digital and social media is relatively new to you, spend some time getting comfortable with them before you start crowdfunding. You will be working with a lot of text creation, image manipulation, and video editing when crafting your crowdfunding campaign. You will also be working nonstop with applications like Facebook, Twitter, blogs, YouTube, and other social media. You don't want to handicap a well-intended campaign by being unacquainted with digital and social media. Spend some time getting familiar with digital media or team up with a partner who can help you out during the campaign.

How Good Is Your Concept?

It is important that your project idea appeal to a lot of people. This doesn't mean that you need to crowdfund something that has blatant mass appeal. In fact, that is probably a bad idea because that sort of project tends to do poorly. You want your project to be unique and interesting enough so you will collect plenty of backers to fund its creation. Just make sure that your project isn't of interest only to a small group of people. On the other hand, if you aren't absolutely sure your project will appeal to enough people to actually get it funded—well, this is when crowdfunding earns its stripes. Run it and you will find out!

Have You Calculated How Much Money You Really Need?

Evidence is coming out now that suggests that a majority of crowdfunded projects are not collecting enough money to allow their creator to "pull it off." In other words, not enough money is being requested to cover hidden expenses: things like unplanned costs, the need for additional help, and other cost overruns. In fact, many crowdfunded companies use all their backers' money during the design phase before they even produce the product. You can avoid this by doing a rigorous cost analysis and applying a worst-case scenario to your financial estimates. Make sure you ask for enough money to actually create and deliver the product to all your backers. Make this your project's financial goal. If you don't, you may lose money when your campaign finishes and you are still obligated to create your rewards and ship them to your backers.

Are Your Rewards Appropriate?

Completing your project is the exciting part for you, but your backers are generally motivated by the rewards you offer, not the design process. Make sure you have good incentives for your backers. You should have a variety of pledge levels that are interesting and unique. Many crowdfunding campaigns are handicapped by a confusing reward structure or one that doesn't provide a sufficient incentive to pledge money.

Is Your Campaign Exciting Enough?

The concept of the elevator pitch is appropriate here. Is your campaign simple and powerful enough that it can be easily understood? Is it exciting enough that people will tell their friends and post it on their own social media pages? Since a majority of pledges come from outside the immediate crowd on the crowdfunding site it is hosted on, it is critical that your campaign be inherently exciting and easy to understand.

Are You Ready for a Huge Commitment of Time and Effort?

Virtually all crowdfunders will tell you that they were unprepared for how much work and commitment their crowdfunding campaigns required. Running crowdfunding campaigns can be a grueling process. If you are going to do one, make sure you can devote enough time to it to make it successful.

CHAPTER 2

Crowdsourcing

Do you remember when crowdsourcing lit up the business press a few years ago? Today you don't see crowdsourcing in the news as much but the concept is doing well, and in fact thriving. This chapter will review how crowdsourcing works and some of the companies that utilize it in their business operations. It will also look into some of the pros and cons involved with crowdsourcing to help you better understand the psychology and behavior of crowds. This knowledge will be useful to you as you design and execute your fundraising or crowdfunding campaign.

Crowd + Outsourcing

Crowdsourcing is simply a portmanteau of the words "crowd" and "outsourcing." Jeff Howe, who first wrote about crowdsourcing for *Wired* magazine back in 2006, is generally credited with coining the phrase. In his seminal 2006 article, he explains crowdsourcing as "the act of taking a job traditionally performed by a designated employee and outsourcing it to an undefined, generally large group of people in the form of an open call." The "generally large group," is, of course, the crowd.

Today, there are hundreds of companies that have leveraged the concept of crowdsourcing into thriving enterprises. Some of them are dramatically changing the business segment in which they operate. For example, iStockphoto has changed forever the way stock photography is created and delivered to clients and customers. It has been truly disruptive in its market space.

> The term *disruptive* refers to an innovation that is so radical and so effective that it essentially displaces an entire existing market network. It also describes innovations that the marketplace does not fully expect, often by delivering goods and services at far lower prices than what currently existed.

Crowdsourcing companies have discovered that when properly used, crowds can outperform in-house talent in many ways and usually at a far lower price. This, of course, makes crowdsourced information tremendously appealing to potential clients. To better examine the ways that this can work, let's examine some of the more successful crowdsourcing companies. This will give you a good perspective on how some businesses are harvesting considerable value from crowds via crowdsourcing.

Crowdsourcing Long Ago

Asking people to assist in collaborative projects certainly isn't an Internet phenomenon. Consider that in the early 1700s, the British government

Chapter 2: Crowdsourcing

performed its own "crowdsourcing campaign" when it realized that it badly needed a solution to a transoceanic navigational problem. The problem involved determining a ship's longitude when out in the open sea. Here's why that was important: To know where they are, mariners need both longitudinal and latitudinal coordinates. Determining a ship's latitude was relatively easy because mariners could utilize the sun's declination (height from the horizon), but longitude was much more difficult.

Because of this problem, ships were getting lost and voyages were often ending in tragedy. Accordingly, the British Parliament established the Longitude Act in 1714, which offered a large cash award to anyone who developed a method to precisely determine longitude at sea. Although no single person actually won the prize, hundreds of contributors were compensated for their proposals and the science of marine chronometers was developed from the ideas that were submitted. This indeed was early crowdsourcing at work.

QUESTION

Was the Bible crowdsourced?
Yes. The word *bible* comes from a Latin word that means "little books." This name was chosen for the religious text because the Bible is actually a collection of sixty-six books written by forty different authors over a period of 1,600 years. The combination of these books is what is known as the Holy Bible, certainly an early crowdsourced book.

Want a little more historical perspective? Back in 1857, the Philological Society of London decided that existing English dictionaries were terribly deficient and that the Society should organize an effort to create a better one. Because the English language had evolved over many centuries and was so diverse, it enlisted the assistance of a very large number of contributors who all submitted "citations" (factual evidence) concerning English words and their use. The creation they were contributing to was none other than the *Oxford English Dictionary*. Although sections of the dictionary were released over time, the construction of the dictionary took "a little while." The actual ten-volume *Oxford English Dictionary* was not released until 1928, some seventy-one years after it was started.

Crowdsourcing Today

Today, crowdsourcing is a huge enterprise generally involving the Internet, and it is changing the way both small and large companies do business. For example, it's no longer necessary to have in-house talent perform many business-related tasks. Nor is it necessary to always seek the talents of dedicated outside business professionals. There is a good chance that what you need, whether obtained in-house or outsourced to dedicated professionals, is available inexpensively from the crowd.

Here's an example: Assume you just started a business and you need a real professional-looking logo. Your options are to go to a professional graphic artist, and pay some $500–$1,000, or you can go to 99designs.com and crowdsource it for about $100. Not only is the savings you enjoy substantial; the actual process is quick and easy. Here's how it works: Once you submit your logo request on 99designs.com's website, you will receive designs from dozens, if not hundreds of artists. You then have forty-eight hours to pick and choose the one you like. From the business owner's point of view, there is not a lot of downside here; you get great, inexpensive logos delivered quickly. Chances are you can reap significant savings and efficiencies simply by searching for crowdsourced talents on the web.

Other Ways of Using the Crowd

The term *crowdsourcing* has become a bit of a semantic umbrella for many other crowd-related activities. Truthfully, there is a bit of overlap between many crowdsourcing methods and the terminology applied to them. Just for background, here are a few of the other variations you may stumble upon.

Crowdvoting

Crowdvoting occurs when the opinions and judgments on particular topics are collected from the crowd. Here's an example: In 2011, Toyota started a voting campaign to get a new name for one of its cars. In six weeks the company received more than 1.8 million votes and the name "Prii" emerged from the campaign. Today Toyota uses the singular form "Prius" as the model name. In Las Vegas, another example has emerged in the field of radio broadcasting. Jelli Radio is creating traditional radio stations for which playlists and other content are suggested entirely from their listeners.

Crowdpurchasing

When large groups of people aggregate to purchase things, they can often receive deep pricing cuts due to manufacturer's volume discounting. There are several websites on the net that facilitate this. It is worth noting that while this concept may provide buying advantages to consumers, it may be considered less than optimum for suppliers who feel that lowball "offers" on their products are often below what is necessary to maintain warranty and service functions. In many cases, knowledgeable suppliers will reject large crowdpurchasing orders for that reason.

Microwork

For a good example of what web-based microwork is all about, visit Amazon's Mechanical Turk site (*www.mturk.com/mturk/welcome*). Billed as a site where "businesses and developers [have] access to an on-demand, scalable workforce," Mechanical Turk is a site where users sign up to perform minor tasks for small amounts of money. Each task, called a "HIT" (Human Intelligence Task), is a small exercise but is a task that requires a human being to perform. The site is especially popular in countries where wages are naturally low and people find the small fees paid on Mechanical Turk worth pursuing.

ESSENTIAL

When famed adventurer Steve Fossett's airplane went missing over California's Sierra Nevada Mountain range on September 3, 2007, microwork was involved in the search. Google, working with Digital-Globe, provided 300,000 images of the area where Fossett's plane was believed to have gone down. Working on Mechanical Turk, more than 50,000 people scrutinized these aerial images for several weeks looking for the wreckage. While this method did not find Fossett, it does illustrate how microwork can be employed to accomplish amazingly diverse tasks.

Crowdcasting

Crowdcasting is a unique way to attract an audience and engage them in a collaborative manner. It starts when an organization announces a prize for an innovation, invention, or accomplishment. Often this announcement is made to a specific audience, not to the entire "crowd" on the web. When applications or responses occur, the organization filters down the audience into an optimum group and then engages them in a particular exercise. Examples of crowdcasting would include certain programs created by General Electric, Whirlpool, and American Express that engage business students to compete by making suggestions for new products and services. In many cases, the winners of these "contests" would receive not only cash prizes but also job offers!

Crowdsourcing Websites

Perhaps the best way to grasp the potential of crowdsourcing is to explore some of the websites that are doing it. The following sites are chosen for illustrative purposes and their level of services differ, but a few may actually assist crowdfunders with designing their campaigns.

Gengo

The concept behind Gengo (*www.gengo.com*) is simple. If you need a document translated, Gengo employs some 4,500 professional translators who will provide translation services twenty-four hours per day/seven days per week. With prices starting at 5 cents per word, the remotely based Gengo contractors will translate articles, websites, documents, just about anything you can imagine. If you have an e-commerce site, you can even engage Gengo to translate customers' queries in real time.

Docracy

Docracy (*www.docracy.com*) is a website where legal documents are posted by the crowd; in this case, a legally trained crowd. As a visitor to Docracy, you will find hundreds of legal documents for free download. The value to those posting the documents is that the legal professionals who post them attach contact information so that if you want additional assistance, you can contact the author directly (for an additional fee, of course). Docracy even allows users to establish personal accounts to store their legal documents for retrieval at any time. In the case of wills and health-care proxies, this is a valuable service.

A frequent criticism of crowdsourcing is that the process exploits the crowd. The argument is that the site clients typically receive high-quality assets for little money and the members of the crowd are poorly compensated for producing the assets. Mechanical Turk, in particular, has received a great deal of criticism. The work on Mechanical Turk is in many cases low paying and mind-numbing, but thousands of willing "Turkers" accept the jobs.

Pricing Prophets

One of the more challenging things businesspeople face is how to price their products. If competitive products exist, at least you have a benchmark when you are trying to determine what a product should sell for. But if your product has differentiation factors (added features, colors, etc.), exactly how much more can you expect people to pay for it? If you have an entirely new product, something that has never seen the light of day, then you may have a real challenge on your hands. Well, the folks at Pricing Prophets (*www.pricingprophets.com*) employ a crowd of people who will assist you with this. It's simple: you upload complete details on your project, pay them $600, and in turn you receive a complete report as to what the crowd thinks your product pricing should be, complete with copious comments attached. While this is an expensive service, it can be considered a bargain in the long run to have your product or service priced appropriately.

Trendwatching

Trendwatching (*www.trendwatching.com*) is an unusual crowdsourcing website that employs more than 8,000 "spotters" around the world constantly watching for new goods, services, and experiences. With a network this large, Trendwatching can inform companies and individuals of things that one would be hard-pressed to stay on top of any other way. The world is a pretty big place, but with a firm like Trendwatching, you have remote agents around the world constantly feeding you information. Trendwatching is a service that is fantastically popular in the fashion industry.

When Crowds Don't Think Well

Under ideal conditions, large groups of people can yield reliable opinions and advice. However, crowds do not always think well. Keep this in mind when you are dealing with your crowdfunding campaign backers, because the information you gather from them via questionnaires and surveys may not always be ideal. The following sections provide context and explain a few ways that information can be affected by common crowd factors.

Leading by Bad Example

Sometimes the decision-making process within groups can devolve toward the opinions of the "leaders," with the "followers" nodding their heads in agreement. Remember Enron Corporation? Just think about how many employees were nodding at that firm. Bottom line is that sometimes groups make poor decisions because they are playing follow the leader, and this can have serious consequences if their data is used for actionable items.

Lack of Context

It is very hard to make decisions in a vacuum. People need context in order to frame their decisions. If you are crowdfunding and watching the waves of comments coming in from potential backers, be aware that most do not have the contextual information that you have to make optimum decisions. In the example of your crowdfunding campaign, it is your job to supply this contextual information in your video and the body text. Paint a complete picture for them about your project and why you are asking them to participate.

Chapter 2: Crowdsourcing

ESSENTIAL

Groups that make business decisions often leave out one ingredient of the mix—profitability! Sometimes the solutions that groups arrive at are highly attractive to the members of the group but not optimum for the company or business involved. Situations like this illustrate the need for leadership that understands the goals of the organization.

No Leaders

Some groups suffer because they have no clear leaders. Some experts believe groups need "someone in charge" or the decision-making will be inferior. With crowdfunding there really aren't any leaders, so you will be dealing with individuals. Always remember, though, that groups can often be swayed by herd mentality. Herd mentality refers to the behavior that groups of individuals exhibit that is often unlike the behaviors of individual members. In many cases herd mentality is influenced by the more vocal, persuasive members of a group but are not the actual group "leaders." Herd mentality often results in poor judgments and decisions.

Limited Demographics

When crowdsourcing, you are usually dealing with a limited demographic. This is simply a given on the Internet. Many studies indicate the typical web user is likely to be white, middle or upper class, English speaking, higher educated, and have a high-speed connection. Moreover, the most active individuals in the crowd are likely to be under the age of thirty and possibly under twenty-five. Of course, you aren't going to be able to change this, but it is best to understand the demographics involved.

Can Crowds Be Made to Think Better?

Crowds and groups do not always think well. Often this is a function of restricted demographics, a lack of decisional context, or leadership issues. When dealing with crowds and groups that are assembled via social media and crowdfunding, you may have a mixture of all three of these issues, perhaps with demographic issues leading the pack.

31

As you might imagine, the topic of making groups of people work together more effectively is of intense interest within corporate environments. When groups and teams work well together, wonderful things can occur. Highly effective decisions and opinions on products, services, and processes can result and can add tremendous value to the company involved. When groups and teams work poorly, however, the result can be poor decisions that provide little value to the company, waste resources, and in the worst case, produce setbacks due to faulty judgments.

It is easy to see why the effectiveness of groups is so important to companies. The solution, of course, is easy. To make groups work better requires informing the group of the need for cooperation, full participation, and commitment to goals. A nice memo or inspirational meeting about this should work, right? Wrong! Getting crowds, groups, and teams to work better is far more deeply rooted than that. It usually requires fundamental changes in the way that group of individuals think and behave together.

There are several academics today who have researched the effectiveness of groups and ways the improvements can be made. In particular, Vanessa Urch Druskat, PhD, Associate Professor of Organizational Behavior at the University of New Hampshire, has written extensively on the subject. Along with her colleague, Steven B. Wolff, Dr. Druskat wrote a seminal paper for the *Harvard Business Review* in 2001 titled "Building the Emotional Intelligence of Groups." Research by Druskat and Wolff identifies three conditions that need to be met before a group operates effectively:

1. Trust among members
2. A sense of group identity
3. A sense of group efficacy

Druskat and Wolff take these three "effectiveness criteria" and integrate them with three different levels of emotional interactions within groups. The key is for groups and individuals to be aware of their emotions and be able to regulate them. The three levels that affect groups are emotions on the individual level, the group level, and the intergroup level.

So what does all this mean for those who are working with the crowd in social ways, and in particular when conducting crowdfunding campaigns? It is important to know that when you assemble a section of the crowd and

Chapter 2: Crowdsourcing

you are relying on them not only for funding but decisions and guidance, limitations can exist. And, if you are conducting crowdsourcing in any fashion, the same may apply. Groups *can* be made to think better, but usually within a controlled environment. In a crowdsourcing or crowdfunding scenario, it may be more difficult. The most important thing to realize is that the decisions and guidance you get from your crowd community should not be taken as absolutely reliable. There may be some biases due to issues of dealing with non-optimum groups.

Companies That Do It Right

There are many websites that are great examples of crowdsourcing done right. Not only do they provide their clients with excellent products and services, they are also good sites to belong to and participate as members of the crowd. Many of these sites have been disruptive in their market space but are not exploitive of their clients and laborers. Following are a few examples to consider, along with an explanation of how they work.

iStockphoto

A crowdsourced company out of Calgary, Alberta, iStockphoto (*www.istockphoto.com*) is a site for professional photographers to upload and sell photos to clients. iStockphoto has become a major supplier of stock photography to the industry. To become a photographer for iStockphoto, you fill out an online form and submit three images for the staff at iStockphoto to consider. If accepted, photographers can upload images to the website along with suggested keywords for clients to search under. When clients download images for use, the photographer receives 20 percent of the purchase price.

Talk about "disruption"! iStockphoto, the crowdsourced stock photo site, wreaked such havoc in the stock photo industry that the industry's most established company, Getty Images, finally ended up buying it. Getty Images CEO Jonathan Klein commented after the acquisition, "If someone's going to completely cannibalize your business, better it be one of your other businesses."

InnoCentive

Located in Andover, Massachusetts, InnoCentive (*www.innocentive.com*) is a crowdsourcing site for scientific research and design (R & D). Scientists can utilize the site to receive financial rewards and even professional recognition for joining groups that are solving complex R & D challenges. On the corporate side, InnoCentive allows companies to "outsource" R & D among a global pool of rich scientific talents. The company does not exist just to assist smaller resource-limited businesses. Large global corporations such as Boeing, DuPont, and Proctor & Gamble also use InnoCentive in major ways.

Here's how it works: Companies that need solutions, called "seekers," post challenges anonymously. These challenges are then reviewed by "solvers" who can submit solutions through the web. If the solution meets the technical requirements of the seeker, the solver receives an award, commonly from $10,000 to $100,000. InnoCentive is a major force in the outsourced R & D marketplace and broadcasts challenges to over 100,000 independent scientists in more than 250 countries around the world.

LEGO Mindstorms NXT

The LEGO Mindstorms NXT (*http://mindstorms.lego.com*) is a robotics tool set that lets users build, program, and personalize robots. When LEGO, based in Denmark, wanted to design its next generation of product, it turned to its customers. The way it recruited assistance, though, was by filtering the crowd. LEGO monitored online conversations about Mindstorms robotics and identified a handful of the most knowledgeable users. These fans were then invited to join private forums where current products and ideas for new ones were discussed. LEGO even invited some of the fans to its headquarters to work for several weeks with product developers. This story was widely circulated on the LEGO enthusiasts' sites and a tremendous following occurred before the product was even released. Today LEGO Mindstorms is a major product line within the LEGO company, due in part to actionable ideas derived via crowdsourcing.

CrowdSPRING

Among marketplaces for crowdsourced creative services, crowdSPRING (*www.crowdspring.com*) is one of the largest. Any business or individual that needs a logo design, website, industrial design, or even copywriting can post the need on crowdSPRING along with an amount that they are willing to pay for the asset. Once posted, the proposal is visible to over 100,000 creatives who submit work for consideration. Buyers then can choose from submissions of actual work, not just bids or proposals. Unlike other online marketplaces that function primarily to match buyers and sellers, crowdSPRING handles full project management, payments, legal contracts, and assists with communications. The company also allows designers to create profile pages on the site for potential clients to view.

Threadless

This website describes itself as an "ongoing T-shirt design competition." The way it works is sheer genius. Threadless (*www.threadless.com*) is a community composed of people who submit T-shirt designs for cash prizes and people who want to buy innovative T-shirt designs. Anyone may join the Threadless community, and members of the community are allowed to submit a design or to vote on others' designs.

To submit their designs, community members download a Threadless template, follow the guidelines for image quality and colors, and upload the designs to the site. The community then scores designs on a zero-to-five scale, with an option to check an "I'd buy it!" box. Designs remain available for voting for two weeks, and the highest-scoring designs are selected by Threadless staff to be printed and sold on the website.

In a typical week, there are at least three new shirts for sale and at least one that's been reprinted due to overwhelming demand. Winning designers receive $1,500 in cash and $500 worth of Threadless T-shirts and gift certificates. In April 2012, 1.18 million votes were placed on Threadless by 22,407 people. During the month, over 6,310 T-shirt designs were submitted.

CHAPTER 3

Raising Funds

A crowd can be employed to research, create, and deliver information that may be difficult and expensive to obtain any other way. A crowd also can be used to finance projects and organizations, not necessarily via crowdfunding campaigns but by "fundraising" in general. Understanding how crowds can be used to raise funds, regardless of the technique employed, will be useful to you when you design and execute your own crowdfunding campaign or raise funds in any other ways.

Fundraising Defined

Fundraising is the process of soliciting and gathering voluntary contributions from individuals, businesses, and other organizations. Although the term is commonly associated with collecting funds for nonprofit organizations, it can also apply to for-profit organizations.

The common perception of fundraising is that it involves a fundraising drive. The concepts of door-to-door solicitations, television campaigns, and direct-mail flyers are commonly seen as "fundraising," but they are just the visible component. There is much more behind the scenes of any fundraising effort. Fundraising, particularly when practiced by larger institutions, is a complete system that requires a lot of work and expertise to execute properly. A haphazard fundraising system just invites unnecessary risk to an organization.

For example, suppose an organization relies on just a few major donors to fund operations. This would be very risky because it essentially puts the entire organization into a state of dependency on just a small number of sources. If one of the donors were to drop out, this could create financial crisis and perhaps shut down operations. Needless to say, assuming this sort of risk is imprudent. The only way to mitigate this possibility is by having a complete fundraising system in place.

Common Fundraising Organizations

There are many organizations that rely almost exclusively on fundraising, or charitable donations, to pursue their missions, so much so that fundraising and the solicitation of resources has become part of the functional structure of the organizations themselves. Most people are familiar with three well-known groups whose mission and fundraising activities are tightly knit.

Religious Organizations

Fundraising efforts have become ingrained in virtually every religious group across the world. Because the very existence of religious organizations requires funding, the process has become part of the daily routines of these groups. In addition to funding internal operations, religious organizations also use the money they raise to help those in need, and sometimes to evangelize and spread the reach of the organization.

Chapter 3: Raising Funds

QUESTION

What is tithing?
Tithing is a controversial concept for many Christian religions. Tithing is an ancient practice based on the belief that members of a religious organization had a moral and religious obligation to donate 10 percent of their income to the church. Some say the principle of tithing is commanded in the Bible, while others believe it distracts from the true meaning of a religion and God. In any regard, most modern religions place tithing in a historical context and use more accepted fundraising techniques to finance their operations.

Political Campaigns

Fundraising plays a major role in American politics. Running a successful campaign is very expensive, which makes fundraising necessary. Add the fact that the legitimacy of a candidate is often seen as directly correlated to the size of his/her coffers, and you can see how integral fundraising is to the political process. Despite the existence of reform laws, campaign financing continues to be a controversial topic in American politics.

ESSENTIAL

Grassroots fundraising is a popular method of fundraising used by political candidates with smaller war chests and less media exposure than their opponents. This method of collecting support has grown tremendously with the emergence of the Internet. Presidential candidates Howard Dean (2004) and Ron Paul (2008) gained a great deal of support via grassroots funding. Today, especially energized by social media, grassroots fundraising has become a powerful tool for communicating with supporters and soliciting donations.

Public Broadcasting

Public broadcasting has a long history of providing programming content that is free from the influence of commercial sponsors. In order to accomplish this, most public broadcasting funding is derived from familiar

PBS Pledge Drives. Pledge drives occur some two or three times per year and typically last one to two weeks. At the present time, PBS collects almost 85 percent of its operating budget during these drives.

Professional Fundraisers

If you are considering raising funds, you should be cognizant of how professional fundraisers work. They employ proven fundraising techniques and they are very effective, but many people find their methods objectionable.

Professional fundraisers are third-party organizations that raise funds for other groups and organizations. They are generally paid for their fundraising services in two ways—either a flat fee or as a percentage of the funds raised. The latter approach is actually forbidden by the Association of Fundraising Professionals, but some organizations still engage fundraisers who are paid a percentage of the funds they raise.

You should note that in the United States there is accountability on the part of professional fundraisers. If you are concerned about a fundraising organization, you can call the office of your state's attorney general or secretary of state and ask for statistics on the organization. The ratio of the funds collected by the professional fundraising company and that given to the charitable organization is a matter of public record, and you can request that statistic among others.

Five Things to Always Do When Fundraising

It takes a while to become a competent fundraiser. However, a lot of it is based on commonsense principles. Following is a list of five basic concepts to keep in mind when you are creating and executing a fundraising campaign.

1. Keep Your Message Short and Simple

Although you want to educate your donors about your cause, do so quickly. Resist the urge to tell a lengthy story about your cause and the extended drama behind it. If you present too much information, potential donors may become bogged down in the details and lose interest. For example, if you are soliciting funds concerning feeding children in a third-world country, your donors are unlikely to take in an extended lesson in the history of the issue, even if the historical background is poignant and emotional.

2. Tell Your Donors What They Are "Buying"

It is far more powerful to tell donors exactly what their money is going toward than just saying they are donating to a great cause. If their $100 is buying a child a new set of clothing, let them know that and show them an image of the clothing. If their money is going toward funding a documentary film, tell your donors that their pledge is helping buy something specific during the filming process. People are more willing to donate when they can visualize what their money is being used for. They want to know that their financial contribution pays for a specific, important piece of the project.

3. Offer Great Incentives If You Can

Donors usually pledge because of the cause involved, but incentives and premiums can be especially beneficial. PBS uses the popular technique of reading donors' names on the air when they pledge during its telethons. This is a great incentive. Plaques and certificates are fantastic, too, because they document a donor's commitment to a cause and can be put on public display. Another great idea is engraving or otherwise placing a donor's name in a public spot for generations to see. For example, many public facility projects raise funds by selling actual bricks with donors' names embossed in the sides to be used in the construction of the facility. Fundraising efforts utilizing techniques like these can be remarkably effective.

4. Convey a Sense of Urgency

As any direct marketer will tell you, it is critical to convey a sense of urgency when you are asking for money. If you are casual about it, people will postpone the decision and are unlikely to follow through with the promised donation. Always put a time limit on the fundraising drive or the time frame to complete the project. If you are soliciting funds to create a supply of fresh water for a remote village in Africa, let donors know that the dry season is approaching soon and the villagers need the water supply before this occurs. Studies have shown over and over again that creating a sense of urgency concerning your project will increase the pledging to your cause dramatically.

> **ESSENTIAL**
>
> A good exercise for any fundraiser is to take a moment and put yourself into your potential donor's shoes. Think about the things that would make *you* want to donate to your fundraising campaign. Chances are that one of the most powerful reasons is "being part of the project." People like to be included in things they feel strongly about. It is very important that you understand this and engineer your fundraising campaign so that every facet of it includes those who pledge.

5. Promise to Stay in Touch

No one likes to be asked for money and then find that's the end of the relationship. Donors want to feel a part of the process after their money is taken and put to use. This does not have to be a major outreach to every individual who pledges to your cause. A newsletter is a great idea, or just a postcard to say thanks. In many cases, simply sending out e-mail updates will keep donors engaged and make them feel included. If you intend to go back to these people for donations in the future, you really have to consider doing this. Remember that it's much easier to obtain a donation from someone who has previously given money to your cause than from a cold donor, so do keep in touch with those who donate.

Five Things to Never Do When Fundraising

There are several things that good fundraisers never do, and you will benefit from remembering them. Again, these are derived from commonsense principles, but sometimes when you get lost in the thick of fundraising, details can slip through the cracks. Keep each item on this "not to do" list in mind when you plan or execute any fundraising program, crowdfunded or otherwise.

1. Never Forget to Emphasize How Important the Donor Is

For you, the fundraiser, the fundraising process is about raising money. For potential donors, this is not the case at all. Potential donors do not have a deep-seated need to give away money. Think about this for a moment: Exactly what does motivate donors? Well, it's really not that complicated; they are motivated by the need to help and to be included in your project. In all aspects of your fundraising campaign, make sure you emphasize that the project needs their unique participation to be successful.

2. Don't Make It Difficult to Pay

Never make your donor choose an inconvenient way to pay. It may be far easier for you to ask for a specific payment type, but the point of fundraising is to make it very easy for the donor. If you are fundraising online, the best method is to use a credit card processing system. This is followed by PayPal and other electronic payment systems. Last choice would be methods that can be put off, such as sending in checks. The problem is that despite people's good intentions, checks just never seem to be sent in. They are put off or put aside and eventually discarded long after the fundraiser has finished.

ESSENTIAL

> Whether you are fundraising or crowdfunding, don't overlook your local media. Local media outlets are always looking for stories of local interest and will likely find your fundraising project interesting enough to cover. Prepare a simple press release about your campaign and send it to every newspaper, magazine, radio, and TV station in your area. After a few days, follow up with the editorial departments to see if they received your press release and to answer any questions.

3. Never Tell Donors to Pledge "Whatever They Can Afford"

An acceptable contribution for some people is $5; for others it's $500. Don't make this a gray area. Ask your donors for specific amounts of money and then tell them what that level "buys." This especially applies to crowdfunding campaigns. In general, a weak method of asking for donations is to say, "pledge what you can afford." A donation request such as this always results in lower donations.

4. Don't Forget to Ask Donors to Spread the Word

In the days before the Internet, spreading the word about charitable causes took a little effort. You mentioned them to people face-to-face or perhaps on the phone. Today, with social media, it's just a couple of mouse clicks away. Be sure to let your donors know they can easily help spread the word and that this is almost as powerful as their donation.

5. Never Forget to Follow Up

After a donor pledges, be sure that you follow up and thank them. This is your chance to cement your relationship with the donors and, ideally, entice them to spread the word to their friends and associates.

Using the Internet as a Tool

Those who are new to fundraising are easily drawn into the belief that fundraising has gone completely online. It's as if nonprofits can stop worrying about grants, pledge drives, and traditional fundraising events, and simply make a website with a huge "Donate now!" button on it. This, of course, is not how it works. Experienced fundraisers will tell you that the Internet has become just another element in the fundraising mix. There's no question that it is a very powerful element, but it must work in conjunction with other fundraising activities.

One of the best uses of the Internet is to keep existing donors in the loop. You can provide reports, fundraising statistics, news, and other information to those who have already pledged. If you are planning a fundraising event, the Internet is a wonderful way to engage pledgers with announcements, invitations to buy tickets online, early previews of silent auctions, and more. Many groups that hold walkathons use software that allows each participant to set up a separate page to use as part of the fundraising pitch. These pages explain the event in general and have a special message from the participant. After the event has finished, the page can be used to deliver details of the event, to display pictures, and to say thanks.

Chapter 3: Raising Funds

ESSENTIAL

Once you start to build an e-mail list of those who are interested in your cause and mission, you can ask for their help in nonfinancial ways. This is a powerful technique for engaging donors. Instead of a "Donate now!" pitch, ask for ideas for fundraisers or creative ways to help build the list of potential donors. People are wary of constantly being asked to donate. If you ask for help in other ways first, it helps build credibility and invites them into the process and the cause.

Another way that the Internet can be used in fundraising marketing mixes is simply in building e-mail lists. The basic idea is that you set up a sign-up form on your website for an e-mail newsletter or other information. Then, over the subsequent months, send out relevant news and information about your work, your mission, and your vision. This is a very effective way to build up a database of people who may become donors as they learn more about what you do.

Popular Fundraising Websites

Groups that wish to use the Internet as a major part of their fundraising mix will find there are many websites available for this purpose. The organizations providing the sites have their own mission: to help fundraisers succeed. Following is a list of several of the most popular sites.

Causes

Fully integrated into Facebook, Causes (*www.causes.com*) allows fundraising organizations to launch and orchestrate online campaigns. Causes is a great way to build communities or "causes" in support of specific issues. Once formed, participants can invite Facebook friends to join their efforts. Existing nonprofits can accept donations through Causes but must be registered 501(c)(3) organizations.

DonorsChoose

This website (*www.donorschoose.org*) is designed specifically for classroom fundraising. Teachers can choose from one of a number of fundraising projects and provide contact information for the parents and children in the class, who, along with anyone else interested, are then invited to donate. The materials for the project are sent directly to the teacher. After the project is finished, those who donated receive photos and thank-you letters from the students via e-mail.

Givezooks!

Givezooks! (*www.givezooks.com*) is targeted toward grassroots and nonprofit fundraising. The site offers a number of fundraising plans that small groups can use, along with options to create custom plans. These could be campaigns, fundraising events, or wish lists. The platform collects $129 per month to use the platform and a small percentage of transaction fees. For small organizations this can be highly worthwhile, because Givezooks! allows you to choose from prepackaged plans and simply get right down to raising funds.

Network for Good

Network for Good (*www.networkforgood.org*) is basically a payment processing engine for fundraising efforts. Integrated into hundreds of websites that exist for socially beneficial purposes, Network for Good uses the DonateNow system behind the scenes. If you have a nonprofit or other charitable organization, you can sign up for the payment processing systems directly.

JustGive

Founded eleven years ago, JustGive (*www.justgive.org*) is a website that allows individuals to find charities to support. The JustGive Guide offers some 1,000 organizations, all thoroughly vetted by JustGive and organized into nineteen categories. The site offers a number of creative ways that individuals can support the causes such as gift cards, wedding registries, and other means. JustGive allows 501(c)(3) nonprofit organizations to set up donation pages and download embeddable "Donate now" buttons to put on webpages and blogs. JustGive does not charge setup costs, but there is a 3 percent fee assessed per donation.

Sparked

Sparked (*www.sparked.com*) is a unique online volunteer network that brings individuals together to support nonprofits and their causes. Essentially this is a crowdsourcing application because instead of giving money, donors give time and other contributions. This could involve things as varied as copywriting, graphic design, help with donor communications—any number of things that donors can remotely do to assist causes. Nonprofits post "challenges" that are distributed to a large volunteer network. Volunteers then can choose the causes and organizations they wish to help.

Jumo

Jumo (*www.jumo.com*) is a social network that connects individuals and organizations and is a registered 501(c)(3) itself. Created by Facebook cofounder Chris Hughes, Jumo's functionality is closely linked with Facebook. Jumo is open to all groups with charitable missions. Nonprofits can easily add their organizations to Jumo, but to receive funds they must provide their employer identification number (EIN—also known as their federal tax identification number). Donations to Jumo are processed via Network for Good, and there is a 4.75 percent fee per transaction.

CHAPTER 4

Crowdfunding 101

Crowdfunding literally means getting a lot of people, "the crowd," to help fund projects, missions, and causes. Although the basic lending concept is as old as time, today the connectedness of the Internet and social media has allowed crowdfunding to become a major trend. As a result, crowdfunding has established a strong beachhead among standard financing techniques and is actually transforming some industries and marketplaces.

Crowdfunding the Statue of Liberty

The concept of groups of people banding together to collectively fund projects is as old as time. Perhaps one of the more intriguing is the story behind the Statute of Liberty and how it was crowdfunded on both sides of the Atlantic Ocean.

The Statue of Liberty was a gift from France to the people of America to celebrate the 1876 American Centennial. As students of history will note, France was a significant ally during the Revolutionary War, providing America weapons, ships, soldiers, and money in their protest against "English tyranny." One hundred years after the revolution, the Statue of Liberty was France's way of celebrating not only the friendship between the countries after the Revolutionary War, but the burgeoning American economy and its major status on the world stage.

There was an arrangement, though. The French were happy to design the statue, bring it to the United States, and assemble it, but the United States was to provide the site and the pedestal for it. As history documents, the French were a little more enthusiastic about the venture than the Americans were. This may have been due to nothing more than a lack of press coverage concerning the venture on this side.

On the French side, the statue was financed by public fees and a lottery. The statue, the internal structure being designed by Alexandre-Gustave Eiffel, the designer of the Eiffel Tower, was a big source of national pride and funds were collected with relative ease.

On the U.S. side, the cost of the pedestal soared, and funds ran out about halfway through. Subsequent fundraising was launched shortly thereafter, but response was tepid. However, in 1885, Joseph Pulitzer and his newspaper *The World* got involved and raised the rest of the funds in a six-month campaign. In the spirit of true crowdfunding, Pulitzer raised $102,000 from over 120,000 donors, much of it in amounts less than a dollar. Pulitzer also publicized stores that offered special fundraising statuettes, which were sold on behalf of the American Committee of the Statue of Liberty for $1 (6 inches high) or $5 (12 inches high).

Types of Crowdfunding

It is important to examine the term *crowdfunding* as it is used today. The term itself is applied to several different ways that crowds can be used to fund projects. It is important that we examine these variations because while they share the common denominator of "crowds" and "funding," they are different techniques. The next several sections will examine the techniques of donation-based crowdfunding, reward-based crowdfunding, debt-based crowdfunding, and equity-based crowdfunding.

Donation-based Crowdfunding

Donation-based crowdfunding is the process of collecting funds from groups of people for specific projects or goals. Strictly speaking, donation-based crowdfunding does not require that rewards be given to those who pledge money. An animal shelter that is collecting funds on its website for a capital improvement project would be practicing donation-based crowdfunding. There would be no expectation of individual rewards from this campaign because funds are being gathered for a specific purpose.

In many ways, donation-based crowdfunding could be considered a subset of standard fundraising. For example, consider the case of political fundraising where a "Donate!" button is located on a candidate's website. This button allows "the crowd" to pledge funds without any intended rewards other than assisting the cause. This would represent donation-based crowdfunding as the funds that are pledged are literally donations.

Reward-based Crowdfunding

Reward-based crowdfunding is what many people identify as regular crowdfunding. Take a trip over to Kickstarter, Indiegogo, or any of the other popular crowdfunding sites and what you will see is reward-based crowdfunding in action. Most of the campaigns on these sites ask people to donate so that a specific project can be undertaken and completed, and many cases offer rewards to donors who have direct connection to the project itself. For example, independent filmmakers usually offer DVDs of their completed films, comic book artists offer copies of their comics, and video game designers offer copies of their games.

ESSENTIAL

> It is said that reward-based crowdfunding has changed independent filmmaking forever. No longer do filmmakers need to beg family and friends for financing; they can go right to those who would like to see the movie and offer a copy in return for financing. While this is true, many indie filmmakers are finding that they still need family and friends, *in addition* to the crowdfunding.

It is worth noting that many of those who pledge reward-based crowdfunding campaigns do not have a solid understanding of the reward-based approach. This is because, in many ways, this type of crowdfunding appears to be a retail model. For example, an independent filmmaker who is collecting funds to produce a movie usually offers a copy of the movie as a reward for pledging. Sometimes this isn't emphasized enough, but it is important to understand: The filmmaker is not "selling movies." After all, the movie isn't even created yet; it is just an idea in the filmmaker's mind. By placing an open call for funding, those who pledge are not buying movies, they are funding the filmmaking process—paying for equipment, travel expenses, food, and all the other expenses that go into making a small film. They are capitalizing the process.

There are two ways in which the confusion between a retail model and a reward-based crowdfunding model can cause concern. The first is the time frame. A filmmaker may not complete the movie for many, many months and that means a lot of time waiting for those who have pledged. The second involves the product. Remember, the movie was in the filmmaker's mind, and it may change during the creation process. As a matter of fact, this is almost to be expected. Things will occur, or be learned, during the filmmaking process that will be integrated into the final product. The important point is that those who pledged for the finished product will still receive a copy of the filmmaker's "vision" when the process is completed.

Debt-based Crowdfunding

Debt-based crowdfunding, also known as peer-to-peer lending (P2P) and social lending, is defined as a financial transaction that occurs between individuals, or "peers," without a financial intermediary involved.

Unless it is in the context of philanthropy, most peer-to-peer lending is a for-profit activity in which lenders anticipate a rate of return for the use of their money. Put into a historical context, lending money to family, friends, and community members is an old concept that predates formalized financial institutions.

The first P2P lending platform to launch on the Internet was Zopa in the United Kingdom in 2005. Just one year later, Prosper launched in the United States. In 2009, Zidisha became the first P2P lending platform to link lenders and borrowers across international borders. Today there are several dozen P2P lending sites, and the amount of outstanding P2P loans had risen from $118 million to $5.8 billion by 2010.

> **ALERT**
>
> The concept of peer-to-peer lending has taken a big hit because of Prosper.com. Prosper was one of the first companies to offer peer-to-peer lending and arrived in 2006 with a lot of fanfare concerning the disintermediation of banks and the democratization of credit. Unfortunately, Prosper was formed just as the recession hit and a lot of its lenders lost money. Some say this is truly unfortunate, because the basic principle of removing financial intermediaries can be a very good one.

P2P lending platforms have evolved to adopt certain functional characteristics. These characteristics can be used to identify an investment style and a platform's overall business model. Following are three investment characteristics that have evolved.

Direct Versus Indirect Loans

Direct lending refers to the practice of allowing a lender to choose a specific borrower to loan money to. Lenders generally do this on the basis the borrower has given for needing a loan and the borrower's credit score rating. In contrast, indirect loans are pooled over many lenders in an attempt to mitigate risk by diversification. Lenders tend to select this sort of arrangement because the risk is substantially less than it is for direct loans. The indirect loan model is essentially the same as a traditional bank model, in which lenders are completely separated for the borrower selection process.

Secured Versus Unsecured Loans

A secured loan is one that has collateral rights attached to the loan. Collateral is something of value that the lender has a legal right to liquidate under certain contractual situations if the borrower cannot pay back the loan. For example, when a bank loans money to someone buying a house, the bank generally retains title to the house as collateral to assure payments are made. In contrast, an unsecured loan is made on the basis of the borrower's credit rating. Unsecured loans are riskier than secured ones, and borrowers often pay higher interest rates to compensate for the risk.

Equity-based Crowdfunding

Equity-based crowdfunding may possibly become the most powerful of the crowdfunding species. The concept is simple. In contrast to pure donation or receiving rewards or payback on loans, equity-based crowdfunding offers the crowd an opportunity to actually buy a piece of a business. They can invest directly in the company and receive shares in it. The advantages to those who buy shares are that they can participate when a company is young and purchase shares that may increase significantly in value.

Originally, the practice of selling shares in any company was tightly regulated by the Securities and Exchange Commission in the United States. These regulations, codified by the Securities Act of 1933, were designed to protect small, unsophisticated investors. For companies to offer sales of equity directly to investors required that the investors be accredited, or have a net worth of over $1 million. This, of course, prevented small investors from purchasing shares directly. For small investors, shares needed to be purchase, through stock exchanges.

In February 2011, a group of businesspeople formed an organization called the Startup Exemption. Their goal was to lobby Washington to update the Federal Security laws so that entrepreneurs could offer early-stage equity via crowdfunding. Their efforts formed the basis of the Entrepreneur Access to Capital Act (H.R. 2930), which was introduced by Rep. Patrick McHenry on September 14, 2011, to the United States House of Representatives. On November 3, 2011, the House passed H.R. 2930 with a vote of 407–17, a rare sign of bipartisan support for a bill in Washington, D.C.

> **QUESTION**
>
> **What is the difference between an "accredited" and "nonaccredited" investor?**
> The definition of what constitutes an accredited investor is spelled out in detail in the United States Securities Act of 1933. In simple terms, when discussing individuals, a person who has a net worth in excess of $1 million (not including his/her residence) or an income exceeding $200,000 per year is an *accredited investor*. This means he is allowed to directly invest in riskier securities such as private placements, hedge funds, limited partnerships, and the like.

Meanwhile, in the Senate, similar legislation was being drafted. On November 2, 2011, the Democratizing Access to Capital Act (S. 1791) was introduced by Senator Scott Brown (R-MA). S. 1791 was similar to H.R. 2930 but lowered the limits that a business could raise and the amount that investors could invest. Debate over both H.R. 2930 and S. 1791 continued for several months. The House forged forward and packaged a number of additional bills into a single bill, H.R. 3606, also known as the JOBS Act. This act was passed by the House on March, 8, 2012. The Senate added several amendments to the JOBs Act and it passed the Senate on March 22, 2012.

President Obama stated in March 2012 that he would pass the JOBS Act as soon as he received it from Congress. On April 5, 2012, he signed the JOBS Act into law. Although the SEC was given 180 days to administer the law, the ability for small businesses to sell equity shares in their companies was allowed for the first time since the 1930s. This is the dawn of a new era in American entrepreneurship.

The Origins of Crowdfunding on the Internet

While some examples of crowdfunding can be found offline, for the most part crowdfunding is an Internet model. One of the first instances recorded on the Internet occurred in 1997 when the British rock group Marillion raised $60,000 in donations from a fan-based Internet campaign. The idea was developed by the fans of the band and was to assist Marillion in funding its North American tour. The campaign had no actual involvement by the band itself and was completely orchestrated by a fan-based organization.

e! ALERT

> On February 8, 2011, Brian Camelio of ArtistShare filed for a patent that covers the business practice of allowing artists to use web platforms for raising investment funds. This patent is an example of the controversial practice of patenting business methods allowed by the United States Patent Office. As the holder of this patent, #7,885,887, Camelio is currently engaged in discussions with crowdfunding businesses that may infringe on his patent. Most notable is Kickstarter, which is asking for the court to invalidate Camelio's patent.

In 2001, the U.S.–based company ArtistShare established itself as the first crowdfunding website for music. It was followed by sites such as SellaBand (2006), Indiegogo (2008), PledgeMusic (2008), Kickstarter (2009), and others. In 2004, the Japanese rock band Electric Eel Shock (EES) raised $10,000 from 100 fans, the "Samurai 100," in return for offering them tickets for any EES concert for life. Two years later, EES became the first band to raise $50,000 (approximately 75,000 U.S. dollars) through the website SellaBand.

Then in 2008, Indiegogo.com was cofounded by Danae Ringlemann and Slava Rubin. The battle cry was to "Democratize Fundraising" by empowering entrepreneurs with the tools needed to raise money for creative projects. Kickstarter.com was launched in 2009, identifying itself as a "new way to fund creativity." Today these are two of the most popular crowdfunding platforms on the planet.

A Typical Crowdfunding Campaign

In this section you will examine a campaign on Kickstarter. If you visit the Kickstarter site (*www.kickstarter.com*), you should be able to find the campaign by typing in the keyword "Planet Tatooine Collectibles" or using this web address: *www.kickstarter.com/projects/legendary/*

rescuing-science-fiction-history. The title of this campaign—Planet Tatooine Collectibles—was chosen to grab attention quickly.

Located above the campaign video you will find four tabs:

- **Project Home:** This is the main tab, which displays the campaign homepage.
- **Updates:** This is where the updates that were posted during the campaign and postcampaign are placed. Posted from newest to last, you can view all the "Public" updates during the campaign here.
- **Backers:** This is a list of all the project backers along with a link to their personal Kickstarter profile pages.
- **Comments:** This is where all the public comments from backers to the project creator are posted.

> **FACT**
>
> Most of the crowdfunding platforms allow you to edit much of your campaign once it's launched, with the exception of your goal amount, campaign duration, and existing pledge levels (you can, however, add additional levels). Once the project is finished, the entire campaign is frozen from editing, so make sure the last iteration is the one that you want archived.

Video

The video was designed to be dynamic and evangelistic. The profile image (the first image on the video) is of a collectible wrist watch and a famous Star Wars film set. The video was crafted in a video slideshow format and edited on a PC with Pinnacle Studio Version 14. The project originators secured images from around the Internet from royalty-free image sites where possible. If necessary, they requested permission from the owners for use of the images. The music also was obtained from a royalty-free site.

Underneath the video you will see a Facebook icon with the number of viewers who "Like" the project. To the right of that is a "Tweet" button that will take you directly to your Twitter page so you can spread the word, and finally an "Embed" button that calls up a dialogue box you can use to design your own campaign widget to embed on other web pages.

QUESTION

What is a "widget"?
A widget is a term used for a piece of code that you can copy and place on other websites to perform a specific function. For example, under a YouTube video there is a "share" button. This button allows you to copy the code for the video and insert it on other webpages as a "widget," or in this case, a stand-alone YouTube video player. Most crowdfunding sites allow you to do the same with their campaigns.

Text

The text located in the body of the project contains the project pitch. It states the perceived problem with current earphone models and the suggestions for better designs. At the bottom of the text, there are questions about what happens after the project is finished, along with a request for "your help."

Results and Rewards

In the upper right-hand side of the campaign, Kickstarter states results of the campaign in large bold text. The Planet Tatooine Collectibles campaign ended with 359 backers and $39,522 in pledges. The original goal was just $22,760. Underneath the results box, the rewards are listed in order of increasing value. The rewards were specifically designed to reflect popular pricing options and to offer an increasing value structure. The rewards for the Planet Tatooine Collectibles campaign were:

- $1—Access to project updates and a hearty "Thank You"
- $17—A Tatooine Certificate
- $37—A Tatooine Certificate and a Tatooine T-Shirt

- $77—A Premium Tatooine Sand Wristwatch
- $107—A Limited Edition Tatooine Sand Wristwatch
- $137—Certificate, T-shirt, and Limited Edition Tatooine Sand Wristwatch

CHAPTER 5

A Crowdfunding Platform Examination

If there were a poll to determine which crowdfunding platform best exemplifies the breed, it would probably be led by Kickstarter. This is undoubtedly due to Kickstarter's high visibility thanks to several stellar campaigns it has hosted. Popularity factor aside, though, the Kickstarter website is well designed and functional and is a good example to look at. This chapter will examine the nooks and crannies of the Kickstarter website and by doing so increase your comfort level of the entire crowdfunding process, regardless of the platform you might choose.

Kickstarter.com

Although not the first crowdfunding platform on the web, Kickstarter (*www.kickstarter.com*) has become the largest and most popular. Many feel this is because it was one of the first to offer the very clever "all-or-nothing" funding goal paradigm. The way "all-or-nothing" works is that donors can pledge for projects but there is no financial obligation until a specific monetary goal is reached. After that goal is surpassed, all the donors' pledges become valid and the project is officially a go. As 2011 came to a close, the following statistics rang up on Kickstarter:

- Launched Projects: 27,086
- Successful Projects: 11,836
- Dollars Pledged: $99,344,382
- Rewards Selected: 1,150,461
- Total Visitors: 30,590,342
- Project Success Rate: 46%

The Kickstarter campaign format is basic and reasonably easy to understand. Not surprisingly, the look and feel of the Kickstarter interface has found its way into the design of many of the other crowdfunding platforms on the web. It might be too strong to say they "copied" Kickstarter; let's just say they pay "homage" to the elegance of the Kickstarter design.

ALERT

It is tempting to try Kickstarter for your first crowdfunding campaign. The site is easy to use and is the largest on the Internet. However, Kickstarter does not accept all projects that are proposed. It has specific guidelines for project acceptance, and some 40 percent of submissions do not make it. If you find that your Kickstarter proposal is turned down, try Indiegogo, RocketHub, or one of the other crowdfunding platforms that typically are more liberal on submission acceptance.

The Kickstarter Introductory Page

When you go to Kickstarter.com you are greeted with a large banner that states "Fund and Follow Creativity." This banner indeed sums up the Kickstarter philosophy of catalyzing creative projects, whether they be media-based, technology-based, or just about anything-else-based. Once you become a little more crowdfunding literate, you will find that a lot of the crowdfunding platforms out there tend to have a particular angle or type of project they prefer. In the case of Kickstarter it's all about "creative projects," and the staff at Kickstarter definitely enforce that requirement in their project selection process.

> **QUESTION**
>
> **What is the difference between a project and a campaign?**
> Just a matter of semantics. Kickstarter refers to its crowdfunding endeavors as "projects." Indiegogo and a few others refer to them as "campaigns." There are also several other definitions in use. Don't get too hung up on the name that is used—they generally refer to the same thing. Just realize that it can get confusing depending on the context in which they are used.

On the top of the Kickstarter introductory page you will see several tabs. These are labeled "Discover," "Start," "Blog," and "Help," followed by several icons. In the main body of the page you will also find crowdfunding projects designated as "Staff Picks," projects that are "Located Nearby," projects that are "Popular," and at the bottom "Curated Pages." One small caveat: the Internet is a dynamic, changing environment for digital information. The specific areas of the Kickstarter site discussed here are likely to change over time, so don't be too concerned if sections are moved or changed.

The Discover Tab

On the top left of the Kickstarter intro page you will find a Discover tab. This tab takes you to the main repository of the projects on Kickstarter. On this page you will see the categories of "Favorite Projects" (as picked by the staff), "Popular This Week," "Recently Successful," and "Recent Updates." On the right-hand side of the page, in the "Featured" list, you will see links that guide you through various categories of projects. These links are:

- **Staff Picks:** A few hundred of the projects that the staff at Kickstarter especially enjoy
- **Popular:** Projects that have generated a lot of interest on Kickstarter for the week
- **Recently Launched:** A collection of projects that have just been launched
- **Ending Soon:** Projects that are within hours, or minutes, of completion
- **Small Projects:** These are modest projects without large funding goals
- **Most Funded:** A gallery of the projects that have collected significant funding
- **Curated Pages:** Completed projects that have connections to specific groups and institutions

ALERT

If you attempt to contact Kickstarter for any sort of reason, you will quickly find out that the site has limited channels for contact, and phone calls are not among them. At various places on the website you will find contact links that you may use to send e-mails to staff, and an HTML form that you can fill out with your questions. However, while you will receive responses in a reasonable amount of time, many times it will be a "boilerplate" response that reiterates Kickstarter's FAQs and other site-based information.

The Blog Tab

On the top right side of the Kickstarter intro page is a Blog tab. The Kickstarter blog is written primarily by Kickstarter employees and is updated every week. There are several weekly blog entries. The titles include "This Week in Kickstarter," "Projects in the News," "Featured Creator," "Trending Projects," and others, depending on the week.

If you are a neophyte crowdfunder, you should spend a few afternoons or evenings perusing the Kickstarter blog. You might say the Kickstarter blog is the heart and soul of this site. You will find opinions on projects, project profiles, commentary, and some extremely insightful statistics.

There are hundreds of blog posts for you to potentially wade through, but the good folks at Kickstarter have broken the blog posts into categories:

- **News:** "This Week in Kickstarter" and "Projects in the News"
- **Profiles:** New projects being launched and "Trending Projects"
- **Data:** Wonderful crowdfunding statistics from Kickstarter
- **Q&A's:** Not an FAQ section, this section profiles various creators in a question-and-answer format
- **Calendar:** A listing of various events around the world with ties to Kickstarter projects
- **Video:** This video-centric section discusses a variety of issues concerning crowdfunding videos
- **Tips:** A must-visit section for beginning crowdfunders; lots of tips and techniques are profiled here
- **Awards:** A good section to visit to see the projects that headline their subject categories

You can also keep up with crowdfunding news by signing up for the Kickstarter newsletter. This newsletter is presently a weekly affair and showcases interesting projects and Kickstarter news. You can also visit archived newsletters on the Kickstarter website that go back to the first issue, July 14, 2010.

The Help Tab

Originally a relatively sparse affair, the Kickstarter Help Center has evolved into a great resource. You will find it broken into three Frequently Asked Questions (FAQ) sections.

Kickstarter Basics

This section covers the topics of "How It Works," "Starting a Project," "Accountability," "Account Settings" and "Odds and Ends." There are some thirty-one FAQ topics here, covering basic and introductory questions you may have with crowdfunding and Kickstarter.

Creators

In this section you will find "Project Basics," "Eligibility Requirements," "Project Submissions," "Rewards," "Fees," "Accountability," "Discover," "Project Media," "Project Updates," and "Amazon & Verifications." There are some 141 FAQ topics here dealing with the details that project creators may want to know before and during their crowdfunding project.

Backers

The "Backers" section is less involved than the two sections just explained, but you should be familiar with it even if you are just a project creator. The reason for this is that you will receive many questions from your backers if you decide to run a crowdfunding campaign. Don't assume they will digest the "Backers" section; most won't even look at it. As a project creator, you need to be ready to answer their questions. The "Backers" section contains three subsections, "Pledging," "Rewards," and "Accountability."

Guidelines

On the lower part of the Help page is a link to the Kickstarter Project Guidelines. You will find that Kickstarter is not liberal about the projects it accepts. The site states that it is a platform for "creative projects," and the staff use that criteria to filter the projects that they do accept. Many a person has submitted a project to Kickstarter and has been denied because he violated one of more of the Kickstarter guidelines. The following sections explain the guidelines so you can make sure your crowdfunding project fits in.

Funding Is for "Projects" Only

Crowdfunding can be used to collect money for a lot of things, but Kickstarter wants its platform to be used just for funding "projects." A project is something with a clear beginning and a clear end. It must produce something. A common submission that Kickstarter sees is "project-like" but really is intended to collect money to start a business. Kickstarter will generally prevent a project from launching if its purpose is to start a business.

Chapter 5: A Crowdfunding Platform Examination

Projects Must Fit Certain Categories

At the present time, Kickstarter requests that projects fit into the categories of art, comics, dance, design, fashion, film, food, games, music, photography, publishing, technology, and theater. A quick glance at this list reiterates the creative focus that Kickstarter wishes to cultivate.

> **FACT**
>
> As noble as raising money for charities and causes is, it just isn't the sort of campaign that Kickstarter wishes to engage in. If you have a social entrepreneurship project or a cause for the social good, there are many crowdfunding platforms designed especially for that purpose. Some examples are startsomegood.com, 33needs.com, and Bzzbnk.org.

Prohibited Projects

There are certain projects that are just not what Kickstarter is all about. For example:

- **No charity or cause funding.** Kickstarter simply isn't interested in raising money for known or unknown charities. Other causes, such as scholarships, awareness campaigns, or social entrepreneuring projects, are also discouraged.
- **No personal funding.** It is not unusual to see crowdfunding campaigns that are established by people who need help paying bills, buying things, paying medical expenses, and the like. While these are genuine needs, they are not the kind of campaign that Kickstarter wishes to launch on its site.
- **Prohibited content.** As noted in the Project Guidelines section (*www.kickstarter.com/help/guidelines*), Kickstarter prohibits campaigns dealing with these areas, among others: alcohol; automotive products; baby products; bath products; beauty products; contests; cosmetics; coupons (discounts and gift cards); drugs; drug paraphernalia; electronic surveillance equipment; energy drinks; exercise and fitness products; financial products (ownership, share of profits, repayment/loans); firearms (weapons and knives); health (personal care products); heating and cooling products; home improvement

products; infomercial-type products; items not directly produced by the creator (things from the garage, repackaged existing products); medical (safety-related products); multilevel marketing programs and products; nutritional supplements; offensive material (inappropriate content); pet supplies; pornographic material; political projects; projects involving acts of violence; projects to sell existing inventory; raffles (lotteries and sweepstakes); real estate; self-help (books, DVDs, CDs); and tobacco products.

Kickstarter School

On the bottom of the Kickstarter Help Center is a section called Kickstarter School. This tutorial does a fine job of stepping you through the process of designing your crowdfunding campaign for best results on Kickstarter. The school itself consists of eight steps, each being just a page in duration. If you are considering a campaign on Kickstarter, you should read through all these pages. Here is a condensed version of what you will learn, along with a few comments.

Defining Your Project

Kickstarter recommends that the first thing you do is define your project. As mentioned previously, Kickstarter is firm on the point that crowdfunding on Kickstarter must be project based. A project is something that is finite; it has a beginning and it has an end. In addition, Kickstarter has a relatively lengthy list of projects that it doesn't allow. Make sure that your proposed project does not intersect with one of the prohibited categories.

Creating Rewards

Creating rewards can be powerful motivation for funding your campaign. It is important that you create tangible, fairly priced rewards. Donors are not always motivated purely by the rewards you offer, but they are important. In the case of some projects, it may be a challenge to decide what rewards to actually offer. Here are a few suggestions:

- **Copies of Your Creation.** If you are crowdfunding for a movie, a show, a music album, a book, or something that can easily be replicated, a copy of your creation is a perfect reward.
- **Creative Experiences.** For special reward, consider special experiences, like a private tour of the movie set, a phone call from the cast, a section of a historic building being restored, a concert in your backyard.
- **Project Mementos.** Personalized pictures from location, the donor's name in the credits, and personalized editions are all unique mementos that have a personal attachment to your project.

Setting Your Goal

Kickstarter operates on an all-or-nothing funding model in which projects must meet their funding goal, or no money changes hands. Projects must set a funding goal and a length of time to reach it. There's no magic formula for determining the right goal or project duration, but the following guidelines should help.

First, what is your budget? How much money do you really need? Be especially careful here; a lot of people have found out that their Kickstarter goal was not enough to actually complete the project. It is easy to get swept away by the magnitude of the funds that you may raise on Kickstarter, but make sure you'll have enough to complete the project and deliver all your backers' rewards.

How long should your project deadline be? Currently Kickstarter allows projects to be from one to sixty days. Research on funding and project duration has shown that longer projects do not necessarily gather more funding. In fact, shorter projects may be superior in many respects. Longer durations can invite potential backers to procrastinate, and often they do not return. Kickstarter recommends that project creators consider projects with a thirty-day duration.

Making Your Video

The first thing that most people do when they see an interesting project title is click the video "play" icon. That is when the project creator's show starts. The video is your opportunity to tell your story and engage your audience. This is the time to get them so excited about what you are creating that they immediately look over the rewards you offer and pledge for one so you can get funded. In a nutshell, the video is critical to the success of your project.

ESSENTIAL

> You will read statistics about project and campaign videos throughout this book. The most common one is this: Projects that include a video rather than just a picture statistically raise 112 percent more funds. Another statistic from Kickstarter involves the success rate, meaning that the project meets its funding goal. In this case, projects that include a video reach their funding goal at a higher rate (50 percent) than do those without a video (30 percent).

Building Your Project

The next "class" in the Kickstarter School covers several other promotional aspects of a crowdfunding project. There are four items to consider here: the project's title, the image you'd like to project, a description of the project, and your bio.

The Project Title

There are a lot of projects on Kickstarter. Choosing a title is no time to be subtle. Of course, you shouldn't go crazy here, but do make a title that shouts out your project and sets it apart from anything else. Make the title interesting enough that people will pause and want to investigate a little more.

The Project Image

Your project image is the first to appear on the video. Just as you do for the other aspects of your crowdfunding project, make the image memorable and make sure it reflects your project. Here's an idea for you: Go to Kickstarter, click on the "Discover" icon, and wade through six to seven pages of projects. Which project images caught your eye? And why did they? Was it the colors? Was it the images themselves? Think about the things that caught your eye and consider using these elements in some form in your project image.

Your Short Description
Your short description appears in your project's widget (the small profile). Kickstarter only gives you space for a couple dozen words so you need to communicate succinctly to your audience what your project is all about and how exciting it is.

Your Bio
Your bio is a very important part of your crowdfunding campaign. Explain who you are and why you are proposing this campaign. The key is to communicate that you are trustworthy and likable.

Promoting Your Project

Promotion is arguably the most important part of your project. What is your outreach program? Kickstarter is a big place—there are thousands upon thousands of projects on the site. The probability that someone is going to stumble upon your project is small. The solution? You have to promote it! Your project needs exposure on social media, blogs, newsletters, RSS feeds, social news; any and all ways that you can promote it.

> **QUESTION**
>
> **What are RSS feeds?**
> RSS stands for Really Simple Syndication. An RSS feed is a document that contains a summary of content from websites such as news sites, blogs, or other sources of information. RSS feeds make it possible for people to keep up with their favorite websites automatically rather than checking them manually. RSS feeds can be received by e-mail, browsers, or a number of stand-alone programs.

Project Updates

Kickstarter gives you a great capability to send updates to those who have pledged your project. It does so with a web form that you can send privately to all backers or allow to be posted on your project page for anyone to see. You absolutely should use this capability and do so regularly. The people who have pledged your project are not passive observers who are simply waiting for a ship date. They want much more information than that. They want to be included in the project and are thirsty for any and all details. Ask anyone who has executed a crowdfunding campaign about the importance of project updates; it's likely that you will be quite surprised. The bottom line is that you want to send updates every few days, regardless of the topic. Your pledgers will expect it, and it isn't hard to do. Keep your backers happy with a constant flow of information during the campaign period.

Reward Fulfillment

When your project closes, the good folks at Kickstarter will post all your backer information (privately, of course) so that you can contact them and collect their information. You can do this by sending messages to your entire group of backers at once or you can e-mail each one individually.

Start Your Project

Not a lot of fanfare is necessary to start a Kickstarter project. No phones calls are necessary, no prior approval needs to be obtained; it's just a click on the "Start your project" link at the top of the Kickstarter pages and you are off and running.

That being said, you may find it useful to think of this process as *crafting* your proposal to Kickstarter. Kickstarter only opens the gate to some 60 percent or so of the proposals it receives, so there is some chance that your project may not be accepted, at least the first time. Kickstarter does allow you to resubmit a project if it is declined, but getting it approved on a resubmission is not a given by any means. Furthermore, Kickstarter often does not give you much guidance when your project is declined other than simply stating, "Unfortunately this project does not meet our requirements." It is usually up to you to scour the Kickstarter site to find out what issue Kickstarter may have with your project. Occasionally, a compassionate customer service representative will give you some insight into the issue, but this is not common. Kickstarter is a busy place, so most responses are succinct and right to the point.

Chapter 5: A Crowdfunding Platform Examination

ESSENTIAL

Some projects on Kickstarter have garnered huge support. Examples are the TikTok watch project, some of the video game projects, and most recently the Pebble Watch project. Take a good look at these projects and try to determine what made them so successful. You will find that the concept played a big part, but equally important is how the project went viral on the web. Examine how this happened and see if you can tap into some of the magic with your project.

The process of submitting a proposal to Kickstarter is a linear one: You will follow eight steps that allow you to build and define your project. Note that you can revisit any step at any time to fine-tune and change things. As a matter of fact, it is almost certain that you will. Keep in mind that this project definition and design process may take you several days, and it probably should. Especially for first-time crowdfunders, this is like visiting a foreign land; you are going to have many, many questions as you proceed. Just realize that this is completely normal and expected. Each step of the project definition process is "saved" by Kickstarter so you won't lose any data. You can come and go over a period of weeks, and as a matter of fact, while you design your project you will almost certainly complete the various sections of your project out of sequence.

The first step is to click on the "Start Your Project" link at the top of most of the Kickstarter web pages. You will find a video that outlines the process and a gray section that explains a few key tenets of how Kickstarter works. After reading the material you find, click on the "Start Your Project" button.

Guidelines

The Guidelines section reiterates the sum of the material that is located in the Kickstarter school and in the FAQs. In particular, funding is for *projects* only; again, projects must fit Kickstarter's categories, and may not involve certain prohibited categories. After you read over these guidelines, Kickstarter requests that you check an "I understand" checkbox. After that, you are allowed to proceed to a button that is labeled "Start Your Project." (Note: you will be asked to enter your password at this point.)

Basics

The Basics section starts off with a header titled "Meet your new project." On this page you're asked to place a project image. This is the image that those who are visiting Kickstarter see first on the crowdfunding project pages. Then you have a sixty-character field in which you can enter a descriptive project title. Underneath that a pull-down menu allows you to specify a category that you feel your project best matches. The last text box allows you 135 characters to make your product pitch. Give the description and pitch for your project some thought. Actually, this applies to the title, too. Both the title and your description of the project are very important. There are thousands of projects on Kickstarter and this is your one chance to get casual viewers to pop in and look at yours. Grab their attention!

FACT

Want to know how to promote your crowdfunding project? Don Hewitt, creator of *60 Minutes*, the longest-running prime-time program on American television, was once asked about the secret to his success. His response was disarmingly simple: "Tell them a story." Hewitt understood that what caught people's attention was the universal interest in storytelling. Use Don Hewitt's insights into human motivation: "Tell them a story"!

Rewards

The next click takes you to the rewards definition page. This section is where you build your rewards, one at a time. You are first presented with Reward #1 and a dialogue box in which you define the pledge amount, the number available (if you have a limited number of this reward category), the reward description, and the estimated delivery date.

Story

After you complete the Rewards section you move on to the Story section. Kickstarter heads this section with the title "It's not just a project, it's a story." If you are new to crowdfunding, you are going to quickly see that garnering the attention of groups of people requires compelling stories. While this does not explain the motivation of every single person in the crowdfunding universe, it does describe the vast majority: They want to know the story behind your crowdfunding campaign. They want to know why it is so important to you and how it fits into their lives.

> **ESSENTIAL**
>
> When you are on one of the many "Start Your Project" sections, you will notice a "Preview" button. This button takes you to a mockup of what your crowdfunding project will look like. Click over to this mockup often just to double-check things. Since this is what your potential donors will see when you go "live," it's a good idea to make sure everything looks right and is easy to understand.

Keeping that in mind, the folks at Kickstarter give you two sections here to express yourself and your passion for your project. The first is via your video, a subject covered previously in the Kickstarter School. The second is your project description. In the description you have the ability to restate your case and perhaps do it a little differently than you do in your video.

About You

This section is all about you. Here is where you post a picture, connect with your Facebook page, write a concise biography, state your location, and post website links. Give your potential donors all the information that you can. Be honest, be likable, and tell people the things that make you who you are. The more people can relate to you and who you are as a person, the more attractive your project and mission will be.

Account

In order to allow crowdfunding, a method of collecting payments must be arranged to collect donations from projects that meet their financial goals. Kickstarter uses Amazon Payments for credit card processing. What this means for you as a crowdfunder is that in order to receive funds, you need to establish an Amazon Payments account and link it to your Kickstarter crowdfunding project. Fortunately Kickstarter guides you through this process and the different steps of verification that must occur before your project and your Amazon Payments account are linked up.

Review

This is just a short section with a checklist to make sure you haven't forgotten anything before you submit your project. Be sure to read each bullet point and verify that you have either done what the site requests or at least understand the issue.

Submit

After you have completed all the sections of creating your Kickstarter crowdfunding campaign, the next step is to click "Submit." Your campaign proposal is sent to Kickstarter staff for approval. After a day or so, you will get a response that tells you whether you get the green light or need to change a few things. It is entirely possible that your campaign may not meet Kickstarter's standards and you will not be allowed to launch your campaign. If this occurs, try one of the other crowdfunding websites. There are, of course, dozens of them. You will find that many of the other sites are similar to Kickstarter in a number of ways, and some may offer additional features and options for you to use.

CHAPTER 6

Other Crowdfunding Sites

The crowdfunding sites you find on the Internet are as varied as the projects and campaigns that people wish to fund. Kickstarter may be the largest site on the web, but as mentioned in the previous chapter, it has a stated specialty—Kickstarter is just for "creative projects." There are plenty of people who wish to raise funds for other needs and, thankfully, a wide variety of crowdfunding platforms are available.

Indiegogo

Indiegogo (*www.indiegogo.com*) is an international crowdfunding site founded by Danae Ringelmann, Slava Rubin, and Eric Schell. Having backgrounds in finance and fundraising, all three of the founders saw an opportunity to help those involved with creative projects find alternate funding streams. The site was officially launched at the Sundance Film Festival in 2008 with a focus on assisting independent filmmakers with fundraising for their projects.

Not long after this high-visibility launch, Indiegogo partnered with MTV New Media and established a program through which promising new television projects could be funded by the crowd and perhaps be acquired by MTV's New Media group after the pilot was made. In June 2012, Indiegogo raised $15 million of expansion capital from Insight Ventures, Khosla Ventures, and Steve Schoettler, Zynga's cofounder. Today, Indiegogo headquarters are in San Francisco, California, and the website has broadened its reach to allow anyone to raise money for virtually any project. As of 2012, it had hosted more than 100,000 funding campaigns in areas such as music, charity, small business, and film.

> **ESSENTIAL**
>
> A major feather in Indiegogo's cap came in April 2011, when it was selected to participate in the Startup America Partnership. A White House–supported entrepreneurial initiative, the Startup America Partnership was formed by the private sector to enact the administration's Startup America campaign. As a partner in the initiative, Indiegogo agreed to offer Startup America Partnership member companies and entrepreneurs the opportunity to raise $30 million in funding at a 50 percent discount on campaign fees through a newly created Startup America Partnership section on the Indiegogo site.

The Indiegogo site is attractive and easy to navigate. When you visit, you are greeted with a large window that cycles through seven profiled campaigns. Underneath that are individual campaign profiles arranged by "Final Countdown," "New This Week" and a larger "Featured Success Story" at the bottom. Back on the top menu bar are three tabs. The first, titled "Browse," takes you to a large dropdown menu with the following six selections:

- **Quick picks:** This tab takes you to a potpourri of campaigns such as "Featured Campaigns," "Final Countdown," "Popular Campaigns," "New This Week," "Near Me," "Success Stories ," and others.
- **Creative:** Here are the major creative categories Indiegogo uses to segment campaigns. Categories include art, comic, dance, design, fashion, film, gaming, music, photography, theatre, transmedia, video/web, and writing.
- **Cause:** Unlike many of the other crowdfunding sites, Indiegogo enthusiastically accepts cause-based campaigns. The current list of categories consists of animals, community, education, environment, health, politics, and religion.
- **Entrepreneurial:** Although just four categories exist in this section—food, small business, sports, and technology—the Entrepreneurial list links you to a large number of interesting entrepreneurs and their campaigns.
- **Locations:** At first you may wonder why the physical location of a campaign creator is of interest. The answer to this is that many campaigns have local or regional interest. For example, a bakery that is running a campaign for a new oven is going to have considerable interest to those who live within its geographical customer base. As a reflection of its international reputation, the locations Indiegogo uses to segment campaigns are Berlin, Chicago, London, Los Angeles, New York, Montreal, Paris, San Francisco, Sydney, Toronto, and Vancouver.
- **Partners:** The last tab of the Browse categories is the partnerships that Indiegogo has arranged. Indiegogo has partnered with quite a few interesting companies.

The next tab on the top menu bar of the Indiegogo main page is titled "Learn." This is roughly similar to the "Kickstarter School" section on Kickstarter. It has sections to teach you how to crowdfund the Indiegogo way. Following are descriptions of the main sections of the Indiegogo Learn section.

Why Indiegogo?

This section is informative and a little bit promotional. The folks at Indiegogo seem to realize that there are many crowdfunding platforms for you to choose from; they explain in a nicely balanced way that theirs is a good platform with much guidance and many tools to help you with your fundraising.

ALERT

> Unlike some other crowdfunding platforms, Indiegogo processes its payments via PayPal. This requires anyone who wishes to contribute to an Indiegogo campaign to have a PayPal account. As soon as your campaign ends, all the funds are immediately released to your PayPal account. In contrast, it takes Amazon Payments up to two weeks to transfer funds.

Features

In this section, the folks at Indiegogo outline the tools and features they offer to those who wish to use their site for crowdfunding. This includes things like messaging forms, comprehensive analytics tools, and other methods to promote campaigns.

Pricing and Fees

Indiegogo outlines its fee schedule in this section. In contrast to other crowdfunding sites, Indiegogo allows you to choose from one of two fee schedules. This feature could be very important to you under certain circumstances. The two fee schedules are:

- **Flexible Funding Plan:** If you reach your goal, you pay 4 percent of the funds collected. If you don't reach your goal, you pay 9 percent of the funds you collected and you keep the remaining amount.
- **Fixed Funding Plan:** This plan is similar to the Kickstarter "all-or-nothing" plan. If you reach your goal, you pay 4 percent of the funds collected. If you don't reach your goal, no money changes hands and the campaign simply ends.

The next tab on the top menu bar of the Indiegogo main page is titled "Create." This section of the Indiegogo website is similar to other sites in the way you are taken through the process of creating a campaign.

RocketHub

RocketHub (*www.rockethub.com*) was launched in January 2010 and was founded by Brian Meece, Jed Cohen, and Vladimir Vukicevic. It is currently the third-largest crowdfunding platform on the web. RocketHub, in general, is for creative projects, which is not a big surprise because the three cofounders are themselves artists: Brian Meece is a singer-songwriter; Jed Cohen is an actor/producer; and Vladimir Vukicevic is a technologist/writer. That being said, the RocketHub website invites campaigns from a much larger universe than just the creative arts; according to the site, it welcomes "entrepreneurs, scientists, actors, artists, composers, dancers, designers, directors, educators, filmmakers, inventors, musicians, painters, philanthropists, poets, politicians, programmers, singers, songwriters, teachers, writers, and more." This is clearly a platform that embraces a wide diversity of creators and their crowdfunding campaigns.

> **FACT**
>
> RocketHub uses two unique words to describe those who participate on its site. First, the people who launch RocketHub funding projects, or upload submissions for LaunchPad Opportunities, are called "creatives." Those who support RocketHub projects and LaunchPad Opportunity submissions by making financial contributions and spreading the word are called "fuelers."

As you learn more about RocketHub, you will find it is like other crowdfunding platforms in some aspects and quite unique in others. For example, RocketHub offers two distinct services for crowdfunders. First, the site offers the ability to run crowdfunding campaigns in a more or less standard format. Like other crowdfunding sites, you can define your campaign, post videos, offer rewards, and converse with interested parties via your own individualized blog.

RocketHub also offers what you might consider a premium service: LaunchPad Opportunities. The way it works is that "creatives" submit their campaigns to the RocketHub team for approval. The RocketHub team and a panel of judges review each campaign submitted. If selected, the applicants receive direct feedback on their campaigns and ways that they can take the entire opportunity to the next level.

The RocketHub Main Page

A visit to the RocketHub main page reveals a crowdfunding platform with quite a number of things going on. The first thing to note about the main page is that it is dynamic. When watching the page you will see the center content switch every ten to fifteen seconds from "Featured Crowdfunding Projects" to "Featured LaunchPad Opportunities." This is simply a profiling of favorites by RocketHub staff in these two categories.

Regardless of the center content, near the top of the page you will be greeted with two large buttons labeled "FuelPad" (which is a formal entrance to the crowdfunding section) and "LaunchPad" (a formal entrance to the LaunchPad section of the site). On the right-hand side of the screen you will see an intriguing item, the "RocketHub Activity" sidebar. This sidebar is similar in concept to the scrolling Twitter feeds except that this one scrolls information concerning the RocketHub site activity on behalf of Creators and Fuelers. An especially unique concept is that you can see the "badges" associated with members of the RocketHub community placed next to their comments and announcements. This helps put the data feed in quick context for viewers.

ESSENTIAL

> The folks at RocketHub believe that education and empowerment are critical parts of the crowdfunding mission. The founders of RocketHub have lectured at Columbia University, General Assembly, Yale, New York University, Berklee College of Music, and other conferences and institutions. They welcome requests to speak at events about the way crowdfunding is changing the artistic, business, science, and academic worlds.

At the top of the RocketHub main page you will see a number of tabs that link you to the core content of RocketHub. There are four of them: "Explore," "Learn," "Partner," and "Success."

82

The Explore Tab

Clicking on the "Explore" button, and then on "View All Projects," will take you to a page with a number of interesting categories you can delve into. On the left-hand side of the Explore page you will find a group of links under the "Status" category. These are "Successful," "Ending Soon," and "LaunchPad Submissions." Directly under that are a series of links to some of RocketHub's larger third-party partners. The last category is where you will find a lengthy list of RocketHub's campaigns, tagged with some very colorful descriptors. Here are just a few of the RocketHub campaign categories:

- Authentic
- Courageous
- Fascinating
- Freaky
- Ingenious
- Inspirational
- Jaw-Dropping
- Mouth-Watering
- Nostalgia
- Rockin'
- Selfless
- Sexy
- Soulful
- Spine Tingling

By design, RocketHub is more than just a place for people to pop in and see what's happening (although that is perfectly okay, too). RocketHub is literally a community of passionate people who enjoy the crowdsourcing and crowdfunding experience.

The Learn Tab

Clicking on the "Learn" button will take you to a page that covers the basics of crowdfunding and the specifics of the RocketHub method. Much of this is reasonably similar to other crowdfunding platforms. In the center of the page are two large, colorful buttons that link to more expansive sections that cover "Crowdfunding" and "LaunchPad Opportunities." It is in this section that RocketHub explains the icons, or "badges," that members of the community are assigned according to participation and interests. The current badges are:

- **Mach 1, 2, and 3:** These badges are for those who have fueled (donated to) projects

- **Supernova:** For those who fuel projects after the projects have hit their funding goal
- **Spark:** Issued to the first to fuel a project
- **Apollo Engineer:** Given to those who have fueled a successful project
- **Explorer:** A badge given to those who have launched their first project
- **Wings:** A badge for creatives who have successfully fueled their first project
- **Magneto:** Issued to creatives who have attracted fifty fuelers to their project
- **Aviator:** Given to creatives who have successfully had multiple projects fueled
- **Afterburner:** For active members of the RocketHub community

The Partner Tab

The third tab located at the top of most of the RocketHub pages is titled "Partner." Clicking on this link will take you to their "Work With Us" section, which is where RocketHub's partnership programs are explained. This section reflects a significant part of the RocketHub vision. Knowing full well that fundraising is a significant part of the process for many creative organizations, RocketHub actively promotes relationships with organizations that utilize fundraising. Organizations that wish to raise funds for projects or operations know that crowdfunding is a method that works well and is being used more and more. The next step is for an organization to determine the best platform with which to raise funds, and there are a lot to choose from. Rather than wait for the organization to stumble onto RocketHub, RocketHub is proactively forging relationships. This allows mutual relationship building, which provides strong advantages to both RocketHub and its partner organizations.

The Success Tab

To the right of the "Explore" tab is the "Success" tab. Clicking on this tab reveals a small dropdown section that profiles a recently successful campaign. Underneath that is a button labeled "Launch Your Crowdfunding Project" and this is the beginning point for those who want to start a RocketHub campaign.

The RocketHub Blog

On the bottom of most of the RocketHub pages you will find a "Blog" link. The RocketHub blog is not just written by RocketHub employees; there are quite a few authors and members of the RocketHub community involved. There are several blog entries every week. Unlike other crowdfunding blogs, this one provides a huge dropdown list of blog entries that will steer you to specific content. If you are considering using RocketHub, the RocketHub blog is a place you should spend some time perusing. As is the case with other crowdfunding sites, you will find out a lot about RocketHub and how it works by reading through its blog entries. You will find opinions on projects from community members, project profiles, and a great deal of interesting commentary.

Peerbackers

Peerbackers (*www.peerbackers.com*) is another crowdfunding website where entrepreneurs can post projects and raise money to fund those projects. It was founded in 2011 by Andrew Rachmell and Sally Outlaw. Peerbackers describes itself as a community dedicated to helping entrepreneurs and innovators get the funding they need to turn a small start into a big finish. The Peerbackers website offers a more or less conventional crowdfunding platform. The site refers to those who create campaigns as "creators," and those who pledge as "backers."

Peerbackers allows you to explore projects according to status: "Closest to Goal," "Most Buzz," "Freshest," and "Ending Soon." The categories in which there are tagged projects include:

- Art/film/music
- Community
- Education/workshops
- Events
- Fashion/beauty
- Food
- Green/environmental
- Health/medical
- Internet/web apps
- Product design
- Mobile apps/gaming
- Not-for-profit
- People to people
- Retail
- Schoolit
- Services
- Technology
- Transportation
- Writing/publishing
- Wholesale
- Other

The folks at Peerbackers suggest there are three key elements that are essential for the success of Peerbackers submissions and campaigns: a passion for your idea that can be communicated easily and vividly, an existing personal network that you can use to jumpstart your backers, and a realistic funding goal that can be reached.

Similar to other crowdfunding platforms, Peerbackers does not require to fee to place a campaign on its site as the founders feel strongly that they do not want to create a financial barrier for entrepreneurs or others to use the funding platform. Instead, also similar to other sites, Peerbackers charges a 5 percent success fee on funds raised to cover its costs. Those who post their ventures are also responsible for third-party payment processing fees via PayPal (typically 2.9 percent).

Peerbackers has a partner program wherein the companies can have a "home base" to use for fundraising activities. Present partners include:

- **The Grasshopper Group:** A company that offers telecommunication solutions for crowdfunders
- **The Adams Center for Entrepreneurship:** Located at the College of Business at Florida State University
- **Act Seed:** Provides online tools for crowdfunders
- **SoMoLend:** Provides additional funding past the crowdfunding stage for entrepreneurs

Quirky

Technically, Quirky (*www.quirky.com*) isn't just about crowdfunding. However, it has an element of crowdsourcing in its business model. Located in New York City, Quirky is an industrial design company to which you can pitch your products. The company solicits ideas for new products via its website, and these ideas are voted on by Quirky members and by company staff. Products that make it through the gauntlet are designed, manufactured, and sold by Quirky. You as a creator or inventor will receive 30 percent of the revenue.

Although this technically isn't pure crowdfunding—with this company you don't control the entire process—the Quirky business model may offer you some distinct advantages. As a creative, you can concentrate on your idea and present it to the crowd for validation. If it makes it through the Quirky process and Quirky accepts your project, you can sit back and enjoy the fruits of your creative talents.

> **ESSENTIAL**
>
> In 2011, the Sundance Channel started a reality TV series called *Quirky* concerning the behind-the-scenes workings at the Quirky company. In each weekly episode, the staff at Quirky sift through the product ideas that are submitted and work with the inventors that submit them. CEO Ben Kaufman and Quirky project "ideators" are a fascinating group to watch in action, and the series enjoys a healthy viewership.

A prospective inventor can submit an idea for consideration for just $10. Every week one or two products are selected. When evaluating products, the Quirky team focuses on the utility of the product, the manufacturing difficulty, and the intellectual property rights. Quirky branded products can be found at most of the top retailers in the country, including Amazon.com; Target; Toys 'R' Us; Bed, Bath and Beyond; OfficeMax; Ace Hardware; Barnes & Noble; and ThinkGeek.com, among others.

When you visit the Quirky website you are greeted with a headline that states "The *easiest* way to bring your ideas to life." This reflects the fact that if the folks at Quirky accept your proposal and go forward, you can relax and watch as the design, manufacturing, and distribution of the product are done for you. This, of course, can be a great thing for those who enjoy the creative process but not the manufacturing and fulfillment processes.

At the top of the Quirky website are a number of links that, due to the crowdsourcing nature of Quirky, are different from most other crowdfunding-only websites.

The Shop Tab

The first tab, titled "Shop," is an online mall where you can peruse many of the products that have been created by the Quirky process. Most of the products are home- and office-related, and many are quite innovative. You will find Quirky products in the following categories:

- Latest
- Gifts
- Power
- Kitchen
- Housewares
- Bed & Bath
- Cleaning
- Organization
- Gadgets
- Back to School

The Participate Tab

The "Participate" tab takes you to a section of the website where you can do two things. First, you can join the thousands of Quirky members who help choose and provide feedback about product and idea submissions. Second, you can submit your product idea to the "crowd" and see what they think of it. For just $10, your idea is seen by thousands of evaluators over a thirty-day period. At any time during this process the staff at Quirky may flag the idea as "under consideration," which means that the staff within Quirky are looking it over in addition to the "crowd." With some luck, this may lead to your idea being accepted by Quirky as an in-house design project.

You have several options after your project is submitted to the Quirky website. At any time during the thirty-day public profiling of your idea, you can edit it. This means that you can change things not only if you think of them, but in particular, if the crowd suggests changes. You also have the option to simply drop the project completely if you feel it doesn't pass the crowd test or for any other reason.

The Upcoming Tab

When products have been accepted by Quirky and are about to launch, they are placed in the "Upcoming" section of the website. This allows you to see what products are new and also gives Quirky feedback on appropriate pricing. The way it works is that you can click on each upcoming product and a complete description and specifications are shown to you. There is also a large questionnaire box that states "At what price would you consider this product too expensive/not worth the money?" This, of course, is a perfect example of crowdsourcing the appropriate price for a product, a very clever feature that Quirky utilizes.

The Learn Tab

Quirky has a great educational section on its website. There is a graphic that explains how the "socially developed product process" works, an elaborate FAQ section, a best practices section, and even a comprehensive section of how-to videos.

The Blog Tab

Quirky has a very nicely designed blog titled "Invention, Inspiration, and What We're Up To." You will find all sorts of small articles written by the folks at Quirky broken down into the following categories: "All News," "Apple," "Video," "Community," "Products," and "Events."

CHAPTER 7

The Keys to a Successful Campaign

It's easy to think that there are lots of crowdfunding dollars out there just waiting to be plucked from the crowdfunding money tree. Just visit any crowdfunding site and you will be treated to a panorama of exciting projects appearing to be just sitting there gathering up copious funding. It sure looks easy, doesn't it? What you don't generally see, however, are the campaigns that didn't do so well, and there are plenty of them, too. The figure varies from site to site, but over 50 percent of crowdfunding campaigns are unsuccessful and fail to reach their funding goal. This chapter will examine some of the things you can do to make sure your campaign ends up in the "funded" category.

Choose the Right Crowdfunding Site

Despite appearances, not all crowdfunding sites are created equal. It's best to match your crowdfunding project and your vision to the most appropriate crowdfunding platform. Fortunately this isn't very hard to do, because the platforms generally let you know right up front what kind of projects they are looking for.

The site receiving most of the recent buzz is Kickstarter. The problem is that Kickstarter is not a broad-based crowdfunding platform. Kickstarter may seem like a site for just about everything, but it really isn't. As mentioned before, the guidelines specifically state it wants creative projects only. In particular, Kickstarter is looking for projects that are creatively unique and have a well-defined beginning and end. If you have a project that is charity based or personal-need based, or a project to launch a business, Kickstarter will almost certainly reject it.

> **FACT**
>
> Most of the crowdfunding websites request that you submit a proposal of your crowdfunding project before it is accepted. Don't be overly concerned if it is rejected the first time around. This is actually quite common. Usually the site will ask you to change a few things or clarify a few points before it meets the staff's criteria, and then you may get the green light.

Don't despair, though—regardless of what you are thinking of raising funds for, there is a crowdfunding site for you. There are sites that accept virtually all projects, there are sites just for creative projects, there are sites for locally based projects and there are sites specifically for starting businesses. It is beyond the scope of this book to list every crowdfunding site out there and their funding foci, but here are a few representative ones, some of which we have examined already:

- **Kickstarter:** For creative projects only; must be based in the United States
- **Indiegogo:** Open to all projects (some subjects are prohibited)
- **RocketHub:** Open to all projects (some subjects are prohibited)

- **StartSomeGood:** Open to all projects designed for social good; can be internationally based
- **Lucky Ant:** Open to all hyper-local projects; must be locally based
- **Appbackr:** Open to software application design projects
- **Wefunder:** A crowdfunding website gearing up for equity crowdfunding
- **NewJelly:** A crowdfunding site for artists
- **Cofolio:** A crowdfunding website to help fund local small businesses
- **Peerbackers:** A crowdfunding site for entrepreneurs "and their dreams"

To find the best site for your campaign you just need to do some research. Visit the popular crowdfunding sites and take a look at their criteria. Look at the current projects to see if any appear to overlap your project. You will also find blogs and commentary about the sites out there that can provide you with some guidance.

Craft a Passionate Pitch

Extremely successful crowdfunding campaigns are driven by passionate pitches. If you want to prove this for yourself, visit several of the popular crowdfunding sites, search on "most successful," and take a look at some of the videos you see there. You will be treated to creative and exciting videos featuring people with a real passion for what they are doing. You, of course, want to do the same. You want to convince your audience that what you are doing is meaningful and that you need their help to bring it to fruition. The most successful pitches have a few things in common.

Tell a Great Story

Some say the golden rule of sales is that "a great pitch is a great story." A great story has a beginning, middle, and an end. Craft your pitch to have a logical story flow to it with the end, of course, being the project brought to reality by successful funding.

Highlight the Unique Aspect of Your Project

While there are many aspects to a successful crowdfunding campaign, to many backers an exciting idea is the core reason for contributing. You need to illustrate in definitive ways how unique and important your project is. For example, if you are raising funds to make a video about the homeless in Chicago, explain why it is critical that this video be made; for example, "By showing the struggles of these homeless families and individuals, real social change can occur."

> **ALERT**
>
> When you craft your pitch, both in your video and in the text, be sure to ask your audience to pledge! That may seem obvious, but many crowdfunders do this halfheartedly. Make sure the viewers know that in order to make your vision become reality, they must become backers and join the cause!

Pitch Yourself

Not only do you want to sell your project and campaign to your audience; you want to sell yourself and your team. Explain why you are uniquely qualified to bring your vision to life. Use your background, your team's background, and any other resources you possess to explain that your project is unique to your team and, with their help, you are going to pull it off!

Establish a Sense of Urgency

You need to build a strong call to action by creating a sense of urgency for your campaign funding. If the sense of urgency isn't communicated right up front, backers may want to "think about it" and come back later. Always remember that "later" often never occurs if your potential backer's motivation and emotions are allowed to cool down. This is one of the reasons why thirty-day crowdfunding campaigns may be the best ones. Thirty days is a short period of time, and many backers will pledge quickly so they don't miss the opportunity.

Establish the Bigger Picture

In many cases, projects can have a big-picture view. In the previous example of a documentary concerning the homeless in Chicago, convince your audience that by pledging to your crowdfunding campaign they can help change lives and indeed, help change the world by shedding light on this pervasive issue. This is the passion that gets campaigns funded.

A Good Campaign Video

Statistics from crowdfunding campaigns point out two things about campaign videos. The first is that you have to have one, plain and simple. The second is that you do not necessarily need to hire a professional cinematographer to make yours. Chances are you are perfectly capable of making your own video.

Let's examine the "mandatory video" part first. All the major crowdfunding sites have statistics unequivocally illustrating the fact that campaigns with videos are over 100 percent more successful than those without. Consider it a given that you want to promote your campaign with a video. Videos are especially effective ways to not only communicate information about your campaign, but also to communicate information about you. People who donate to crowdfunding campaigns often do so because they want to see not just the project succeed; they want you, the creator, to succeed. This is a wonderful human behavior you are tapping into—empathy from the crowd. Believe it or not, there are potentially a lot of people who want to see you succeed, and they will help you out.

> **ESSENTIAL**
>
> When crafting your campaign video, keep the special effects to a minimum. Most editing programs today are laden with special effects like flying text, spinning transitions, chroma-keying, and lots of other fun video stuff. However, these effects are unlikely to impress your audience because they add little to the content of your video pitch. In most cases, simple fade transitions and minimal title animations make for a much more effective campaign video.

The second issue involves the quality of the video. Don't be overly concerned about the "professional" aspect of your video. Most crowdfunding videos are reasonably well produced, but often the more homespun videos made by the project creators themselves are as effective.

So, how do you decide how professional your video needs to be? As a general rule of thumb, if you are trying to raise funds for an artistic project, you probably should consider a more professionally made video. Your audience, after all, may be a little concerned if you are pitching a documentary film and your campaign video is shaky and out of focus. However, if you are pitching something more technology oriented, your potential donors may be more interested in your description of the project and what you are like as an inventor than the quality of the video.

A Proper Funding Goal

Every crowdfunding project has a funding goal. With crowdfunding platforms that use "all or nothing" funding, establishing your funding goal is an important decision. If you set your funding goal too high, you may not collect enough backers to meet your goal. When this happens, the campaign simply ends and no money changes hands. If you set your goal too low, there are other issues. Let's take a look at both of these scenarios in order to give you a framework to use as you establish your funding goal.

> **FACT**
>
> There are two general methods used in campaign funding: all-or-nothing funding or flexible funding. All-or-nothing funding means that you set a financial goal for your campaign and unless the goal is reached, no money is exchanged. In other words, your backers' credit cards are not charged when they pledge; they are "held on reserve" until you meet the funding goal. If you don't reach that goal, the cards are not charged and the campaign simply ends. With flexible funding, a goal is usually stated but the backers *are* charged at the time they pledge.

Funding Goals Set Too Low

It is tempting to set a funding goal too low because you think it would be easier for backers to reach the goal, which may encourage early pledging. Also, you may think it will seem like you are "greedy" if you set your funding goal too high, and this too may cause you to set a lower goal. Both of these conclusions can get you into trouble.

First, backers rarely look at a funding goal and draw conclusions from it. It is true that it may seem to be a stretch to meet a very high funding goal set on an all-or-nothing funding platform, but feedback from backers concludes that most are far more concerned with the project, the person behind it, and the rewards than the probability of reaching the goal. Frankly, if the project is exciting enough, most feel that additional backers are going to flood in and the goal will eventually be reached anyway. This is especially true if your backers feel compelled to go out and spread the word to assure that the goal is met.

The same applies to the idea that a higher goal may make you seem "greedy." Common sense says that creators need to collect enough money to not only create the project and deliver the rewards but also to cover hidden expenses and any additional costs they may incur. For example, consider a project such as making a documentary DVD. The probability that a filmmaker will run into unforeseen expenses during the filming is close to 100 percent. A car might break down, an extra lunch for the crew may be necessary, or an extra camera might be needed. These are the unknowns that can add money to your project's creative budget quickly. You need to build these contingencies into your budget. This is not being "greedy."

ESSENTIAL

Many crowdfunders find that establishing a funding goal is the hardest part of developing a campaign. Do your research. Look at a number of finished campaigns that are similar or in the same subject category as yours. The number of backers they obtained and the reward levels they offered can help guide you with your decision.

Funding Goals Set Too High

The main issue with setting your goal too high is simply that you may not reach your goal. Regardless of how exciting your project is and the people involved, you may not get enough backers to make your project become a reality. With an all-or-nothing funding situation, this means the project just comes to a finish and no money changes hands. The project creator then, depending on the crowdfunding site being used, may have the option of relaunching with a lower goal. However, when projects are relaunched (usually with lower goals), they may carry a certain stigma and fail to regain their original momentum. It is hard to say why this is, but it seems that backers may draw a conclusion that something isn't "what it seems" and thus fail to pledge again. The bottom line is that you would like to avoid running the same crowdfunding project twice.

Setting Your Funding Goal Properly

So what is the best funding goal? This is a tough question, but many feel it is best to set it at the lowest level at which you can be reasonably assured that you can deliver on your rewards. Then you will have a sort of "break-even" point established. Estimate what it will actually take to complete your project, *factoring in all possible extra expenses that might occur.* Is this worst-case approach necessary? Feedback from crowdfunders across multiple crowdfunding sites suggests that many did not build enough cushion into their funding goals and when they hit snags, they didn't have the money to overcome them. Make sure you set a conservative break-even goal.

A good way to double-check your funding goal is to look at similar crowdfunding projects and roughly gauge how many backers were attracted to them. Using this number and the cost of your rewards will help you calculate what a reasonable breakeven would be for your campaign. Of course, no two crowdfunding projects are the same, but try to find a few that are as reasonably close to yours as possible.

An Effective Reward Structure

The reason that people pledge to crowdfunding campaigns is not solely to "get stuff" but to participate in the creation of something new and exciting. While they are happy to receive campaign rewards, especially if the rewards are a sample of the project itself, backers often are just as excited to be part of the process. There is a sense of community among those who help bring crowdfunding projects to life.

That being said, many backers will look at your crowdfunding campaign and its reward structure with a retail mindset. It's unavoidable. For example, a DVD of a recently released movie that sells for $2 is a considered a

Chapter 7: The Keys to a Successful Campaign

bargain, but the same DVD selling for $200 is not. This sort of value judgment becomes almost hard-wired into people. Accordingly, it is best to keep a loosely based retail framework in mind when you design your reward structure and pricing, even though in many cases you are making things that are absolutely unique.

Offer Your Rewards in Multiple Tiers

The retail giant Sears hasn't offered products in a "Good, Better, Best" format for more than 120 years just because it sounds like a nice slogan. The offering of incrementally priced tiers correlated with increasingly attractive features is a retail concept that simply works. Perhaps it's just retail conditioning or perhaps it taps into something deeper, but this structure permeates most retail pricing strategies. Use this structure when you design your reward structure.

Offer simple rewards in the lower-priced tiers and increasingly more attractive rewards as the tiers increase in price. Separate the tiers with comfortable price margins. For example, don't offer two tiers at close to the same price unless they are essentially the same reward with a minor change, say in color or some other minor customization.

ESSENTIAL

> For your upper-priced tiers, you don't necessarily need to offer exotic product features or tangible items at all. Many crowdfunders offer special experiences as their highest-tier rewards. For example, musicians may offer to write songs specifically for their upper-tier backers, or filmmakers may put the names of their backers into the credits of their film productions as "executive producers."

For the top tier levels, you may want to offer something very unique and exclusive. Here's an example: Robert Noble Sack is an artist who executed a crowdfunding campaign on Kickstarter during the summer of 2012 for handmade ceramic "Garden Gorillas." He designed his tiers like this:

- $10   8.5" × 11" Garden Gorilla Print
- $25   Garden Gorilla T-Shirt

99

- $120 12" Fired ceramic Garden Gorilla (brown or black)
- $135 12" Fired ceramic Garden Gorilla (blue or green)
- $150 Custom-engraved 12" fired ceramic Garden Gorilla (brown or black)
- $165 Custom-engraved 12" fired ceramic Garden Gorilla (blue or green)
- $250 Custom-engraved 12" fired ceramic Garden Gorilla with fine detailed hair (brown or black)

The value that his backers receive increases as the tier level increases. His most expensive tier was an exclusive item: a custom-engraved Garden Gorilla with extra details.

Some backers are especially interested in unique experiences. If you spend some time looking over the top-tier rewards on any of the crowdfunding sites, you will see some very interesting rewards. Filmmakers may offer a dinner with the cast and crew of their video project; some comic book writers will put you in the plot of their stories as a character; and many artists will incorporate you into their visual media project. By all means, consider offering a top "experiential" tier. They are unusually popular and can provide you with substantial additional funding.

Offer Your Rewards in the Most Popular Price Tiers

Kickstarter recently released some statistics that show the popularity of various tier pricings on its site. The most popular tier price on Kickstarter is $25, with 18.41 percent of all backers choosing this option. It therefore would make a great deal of sense to offer pricing for your rewards centered around this $25 range, if you can, with some of your tiers below this price and some of your tiers above. After the $25 level, the next most popular pledge levels are:

- $50: 13.57 percent of total backers pledged
- $10: 12.12 percent of total backers pledged
- $100: 9.52 percent of total backers pledged
- $20: 8.41 percent of total backers pledged
- $5: 6.37 percent of total backers pledged
- $30: 4.22 percent of total backers pledged

A Comprehensive Outreach Plan

Many beginning crowdfunders believe that simply putting a well-designed campaign with attractive rewards on a crowdfunding site is all they need for crowdfunding success. Some people think that crowdfunding sites are swarming with people who just love to fund things. Well, this is not the case. There are a lot of people who visit crowdfunding sites to see what's new and interesting, but few go there with the intention of "spending money." They go there to look around. Crowdfunding campaigns are successful because people are driven to the site from other sites around the Internet. This occurs because of mentions and recommendations on social media, public relations efforts, and other endorsements.

It's critical that you have an outreach plan in place before you start your campaign. This cannot be stated strongly enough. You should identify the media that you wish to engage and have a plan for how to do it. In fact, you should have this all in place before you actually begin your campaign. Why? Because most campaigns are generally thirty to sixty days in length, and the time seems to go pretty quickly. Chances are you won't have time to assemble an outreach campaign during your crowdfunding campaign because you will be too busy. Do it beforehand! Here are just a few of the techniques that you will want to consider:

- Announcements on social media such as Facebook, Twitter, YouTube, and others
- Press releases to appropriate blogs, microblogs, and other online organizations
- Postings on social news services such as Reddit, Digg, StumbleUpon, and others
- Pay-per-click (Google AdWords) campaigns

Assembling a strong outreach campaign before you launch your crowdfunding campaign will ensure that some activity and pledging will occur immediately after launch, which will in turn encourage further pledges. This is a well-known human behavior; when people see that others have an interest in something, they will pause to take a closer look. Tom Dawkins from StartSomeGood explains it by asking a question: When was the last time you saw a street musician's donation bag or hat without a handful of change or bills in it? Chances are you never have, because street musicians understand this behavior well. They make sure to put some money in the hat themselves because it validates that what they do is worthy of your donation.

Your Campaign's Duration

Wouldn't it seem that the longer you run your campaign, the more money you would collect? After all, it takes a while for the word to get around and for backers to visit. Yes, it usually would seem that a longer period of time is better—but not when it comes to crowdfunding campaigns. Believe it or not, the duration of a campaign has little to do with how it performs. It seems counterintuitive, but statistics bear this out.

When the folks at Kickstarter plotted pledges versus the duration of various crowdfunding campaigns, they found that all of the campaigns start off rather strong; hit a "trough," when interest and pledges slack off; and then pick up at the end. It would appear that when a project launches, the creator is actively spreading the word and hopefully engaging an outreach plan full force. Then, after a period of time, the project settles into a more normal rhythm. At the end, the creator and the existing backers start beating the drums again to drive the project above the funding goal.

Additional Keys to Success

Of course, there are many facets of a crowdfunding campaign that contribute to its success. As crowdfunding becomes more mainstream, there will be more statistics and information available to provide guidance. An especially good way to assemble the factors of success for your crowdfunding campaign is to visit a number of crowdfunding websites and read through their educational materials and blogs. This is where the most recent statistics are. You should look for external blogs and collect opinions from knowledgeable crowdfunders posting on those as well.

CHAPTER 8

Using Social Media for Crowdfunding and Business

For virtually every business, utilizing social media is not an option, it is a necessity. Social media allows your business to get involved in interactive conversations concerning your business, your brand, and your customers. By doing so, you'll acquire new customers and retain existing ones. Also, chances are very good your competitors are online already, and you can't afford to be left behind.

If you're new to using social media for business, you're not alone. However, if you are about to raise funds via the Internet or crowdfunding, you need to establish an online presence as soon as you can. Social media must be an integral part of your campaign's outreach and donor acquisition plan.

What Is Social Media?

Most definitions of social media are somewhat academic. This one is from Wikipedia: "Social media includes web-based and mobile-based technologies which are used to turn communication into interactive dialogue among organizations, communities, and individuals." While this definition is technically correct, it lacks direct meaning. Here is an alternate, more simplistic definition, suggested by the author: "Regular media is like a one-way street where information flows from content creators direct to the consumer. Social media, however, is like a two-way street where you can engage in an interactive dialogue with customers, fans, and those that are interested in what you do."

FACT

A recent Nielsen study revealed that 14 percent of consumers trust standard advertisements, whether online or via traditional media, versus a 78 percent trust of peer recommendations. This is an especially powerful aspect of social media. Besides social media's wide reach, the effect of peer recommendations is tremendously effective when endorsing products, services, brands, and companies.

What Can You Do with Social Media?

If you are new to using social media for business, it is easy to get intimidated with all the jargon and concepts involved. In fact, some small business owners are so put off that they resist getting involved. This is a mistake because social media can do some wonderful things for your business. You will be able to:

- Spread your content and expertise to a new audience
- Build a community of people who will act as evangelists for your company and products
- Reach new customers in the channels they use to communicate
- Involve your customers and prospects in product definition and design

- Be seen as a knowledgeable leader in your industry
- Hear what's being said online about your brand, products, or business

Needless to say, these are all things that business owners will find attractive. The question is, how do you jump on board quickly when the whole process seems so complex and the landscape is covered with social media platforms? The answer is that you need to have a social media strategy.

Your Social Media Strategy

There are many ways to integrate social media into your business or to use it when crowdfunding. At first it's tempting to think that you have to exploit all facets of social media because it's all good for your business or crowdfunding campaign. While this approach will yield results, it is best to look at each platform and define specific goals that you would like to achieve. As you will discover through reading and research, all the platforms are different and can help you achieve different goals. To make sense of all the options, most professionals suggest that you craft a social media strategy that makes sense for you and your enterprise. This cuts down on experimentation and lays out a pragmatic framework that you can follow. Determining the best strategy will take a little bit of work and time, but will result in a plan that's tailored to your goals.

ALERT

> Unless you have a lot of friends, employees, or acquaintances to constantly monitor your social media, don't jump onto every social media platform you can find. Many of those that frequent social media are criticizing companies that establish broad social media strategies and don't have the resources to take care of them. Remember that these are interactive forums and if no one answers questions and concerns, it may seem that your business doesn't care.

The remainder of this chapter will quickly review the major social media platforms and a few of the options that you may want to include in your social media strategy. You might want to consider this a good starting point for your social media education if you are new to the topic. The web, of course, contains a multitude of other resources to continue your education.

Starting a Website

If you are considering fundraising or crowdfunding you may want to have a website "home" on the Internet. When people read about you or see links, they are going to want to click through to your website to see what you are all about. For businesses, however, having a website is essentially mandatory. Existing customers, potential customers, and everyone else will expect to see one. For those that are "website homeless," here are the basics to get up and running.

Get a Domain Name

If you don't have one, the first thing you need is a domain name. A domain name is the name you want to give to your website. For example, the domain name for Adams Media, the publisher of this *Everything® Guide to Crowdfunding*, is *www.adamsmedia.com*. To get a domain name, you need to find a domain name registrar, choose the domain name that you would like to have and then pay an annual fee. Fees are generally $8–$12 per year and there are dozens of registrars that you can choose from.

ESSENTIAL

If you are looking for your first domain name, you will quickly find out that most common names are taken. Registration of domain names started in 1995, and companies jumped in quickly to secure the "good" names. Don't despair, however, if you find that all the names you would like are already taken. Use some creativity and get a name that is unusual or is a series of words. There are several sites on the Net that will help you choose unusual domain names.

Choose a Web Host

A web host is basically a company that has many "servers" (computers) connected to the Internet. When you sign up for an account on a web host, you are basically purchasing a spot on one of the servers that you store your web pages on. This allows anyone in the world to be able to connect and interact with them. Today, most web hosting companies are very affordable, often $5–$10 per month to host your website. A few of the larger web hosts are:

- GoDaddy
- 1and1
- HostGator
- Bluehost
- HostMonster

> **ALERT**
>
> **What is the most important thing to look for in a web host?**
> There are hundreds of web hosting companies and many of their hosting plans are similar. If you aren't a web design professional, there is one primary thing to look for, however, when choosing a host: how you contact their customer support. The best companies offer not only FAQs and e-mail support, but actual phone call support. This can make a huge difference.

Design Your Website

Once you have secured your domain name and web host, the next step is to design your website. You have a couple of choices; you can design your website yourself or you can get a professional to do it for you. The advantage of using a professional is that you will get a nice-looking website up and running quickly. The downside is that it will cost you some money. Doing it yourself offers the advantage of little or no cost, but it will take you time to learn how to make and troubleshoot your site.

eV FACT

> Many of the web hosting companies offer "template sites" that you can customize yourself online. These sites do not require any knowledge of website programming (HTML, PHP, Java, etc.), as it is all done for you. All you have to do is pick a design you like, click on various dialogue windows, and insert text and images. In many cases these sites are perfectly acceptable for small businesses, and they allow you to be up and running quickly, usually within hours.

Test Your Website

It may seem redundant to have a separate heading for testing your website. Isn't this done during the design cycle? Well, yes it is, but many new webmasters neglect to test their new website on all the major browsers. Once you get your website up and running, be sure that your website behaves well on the following browsers:

- Internet Explorer
- Google Chrome
- Firefox
- Opera
- Safari

In general, be sure to load your entire website and see if there are any problems with graphics and page-loading issues. Not all browsers act the same but you don't want any outlandish problems occurring. If you do discover something problematic, you can often find out what the problem is by describing the problem in a Google search. Again, this is a good reason to get a professional web designer involved; that person will be able to do all this testing and can save the small business owner a lot of trouble and time.

E-Commerce

If you are selling products or services, you will need some way to collect money. In the old days of the Internet you had to sign up with expensive third-party credit card processing companies that were integrated with web design firms. Today things are far simpler. There are plenty of companies that will allow you to process credit cards and accept other forms of payment right on your site. Here are five of the major credit card and payment processing companies:

- Amazon Payments (*https://payments.amazon.com/sdui/sdui/index.htm*)
- PayPal (*www.paypal.com*)
- Authorize.Net (*www.authorize.net*)
- VeriSign (*www.verisign.com*)
- IntelliPay (*www.intellipay.com*)

Blogs

"Blog" is a shortened version of "weblog," a term used for unique websites that maintain ongoing discussions and a chronicle of digital information. A blog is generally a personal website featuring diary-type information within a visually pleasing format that reflects the owner of the blog and his or her personality. You can find blogs on virtually any topic, and some boast very large communities of readers. Generally speaking, all blogs tend to have a few things in common:

- A main content area with articles listed chronologically, newest on top
- An archive of older articles often arranged in a tree structure for searching
- A message box for people to comment on the articles
- A list of links to other related sites, sometimes referred to as a blogroll
- One or more RSS news feeds

On a blog, the content consists of posts or entries that the author writes. Some blogs have multiple authors, each writing his or her own articles. Blog owners can easily invite others to contribute to their blog. Typically, blog authors compose their articles in a web-based interface built into the blogging system itself. Here are several ways that blogs can assist your social media business presence:

- Position your company as an expert source of information
- Develop a new communication channel with customers

- Allow a forum for "thoughts" such as new products, philosophies, and commentary
- Help enhance the visibility and presence of your business amongst the competition

ESSENTIAL

One of the very strong side benefits of having a business blog involves Search Engine Optimization (SEO). SEO is the process whereby search engines rank websites according to content. Websites with more "relevant" content are ranked higher on a search engine page. As it turns out, search engines take blogs into high consideration when determining search results ranking. This means that having a good strong blog with lots of links and articles will improve your visibility when people are searching for the things that your company does.

Facebook

Few people on the Internet fail to recognize the importance of being on Facebook. Along with Twitter, Facebook is a major social networking site and a "must be on" for all businesses. Today the statistics concerning Facebook usage almost defy imagination. At the end of March 2012, Facebook had 901 million monthly users with 526 million users active every single day. During the beginning of 2012, 300 million photos were uploaded to Facebook every day and the platform currently tabulates 125 billion friend connections.

Unless you have a real good reason not to (and there are very few reasons not to), you really have to have a Facebook page for your business. If you don't, it sends a "what's up with that" signal to anyone visiting your website or your crowdfunding campaign. Here are a few things that every small business and those who are crowdfunding should consider doing on Facebook.

Create a Fan Page

Most businesses today have Facebook fan pages. It should be your central point for business on Facebook. On your fan page, you can interact with customers, make announcements, post images and updates, and launch new products and services. With a little work and some time, your Facebook fan page will become a robust community that will provide you new customers, support existing ones, and provide you valuable feedback on your products and services.

FACT Facebook offers you "Facebook Insights," a built-in analytics package that you can use to analyze your fan page. Facebook's analytics will help assess the performance of your page and tell you what content resonates the best with your audience. You can view metrics such as the total "likes" your page has collected, the number of unique friends your fans have, and the total reach of your page. This information is valuable and can help guide your business strategy.

Add a "Like" Button

When Facebook users click the "Like" button on your Facebook page, all their friends will be notified of the "Like" and the effect is almost viral. Definitely encourage people to "like" your product, brand, or crowdfunding campaign and you may see a great deal of traffic back to your site from those who want to see what the originator found of interest.

Create Facebook Ads

Although they aren't free, Facebook ads can be very effective ways to advertise your business, and you can easily set them up yourself. On the right-hand side of your news feed, you will find a button labeled "Create an Ad." After you define your ad, you can instruct Facebook to send it to an external URL or to your Facebook page. The last steps allow you to define your target audience and set your advertising budget. For many small businesses, Facebook ads may not be in the budget, but you should know they are available. If at all possible, you may want to try a few trial ads to see how they work out.

Add a "Subscribe" Button

If you have a profile page on Facebook, you can place a "Subscribe" button on other pages, such as your fan page and other website pages. One main benefit of the Subscribe button is that it allows other users to receive the public status updates of your profile page in their news feed. This occurs without having to be "friends" with them. This is very similar to Twitter's "Follow" button, which allows users to see the news feed of those they are following.

Twitter

Twitter, the second biggest social networking site on the Internet, describes itself as "a service for friends, family, and coworkers to communicate and stay connected through the exchange of quick, frequent answers to one simple question: What are you doing?" While that may be a great definition, it might be easier to just think of Twitter as a new form of online communication that occurs in 140 characters or less. Not only does Twitter present communication in a new shape—quite literally, because users have developed a lot of interesting shorthand and special characters to deal with the character limitation—it's also a platform for listening to the communication of others in new ways.

Here's a quick overview of Twitter: Every tweet has a username or handle (preceded by the @ symbol) and a maximum of 140 characters of text. To share a message with people "following" you, type your message and click the "Tweet" button. If you want to forward a tweet that you received to your followers, click "Retweet." Here are a few best practices that small businesses should consider when using Twitter.

Define Your Goals

Twitter is a quirky sort of communication tool that allows you to communicate easily with other Twitter users, but it may not be the best site to mine for customers. It is more powerful to join or establish communities that exchange information. Once you become an established member of a community, followers will be more interested in finding out about your business.

Set Up a Business Page

For those who do decide to use Twitter as part of their social media plan, it's best to set up a business page. Twitter makes this easy to do with a well-designed page design interface that allows easy customization. When finished, your business page will provide a nice attractive location for those who want to see what your business is about.

Build a Good Community

Like the other forms of social media, on Twitter you are generating content and people are following you to see what is going on and usually comment and interact with you. The key to making this really effective is to have interesting and influential people following you. If you can achieve that, your community will take on a vibrancy that serves everyone well. Establishing a great community takes some effort on your part, but the result is worthwhile. Start by searching for interesting, relevant users in the Twitterverse and then sign up to follow them. When you retweet those users' content to your membership, those users will likely follow you at some point and become members of your community. Over time you'll find that you need to purge some followers because they're using Twitter to send spam, offer adult content, and other such things. Twitter allows you to block, report, or simply delete such users. Doing this periodically will make your community more desirable.

> **ALERT**
>
> Communications on Twitter are best when they occur in real time. Unlike other social media platforms, Twitter communications can seem like a direct line between people. The difference between a rapid response to tweeting and a delayed one can be huge. This means that in a larger company you may want to designate several employees as "Tweeters." It can keep the information flow more instantaneous and responsive.

LinkedIn

LinkedIn is a social network for professionals. With more than 160 million users (as of March 2012), the platform is favored by professionals around the world, including job seekers, human resource departments, sales, business development, and professionals of every sort. LinkedIn counts executives from all 2011 *Fortune* 500 companies as members and its corporate hiring platform is used by 82 of the *Fortune* 100 companies.

You should consider having a company page on LinkedIn or, at a minimum, personal pages for executives and company staff. Being on LinkedIn makes your business and staff look professional. Following are a few things that businesses should consider doing on LinkedIn.

Create a Company Page

Once you sign into LinkedIn, you will find a tab on the toolbar labeled "Companies." From here you can click on "Add a Company" and add your business information. When people search for your company or your staff, the search engine on LinkedIn will connect them to your company page and staff pages.

Create a Products/Services Tab

Once you have your company page established, you can place write ups for your products and services, and LinkedIn members can share and recommend them. LinkedIn also allows you to create a banner of images in slideshow format at the top of each page.

Link to It

Put links to your LinkedIn page in your e-mail signature and other online pages. These links can lead to your other social media, a blog, or other relevant sites.

Google+

Launched June 28, 2011, Google+ is a social network operated by Google, Inc., that integrates across a number of Google products, including Google Buzz and Google Profiles. One key element of the Google+ platform is a focus on sharing within subgroups of your main social group. Google calls these subgroups "Circles." Circles are simply small groups of people you can share with, each with familiar names like "friends," "family," and "coworkers."

Google has also created a section within Google+ specifically for viewing, organizing, and editing multimedia. The photo tab in this section takes a user to all of the photos she has shared with others in addition to the ones in which the user is tagged (where a mouse-over of a person's picture reveals a link to their profile page). This section is not just for photo tagging, however; Google+ includes an image editor, complete with photo effects, and various privacy and sharing options. Following are several things you can do to utilize Google+ in your business.

ALERT

> Google+ offers a tremendous amount of value for a social networking platform, but some businesses are reluctant to add it to their social marketing mix. They argue that they maintain highly engaged audiences on Facebook and Twitter and find only a small number of their customers are on Google+. This will undoubtedly change as Google+ becomes more familiar to users and is integrated into more of the social dashboard applications.

Create a Google+ Page

Google allows you to create a large variety of theme-based Google+ pages. Like most Google products, the interface is clean and easy to understand. Like other profile pages, it will ask you to post a profile photo, a tag line, and bio information.

Start a Hangout

Another interesting feature Google+ offers is called "Hangouts." This is Google's new inter-group chat feature. Here's how it works: A user clicks "start a hangout" and then shows up in an empty chat room. At the same time, a message goes out to others in the user's circles that their buddy is "hanging out" and they are invited to join the video conversation.

Google Hangouts gives you a perfect way to engage your customers and get personal with them in an intimate setting. Try hosting a hangout with certain customers once a week. It's likely that you will establish a terrific bond with those who participate.

Affiliate Marketing

Once you understand affiliate marketing, you will find you better understand the way the Internet behaves. Affiliate marketing is everywhere on the Internet, and whenever you search for things, particularly products and services, you are going to bump into it.

How Affiliate Marketing Works

When you use a search engine to look for a product or a service, the results are likely to include links that take you to special pages where the product will be discussed. These are landing pages that are designed by affiliate marketers who are trying to lead you toward a merchant with whom they have a business arrangement. Here's an example: Type "Sony Camcorder" into a search engine. You will find not only links to Sony and authorized Sony merchants, but also links to websites with names like sonyreview.com, comparecamcorders.com, and so on. Those last two links are landing pages designed by affiliate marketers that are offering you value-added information about Sony camcorders and a link back to a merchant (a Sony dealer) in the hope that you will click through and then purchase a camcorder. When this occurs, the owner of the landing page, an affiliate marketer, gets paid a percentage of the sale.

Perhaps the best way to visualize affiliate marketing is that for an Internet merchant, it is like "outsourcing" your sales staff. Instead of having people that work within your organization performing sales functions, you hire "affiliates" to do it for you. For some product categories, it works very well.

Getting Started with Affiliate Marketing

Getting up and running with affiliate marketing is relatively easy. There are companies called "Affiliate Networks" that handle most everything for you. These companies oversee most of the affiliate process; they help with the link structure, track sales, and distribute commissions. The top two affiliate networks are Commission Junction and LinkShare. Others are ShareASale, PepperJam, and Google Affiliate Network (GAN).

Websites or merchants that accept affiliates usually say so on their homepage. Often this is down on the bottom navigation bar where you will see a link that says "Affiliate Programs" or something similar. Most merchants will already be signed up with one of the third-party affiliate network companies, but some do it in-house themselves.

Learning the Ropes

There are plenty of resources on the web to help you learn about affiliate marketing. One of the best is a forum called ABestWeb (www.abestweb.com). With 60,000 members, ABestWeb is the world's largest affiliate marketing forum. Not only you can find information on everything affiliate there; several successful affiliate mentors will share information with you as well. James Martell is one who shares his expertise via free downloadable eBooks and on his blog. In addition, by executing a Google search, you will find many others that share valuable insights into affiliate marketing.

Reddit

Reddit is a social news site where users determine what news becomes the highest ranked or most visible on the site. The way it works is that registered users submit links or text about anything that they feel might be of interest to other users. After posting, other users on the site vote the submission "up" or "down" and their voting determines the post's position on the Reddit pages. Basically the "crowd" determines what news they want to display, not only to themselves but to the world at large.

Like other social media, communities form around certain topics on Reddit. The members of these communities, sometimes referred to as "redditors," customize the content that appears on the front page of their individual "subreddit" communities. The rank of submissions within these subreddit groups is determined by the ratio of the up votes to down votes factored by the total vote count. Because this process is dynamic and ongoing, each day submissions cycle through the front pages of the subreddit pages. Note that users, in addition to voting up and down, can also comment on other user submissions, and Reddit also allows the comments themselves to be up-voted or down-voted.

FACT

Secret Santa goes viral! In 2009, users on Reddit started the largest Secret Santa program in the world, which still operates today. For the 2010 holiday season, 92 countries were involved in the Secret Santa program. There were 17,543 participants, and $662,907.60 in gifts were exchanged between absolute strangers.

Reddit is known for its large and diverse user community. According to the Reddit blog, more than 2 billion page views were served up in December 2011. Because of an enormous user base, the site now supports subreddits that serve as content niches for just about anything you can imagine. In fact, the Reddit blog claims that there are active subreddits for almost every city, university, TV show, video game, sports team, image choices, flavor of politics, and even every world problem. For those who are fundraising or crowdfunding, locating a subreddit via the Reddit search function that would be interested in what you are doing would be time very well spent.

Managing the Social Media Beast

Are you overwhelmed yet? One of hardest challenges for people jumping into the world of social media is to determine how to accomplish the seemingly endless tasks that social media presents. The best way to approach this is to create a formal social media strategy and then, after all the social media platforms are set up, have a daily and weekly checklist. Of course, every business's checklist will be different because no one company is going to have the exact same social media strategy as another. However, by developing a reasonable checklist based on your individual strategy, you will be able to tame the sometimes unruly social media beast.

John Jantsch, author of *Duct Tape Marketing: The World's Most Practical Small Business Marketing Guide*, suggests that you break your social media "to-do" list down into specific tasks that are performed twice daily, daily, and weekly. By doing this you can make your social media job easier to understand and perform.

CHAPTER 9

Pay Per Click and Crowdfunding

Pay-per-click (PPC) advertising refers to an Internet advertising model that is used to direct traffic to websites. It is remarkably attractive because advertisers are only charged when potential customers "click through" to their websites. Google AdWords is the most popular PPC method on the Internet, but other companies do offer alternative versions of it as well. At the present time, PPC methods are infrequently used for crowdfunding, but their use is growing fast.

Two Types of Advertising

The only thing simple about advertising is its dictionary definition: "the act or practice of calling public attention to one's product, service, or need." The practice of advertising, in particular doing it effectively, is a true combination of art and behavioral science. Indeed, people devote entire careers to the practice of advertising and, even then, will confess it is a continuous learning process. To be a successful crowdfunder, you don't need to know everything about advertising, but you can learn about some of the most effective ways to use Internet advertising to promote your crowdfunding campaign.

In broad terms, there are two types of advertising: brand marketing and direct marketing. *Brand marketing* works by building name recognition in a product or service. *Direct marketing* is a more immediate form of advertising that focuses on rapid responses to wants and needs. Understanding the difference between these two advertising methods is important.

Brand marketing is literally building an awareness of a product through repeated and prominent advertising so that when the need for that product or service appears, people will know what brand they want to buy. Most of the advertising you receive on TV, radio, newspapers, and magazines is brand marketing. So are billboards, signs, and other methods that inform potential purchasers of all the positive characteristics of your product or service in an informational way.

Direct marketing is different. It is far less about building awareness for future purchases than it is about solving more immediate wants and needs. A sign in a store that says "50 percent off today" is direct marketing, and so is a flier in the mail that has an offer that must be redeemed within thirty days. These offers are not focused on brand awareness; they are focused on solving current needs and attaching a time frame for doing so. The ultimate direct marketing can be described as offers that occur as a result of search engine queries. The connection between the search involving a person's wants and needs and suggested solutions can be just seconds apart.

> **ESSENTIAL**
>
> Search engines are complex computer programs that scour the web looking for and indexing digital content. While the processes by which they operate are closely-held secrets, what they do is rather simple. They are designed to deliver links and content that are "highly relevant" to your query.

Chapter 9: Pay Per Click and Crowdfunding

What Search Engines Do

It's important to realize that every time someone executes a search on Google, or any of the other search engines, that person is trying to obtain information about something that's important to him at that moment. Often the search is done to solve a problem or satisfy a need. Just think about the last time you searched for something on Google (if you can't remember what it was, check the "history" list on your browser). Chances are that you were looking for something that was significant to you, something you wanted to know about; in other words, it was not just a casual entry out of sheer boredom.

Here's a quick look at how your browser behaves when you type something into a search window. This example will refer to a Google search because most Internet searches occur through Google.

> **QUESTION**
>
> **How do the various search engines rank in popularity?**
> According to ComScore, a digital marketing intelligence firm, in early 2012 Google led the pack with 66.2 percent of all Internet searches occurring on its site. Next was Bing with 15.1 percent and Yahoo! with 14.1 percent. Bringing up the rear was Ask with 2.9 percent and AOL at 1.6 percent.

Let's assume that you live in New Hampshire and your Ariens snowblower is broken. You need a new drive belt. On the Google homepage, you would type in "ariens parts nh" in an effort to find an Ariens small-equipment dealer nearby. In response to this query, you will see the search engine response page (SERP) that Google delivers to your browser. You will find there are two mechanisms at work here. The first is the list of highlighted links to the left-hand side of the screen. These are called "natural" or "organic" results. They are the listings that Google serves up at no charge to anyone and they are sorted according to relevancy. On the right side of the page are the sponsored ads, which are links that advertisers pay for in the Google AdWords program. These ads are generated (written) by advertisers, but the content offered on the advertisers' websites and relevancy to your search is tightly monitored by Google.

FACT

> *Relevancy* refers to the nature of the content and links that Google serves up whenever queries are entered into its search engine. Google wants to provide you with excellent, relevant information about what you are looking for and by doing so, it hopes to become your favorite search engine. Originally search engines served up the links and ads that made the most money for them. Google realized that such poor search results compromised the users' experience and changed that model long ago.

Organic and Sponsored Searches

The organic results on a Google response page are the listings that are to the left of the SERP page, headed up with blue links, and served up by Google in order of relevancy. Google calculates a link's relevancy by analyzing where it goes, the content it finds, the site's reputation, what it finds for links from other sites, and other criteria. All of these factors are important to Google because it not only wants you to find the information that you are looking for; it wants it to be very high quality.

Since the ranking of links and sites is very important to capturing traffic, a very popular process called search engine optimization (SEO) has evolved. It refers to the process of optimizing the content and other variables on your website so that it "ranks high" in the organic search results. The science behind this is complex and constantly changing but there are things that you can do to your website that will improve its position in search engine rankings.

Sponsored search results are the ads on the right hand side of a SERP page and sometimes above the organic results. These ads are the front end of Google's AdWords program. They are specially formatted ads that you pay Google to place on a search result page when certain "keywords" are entered into a search. In our example of the snowblower search, the keywords would be "Ariens," "Parts," and "NH." Google, armed with millions of servers, processes all the keywords that people enter when searching for things on the Internet and serves up the sponsored ads that it feels best matches the needs of the person searching.

Chapter 9: Pay Per Click and Crowdfunding

ESSENTIAL

> One of the factors that makes Google AdWords and other PPC systems so effective for advertisers is "immediacy." This refers to the fact that when someone expresses the need for information, a result can occur within seconds. Contrast this with brand marketing techniques in which endless TV, radio, or print ads attempt to build knowledge about a product or service. With a PPC system, you have "instant yellow pages"; when a person needs something, she can receive an answer within seconds that addresses that need.

How Google Ranks Ads

People tend to click on the sponsored ads that are listed in the top positions on SERP pages. According to Search Engine Watch, a website for search engine professionals, sponsored ads that are in the number one spot receive 36.4 percent of all clicks, those in the number two spot receive 12.5 percent, and it goes down from there. So how do you get listed at the top of the sponsored listings? Is it a matter of paying more money than the other advertisers? Well, money is a factor, but there's more to it. Google has a unique way of determining where sponsored ads rank in listing order on SERP pages, and it involves both a cost-per-click (CPC) bid and a quality score. The best way to explain this is to illustrate the formula that Google uses to determine the rankings of sponsored ads:

Ad Rank = Maximum Cost-Per-Click Bid (Max. CPC) × Quality Score

The first factor in the equation, the CPC bid, is the amount of money that you are willing to pay for a "click-through" on your ad. (A click-through is when a person sees your ad, clicks a link on it, and is brought to your website or other destination.) Let's look at the snow blower parts company again. The company realizes that when someone goes to Google and types in the search field "ariens parts nh" that there is a high likelihood that this person is in New Hampshire and is looking to buy Ariens parts very soon. Because of this, the company would like its sponsored ad stating "We Stock All Ariens Parts!" to be shown whenever someone types in "ariens parts nh."

The question is, how much is that "lead" worth? How much should the snowblower company pay for that click? Well, it depends, but chances are it's less than a dollar and may yield a sale of $20 or more.

> **ESSENTIAL**
>
> What is tremendously appealing about PPC advertising is that advertisers are only charged when someone clicks on their ad. They are not charged per impression (an impression is each time an ad is displayed on a SERP page). This is tremendously valuable to advertisers for two reasons: First, they aren't charged when their ad is displayed and nothing happens. Second, it filters inquiries. People who click through are more qualified because they found the ad copy interesting enough to click through.

The second factor in the equation is the quality score. The quality score is a semi-obscure factor assigned by Google and is generally correlated to how relevant your content is. If you have a link destination that has great, relevant information concerning a certain topic, Google will give that link a high quality score for searches involving that topic. If your content is weak, Google in effect penalizes you with a low quality score. All of this is designed to improve the quality of searches for Google clients and works just fine for commercial enterprises once they understand how the system works.

Interestingly, the top sponsored ad ranking does not always go to the person who bids the most money. If you examine the formula again, you can see that a site with a high quality score can actually outrank one with a higher bid amount. Google has designed the system so that both factors are relevant to the ranking that a sponsored ad receives.

Setting Up a Google AdWords Program

Google has made it very easy to set up an AdWords campaign. The site offers robust support with detailed guides, interactive videos, and a lot of other helpful assets. Since AdWords represents almost 97 percent of Google's total revenue, some $32.2 billion per year, it is to the company's benefit to design the entire AdWords program to be extremely user friendly, and it is. An effective AdWords campaign can help you direct potential pledgers to your crowdfunding project. Here are some things to think about before you set up your AdWords campaign.

Learn about Google AdWords

Whether it is through Google or using other informational resources, spend some time learning about how AdWords works. While Google AdWords can be a very effective way to advertise, that doesn't mean you can just jump in blindly. Learn what works and what doesn't before you plunge.

Do Your Keyword Research

Try to think of the main keywords that potential donors might enter into a Google search page that are related to your crowdfunding campaign. Use the keyword research tools to see how many people have searched on your keywords in the last few months. This will give you a rough idea of the size of the population you are tapping into.

Create Ad Groups

You should consider creating an ad group for each main keyword or keyword phrase. There are several sites that can assist you in developing additional keywords related to your main keywords. This will enable you to target potential donors who are specifically using those words for searching and see which keywords are the most effective.

Write Compelling Ad Copy

The goal is to catch the eye of potential donors. Look at the ads people are already placing on Google to give you an idea of what is effective. Consider using your main keyword or keyword phrase in the title of your ad.

Create Your Google AdWords Account

Google charges $5 for an AdWords account. After that, decide how much you are willing to pay per click and per day. You can choose a maximum CPC from $.05 to $50 and set a daily budget as well.

Monitor and Modify Your AdWords Campaigns

Start with two or three ad groups. Make changes to your ad copy, keywords, or bid prices to improve your click-through rate. Google automatically tracks the click-through rate for each of your ads so you can easily compare the effectiveness of changes.

FACT

> A key metric in PPC advertising is an ad's click-through rate (CTR). The CTR is calculated by dividing the number of clicks by the number of impressions (the number of times your ad was shown), and then multiplying that number by 100. For example, let's suppose you got 61 clicks out of 1,243 impressions. The formula works out like this: 61 ÷ 1,243 = .049 × 100 = 4.9%, which is considered a fairly good CTR.

Picking the Best Keywords

One of the more challenging aspects of creating a Google AdWords campaign is choosing the right keywords. It would seem that if you are looking to direct traffic to a crowdfunding campaign concerning something specific, let's say, a documentary about mercury in food products, the keywords would be obvious. Wouldn't they just be the words "documentary," "mercury," and "food"?

Well, that's not a bad start, but ask yourself this: Is everyone who might be concerned about this issue going to type those exact three words into a Google search field? What about words such as "DVD," "movie," "poisons," "fish," "processing," and "seafood"? All of these may be words related to the issue, along with various phrase combinations and permutations. Do you see the challenge? Welcome to the wonderful world of keywords.

To get a better understanding of the task ahead, consider what facets of your crowdfunding campaign are under your direct control. Your text, video, reward selections, and dozens of other creative decisions are areas where you can completely take charge. However, this does not extend to your keywords. Your job when working with keywords is not to *specify* them; it is to *discover* them. This is a very important difference. Your job is to discover what keywords are already being used or are likely to be used by others.

e! ALERT

> It is important that anyone who practices commerce on the Internet to understand "market empathy." This is a relatively new term that denotes an awareness of other people and the way they think and act. Many an entrepreneur has succumbed to the fallacy that everyone else shares his or her specific wants and needs.

Fortunately, once you understand the research that needs to be done, you will find that the art of doing this is well developed and you have a lot of resources at your fingertips to help. Some of these resources are provided by Google and some are available from third-party websites around the Internet.

You will also find that keyword selection and utilization is a dynamic process. Those who are successful with AdWords campaigns generate large lists of keywords and they run campaigns in specific ad groups to see how effective they are. Certain keywords will be effective and will stay, while others will prove not as good and will be discarded. This sort of fine-tuning is a normal part of running an effective AdWords campaign.

Making Keywords Work for You

To help you direct the highest-quality prospects to your website, Google provides you with a number of tools that affect the way your keywords are used during an AdWords campaign. There are quite a number of techniques for you to consider, but we will limit our discussion to the two most powerful ones: keyword matching and negative keywords.

Keyword matching refers to the way that Google uses your keywords when it is looking for "matches." Every time someone types something into a search field, the servers at Google decide whose sponsored ads to display and in what order. Google's servers are essentially asking, "is this a match?" You can help determine the likelihood of a match with your campaign's match options. Google offers you four types of options: broad matches, phrase matches, exact matches, and negative matches.

Broad Matches

When you specify a *broad match* on a set of keywords, Google's servers will look at your specific keywords and similar keywords too. The reason this option is called broad is that it will capture a lot of keyword and phrase variations and trigger them to display your sponsored ad. In the case of the New Hampshire–based snowblower parts company, "ariens," "parts," and "nh" are three keywords. A broad match might trigger the company's ad not only when these words are typed but also when other related words are typed. All of these words are highly related to what a person searching for Ariens snowblower parts might be entering as a Google search query.

Phrase Matches

A more restrictive keyword search is a *phrase match*, which looks for the presence of all the keywords you specified in your AdWords campaign. A phrase match involving the snowblower parts company would trigger a sponsored ad when all three keywords, "parts," "ariens" and "nh," are typed in plus any other words. For example: "need ariens snowblower parts in new hampshire." Note that the order is not important, nor are extraneous words. As long as the Google search algorithms see those three specific keywords, it may trigger the display of the parts company's sponsored ad because it is a "phrase match."

ESSENTIAL

If you are working for a nonprofit or an organization that serves the common good, you may be eligible for free AdWords. Google has a wonderful program called Google For Nonprofits that offers a wide variety of Google programs at low or no cost to those that qualify. In particular, you may be able to arrange AdWords campaigns to direct traffic to your nonprofit website and not have to pay for clicks.

Exact Matches

The most restrictive search criteria occurs when you specify an *exact match*. When someone types in "parts," "ariens," and "nh"—specifically these three words and in that exact order—a match occurs. This is obviously a very restrictive match and indicates that the advertiser is looking for very specific searches. You will find that ads may be triggered infrequently when exact matches are applied, but when they are triggered, it is done so by a highly qualified prospect looking for something very specific.

Negative Matches

Another match option that Google offers you is the ability to prevent your ad being triggered because of negative keywords. Negative keywords indicate that someone is most likely searching for something not related to your AdWords offer. For example, suppose you have a small clothing boutique that sells a wide variety of women's clothing and you carry everything except shorts. When this business sets up its AdWords Campaign, it should specify "shorts" as a negative keyword so that if someone types that into a search string, the boutique's sponsored ads won't be displayed. Another example involves common word confusion. Suppose you have a home business making the world's finest bat houses. You may want your ad to be shown to those who type in the keywords "bat" and "house," but you don't want the ad to be seen by those who type in "baseball," "softball," or other words that indicate the bat they are talking about is a wooden implement, not a little animal with big ears. In the case of our snowblower parts company, you may want to use the word "new" as a negative match because our snowblower parts company does not sell "new" snowblowers, just parts. In general, it may be helpful to conceptualize negative keywords as your frontline filter. When properly employed, they keep the unqualified prospects away.

> **FACT**
>
> Google AdWords professionals say that one of the biggest mistakes beginners commit is forgetting to use negative keyword exclusions when setting up AdWords campaigns. Your AdWords campaign will be much more effective when you employ negative keyword exclusions.

If you're new to the world of AdWords campaigns and Internet advertising you may think that you shouldn't restrict searches with negative keywords. You might fear it will reduce the traffic to your site. Resist this temptation. Consider this mantra: "Positive keywords bring traffic, and negative keywords filter traffic." Your goal should be to use both for optimum effect.

Writing Magnetic Ads

After you've examined the mechanism that serves up your sponsored ads on SERP pages according to keywords and keyword match options, the second part of your job is to craft compelling ad copy so that people can quickly see what you are offering. Many AdWords experts consider this the most critical part of a campaign because you really have just a few seconds to grab people's attention before they are off looking at other ads.

A Google sponsored ad has three main parts. At the top is an ad title, which is a blue clickable link. Underneath that is a green URL (web address), and the two remaining lines of text are the ad copy. Spend some time looking at a lot of sponsored ads, noting things that you like and things that you don't. Note what catches your eye and things that seem neutral. Also, take a look at some on Google that cover good sponsored ad practices. Here are a few things to consider before creating an ad.

Carefully Choose Your Ad Copy

Your sponsored ad serves as your company's introduction to potential customers. Its structure and crafting indicate the quality of your company and your offer. It helps users to decide whether to click on your ad or travel elsewhere. Before you start a Google AdWords campaign, take time to learn as much as possible about good sponsored ad copy.

Put Your Keyword in the Copy

Since it is the keywords that lead to the sponsored ad's appearance on the SERP page in the first place, why do so many ignore the keywords in the ad copy? Again it seems obvious that you would include the keywords you have paid for in the ad, especially in the headline. Use common sense and put your chosen keywords in the ad copy.

ALERT

> Don't color your sponsored ad with symbols, gimmicky language, and superlatives ("Absolutely the world's best," "The cheapest you will find"). Also avoid the repetition of words and phrases for effect ("Sale, sale, sale . . ."). If you do use techniques like these, Google will likely not allow your ad to run. AdWords experts also suggest that you avoid antiquated phrases such as "click here" or "link," since virtually all computer users know how hyperlinks work.

Differentiate Your Ad

Unless you have chosen really unique keywords, you are likely going to have your fair share of other people's sponsored ads to compete with. Obviously you want to differentiate your ad from the others, by color, wording, or other ways while also making it just as appealing to click on.

Check Grammar and Spelling

Is there anyone who would let sloppy grammar or spelling slip by in an ad that they paid good money for? Well, it happens more often than you would think, particularly in respect to grammar. And this issue highlights one of the main concerns on the Internet to begin with: the issue of trust. Why should any Internet user trust a site that can't even spell and/or structure a sentence properly? Be smart and double-check your spelling and grammar, particularly if you are starting up a large, expensive AdWords campaign. Don't destroy your readers' trust before they even finish reading your ad.

Provide a Clear Call to Action

What is it you want visitors to do when they arrive at your website? Learn about your cause? Buy something? Join your campaign? Subscribe to a newsletter? Whatever it is, include a "call to action" statement in your ad copy. "Learn more," "Order now," and "Subscribe to our Free Newsletter" are all examples of call-to-action statements.

Remember That You Are Going to Change Things

Don't feel that you have to create the perfect sponsored ad the first time you jump into the game. Most successful PPC ad campaigns are a result of experimenting with different versions of ad copy and tracking the results to see what worked best. There is nothing wrong with poor results when you start as long as you learn from your mistakes and improve your campaign using this knowledge.

Split Testing

Split testing is one of the most powerful techniques in e-commerce. It allows you to experiment with dozens of parameters in your AdWords campaign and fine-tune the whole campaign for peak performance. Sometimes you can increase your response rate 200–300 percent or even more.

Split testing, sometimes referred to as A/B testing, is a process of testing out different versions of a promotion to see which one performs best. The promotion could be a direct mailing, a highway billboard, a webpage, or an e-mail. You use split testing when you want to find out how response results can differ based on changes to an original offer.

Let's take a 10,000-piece direct mailing for an in-ground swimming pool promotion, for example. You could test the difference between two different offers; one is for 10 percent off and the other is for a free automatic pool cleaner. Here's how the test works. Within the same geographic area, you send out 5,000 fliers offering 10 percent off and a second 5,000 offering free pool cleaner. Each of these offers has a different phone number assigned to it so that within a few weeks, you know exactly which offer has the best pull.

Why do advertisers use split tests? Because even the experts get it quite wrong sometimes. Here's a true story: A major advertising agency was working on an ad campaign for a big client. The agency developed several different versions of the ad and then asked its stable of experienced, well-paid ad executives to weigh in as to which would perform better. After each executive had picked the ad he thought would be the winner, the agency ran the complete promotion including all the versions and tabulated the results. Of the dozen or so executives it queried, not a single one chose the ad that actually performed the best! This is why split testing is so crucial. No matter how well you think you know your market, there will always be things you have to test to discover.

Split Testing AdWords

As you have learned, there are dozens and dozens of choices that you need to make with an AdWords campaign. Choices range from keyword selections and keyword matches to ad copy, ad ranking, and dozens of other variables. Potentially all of these variables could be tested, and you should certainly consider some of them because you never know what you will discover. There have been stories of one single word doubling the conversion rates of an offer! Other stories illustrate that changing something seemingly very minor, such as the color of the text on an order button, can dramatically increase conversions too. This is why split testing is such powerful stuff.

You can do split testing in various ways. With Google AdWords, you'll find there's a split testing system built in. If you're split testing something involved with a crowdfunding campaign, you certainly want to track variables like your keyword selections and ad copy.

One last note: split testing works better with a fairly large number of visitors. If your volume of visitors is low, your split testing numbers may be somewhat inaccurate and it can often take longer to get statistically valid results that you can use. Nevertheless, split testing even with low volume is usually better than not doing it at all.

CHAPTER 10

Using Twitter for Promotion

Of all the tools in your social media arsenal, Twitter is one of the most important to use for business and for crowdfunding. With over 500 million registered users in mid-2012, the "Twitterverse" contains thousands of people who will be interested in what you are doing no matter what it is. The key is to find people who are interested and connect with them.

Introducing the Twitterverse

Twitter is nothing more than a communication system where people exchange information in 140-character messages called tweets. Some call it a "micro-blogging platform" where communities and groups can form and interact with each other by exchanging messages on a frequent basis.

While these definitions are useful, they don't give you a real feeling for what Twitter really is. Consider this analogy: Twitter is a collection of millions of communities all talking among themselves and you can listen in on any one of them. As matter of fact, you can listen to all of them . . . at once. That's right, all the information flow in every community is aggregated into a "Public Timeline" where you can see every tweet . . . from every person . . . in every community . . . as it occurs. It's a mind-boggling concept.

FACT

> A few statistics to put the magnitude of the Twitter platform into perspective: The record for most accounts created in one day occurred on March 12, 2011, when 572,000 accounts were created. The current tweets per second (TPS) record was set during Euro 2012, the major soccer tournament that wrapped with Spain taking home the coveted Euro Trophy. Soccer fans generated over 15,000 tweets per second during this event.

In this avalanche of data there are thousands of people you will want to connect to. These are people you would like to have in your own community—a community of customers and advocates for your business that you can interact with, offer products and services to, and collect feedback from.

The general way to gather information from Twitter is to "follow" certain people or organizations. When you do this, their tweets are pulled from the pile and posted on your Twitter page, where you can read them. The way you build your community is to get people to follow you, which makes them "members" that you can send tweets to and interact with.

In the early days of Twitter, the concept of "communities" was less prominent. It was originally conceived as a simple messaging platform. Today, it has become a major social media platform with communities exchanging links, engaging in conversations, and even broadcasting real-time accounts at the scenes of disasters, accidents, or other newsworthy events. Some say that Twitter will grow into the number one social media platform in the world in the near future.

Why People Use Twitter

You already know that Twitter is a wonderful micro-blogging platform where short messages can be communicated among millions of people. But what are the reasons people give for using Twitter? What utility does it provide?

To Send Quick Messages

In its most basic sense, Twitter allows you to send quick SMS (text messages) between devices. While most smartphones today offer standard SMS texting, doing so via Twitter allows a greater control of the protocol with many different applications available to organize and arrange messages.

To Build Robust Communities

Because it's a *social* media, Twitter allows robust communities to form and members to interact with each other. In a way, each user starts his own Twitter community when he establishes an account and starts to use it.

> **QUESTION**
>
> **What is SMS messaging?**
> Short Message Service (or SMS messaging) is really just texting. When you send a text from one cell phone to another, you are using the SMS protocol. SMS messaging is the most widely used data application in the world, with over 3.7 billion active users. SMS messages are generally treated as lower-priority traffic, and various studies have shown that around 1 to 5 percent of SMS messages are lost entirely, even during normal conditions.

To Share Life

Some people, most notably celebrities and other high-profile individuals, use Twitter to share their lives with their followers and anyone else who tunes in. They can tweet what they're thinking at the moment, things they are observing and experiencing, and send links to articles and images that interest them as they find them. Twitter provides a close link to anyone who chooses to tweet personal thoughts and experiences.

To Stay in Touch

Some people use Twitter as an active address book where contact information for old friends and new friends can be rapidly stored and accessed. You may find that you constantly use Twitter this way as you meet and interact with new people.

The Anatomy of a Tweet

Communicating via Twitter is easy but a little less conventional than communicating via e-mail or SMS texting. There are some unique parts to a tweet, and you will need to master some jargon. Fortunately, understanding all these conventions will come very quickly as soon as you start using Twitter. In fact, virtually everyone who uses Twitter has come to appreciate the shorthand and conventions involved because the whole system is such an efficient way to communicate with people. Here are some of the important parts of a tweet:

- **Hashtag:** A hashtag is any word that is preceded by the # sign. The use of hashtags was started by users of Twitter several years ago to allow users to organize conversations around certain topics. When you click on a hashtag, the Twitter search function will locate all the tweets in the Twitterverse with that hashtag in it. For example, #onedirection will bring up conversations about the British boy band One Direction.
- **@Mention:** Sometimes you want to tweet somebody but you want all your followers to be able to see the tweet, too. So, instead of just replying, use a mention. Include the @username of whomever you want to mention in your Tweet, and it will appear in the Mentions section. By nature, @replies are public. If you want to send a private message to someone, use a direct message. Direct messages (DMs) are private messages sent to specific recipients. No one else can see them.

- **Reply:** You can reply to a tweet by clicking on the "Reply" button. When you reply, your response is public, and will show up in your profile page timeline and the timeline of the person to whom you are responding. Your reply will also be visible in the home timelines of people who follow both you and the person to whom you sent the reply.
- **Retweet:** Retweeting is becoming a major activity and the folks at Twitter have made it easy with a "Retweet" button. When you click on the button, you can resend original messages that you have received or found to all of your followers.
- **Shortened URL Links:** With only 140 characters available you don't want to copy any lengthy web addresses (URLs) into your tweets. Fortunately Twitter has an automatic URL shortening service that takes any web address and shrinks it down to nineteen characters. For example, a large URL like: *http://www.nytimes.com/interactive/2012/09/02/nyregion/a-history-of-new-york-in-50-objects.html?smid=tw-nytimes*, can be be shortened to a short URL like: *http://yfrog.com/ke7romoj*.

When you use Twitter, you are identified by your username or handle. These are typically formatted as "@username"; for example, the handle for the author of this book is @thosyoung. As the differentiation between online and offline identities becomes closer, it's best to choose a handle that is short, easy to remember, and not obscure. The days of using handles like "studmuffin67" in anonymous chat rooms are long gone. Social media today demands more transparency.

Twitter Third-Party Applications

Third-party applications are platforms that interface with Twitter and allow you to perform Twitter activities. Many users prefer the third-party applications because most are designed to allow you to view many Twitter activities at once. On the Twitter main page itself this is not the case; you have to click tabs to see all of your activity. An additional benefit of many of the third-party applications is that they are customizable. You can place different columns and feeds where you like for optimum viewing. Several of them even allow you to view Facebook pages as well as Twitter. This allows users to manage the two biggest social media platforms on one screen. Here are several of the most popular third-party Twitter applications to consider:

- **TweetDeck** is a browser-based Twitter application for power users. It offers a multicolumn view and great filters to enable you to monitor multiple Twitter accounts. TweetDeck also allows you to write and schedule tweet postings, and you can use as many Twitter accounts as you can create.
- **HootSuite** is a social media dashboard designed to manage multiple social media profiles. Among its many other features, HootSuite allows you to keep track of tweets, mentions, and DMs, and it can also auto-update profiles via RSS feeds. The free version of HootSuite supports up to five social network profiles.
- **Twhirl** connects to multiple Twitter accounts as well as other social networks (in particular, Facebook, MySpace, and LinkedIn). It's a free application that covers the basics and may be a touch easier to use than others.
- **Twitterrific** is a hugely popular Macintosh application that received MacWorld's Twitter Client of the Year award in 2010. You can use Twitterrific as a browser-based application and on your iPhone and iPad. It includes features such as easy translation of foreign-language tweets, multiple account support, keyboard shortcuts, and a choice of themes.
- **Sobees Desktop** is another social media dashboard with support for not just Twitter but also for Facebook, MySpace, and LinkedIn. It's aimed at social butterflies—"check your MySpace friends' activities and update your own mood" is one of the selling points—but it's quite clever and because it's currently in beta, it's free.
- **Echofon** can be used on almost any platform. There are desktop versions for Macs and Windows, iPhone and iPad apps, and Android versions. The free version is ad supported, but the ad free is a reasonable $9.99. The desktop apps sync effortlessly with their mobile cousins and can support multiple accounts.
- **Digsby** helps you manage all of your IM, e-mail, and social network accounts from one application. Digsby lets you communicate via AIM, MSN, Yahoo, ICQ, Google Talk, Facebook Chat, and Jabber with one simple "buddy list." It provides notifications when new e-mails arrive and lets you perform actions such as "Mark as Read" or "Report

Spam" without having to go to your inbox. Especially convenient are pop-up notifications that keep you up-to-date on what's happening on your social networks and news feeds of recent events for Facebook, Twitter, LinkedIn, and MySpace.

- **Tweetree** has developed what many say is a more user-friendly online interface than Twitter. The biggest difference is that Tweetree puts posts into a tree so you see someone's original post and the subsequent replies. It's a small feature but one that has a major impact on how you use Twitter given there's no need to provide a reference to the original tweet. Another great feature is that Tweetree inserts video and image if someone includes a link in their post. For example, if you link to a video, the video appears within the stream.
- **Twitpic** is a platform that allows users to easily share photos on Twitter. You can post pictures to Twitpic from your phone or through the website itself. Some Twitter applications have built-in support for Twitpic that is extremely useful. Twitpic is often used by journalists to upload and distribute pictures in real time as an event is taking place.
- **TwitterFon** is a free and functional Twitter client. It's basic compared to some of the ad-supported apps like Twitterrific, but it works perfectly for most Twitter users. With TwitterFon you can tweet, post pictures and photos, and post links from Safari using bookmarklets. The interface is fairly simple. Navigation is via the five buttons located at the bottom of the display, and you can follow links or pictures in tweets by clicking on link icons.

Getting on Twitter

The first thing to do is sign up for a Twitter account. Its free. Visit *www.twitter.com* and you will be greeted with text that asks "New To Twitter? Sign Up." This will lead you directly into the Twitter sign-up process. One of the first things that Twitter will ask you is to choose a username. If you are establishing a personal account, choose something unique but not embarrassing. If it's available, try to get your real name. If you are establishing a Twitter account for your business, then you should use your business name or something close if the name is already taken.

ESSENTIAL

Are you not on Twitter with a personal or business account yet and don't plan to be for some time? Sign up now anyway. Here's why: With the phenomenal success of the Twitter platform, you want to secure your username or handle as soon as you can. Just like the issue with domain names, popular names are taken quickly and getting the one you would like will become more difficult as time goes on.

Next, it's time to create your profile. You get one image or avatar and 160 characters to explain who you are and what you do. For business accounts, it's a good idea to visit a number of other Twitter business pages just to see what some of the others look like. You will find that most businesses have nice-looking Twitter account pages for obvious reasons. Try to pick a background and color combinations that are tasteful and professional.

Before any promotion of your new Twitter account, write twenty tweets to fill out the first page, spacing them at least fifteen to thirty minutes apart from each other. After that, continue to tweet every day, four to five times a day for the first few weeks. Later, you can taper off and hopefully lots of new followers will start to fill in. The object of doing it yourself for the first few weeks is to make the account look active.

Finding People

The key to Twitter is to connect to people who are interesting to you. Many people use the platform just for personal purposes, such as to stay in touch with family and friends. Businesses, however, want to build large, flourishing communities of customers and advocates, all centered around their core products, services, and/or mission. In the case of crowdfunding, project creators want to rapidly build up a community that supports their crowdfunding campaign and promotes it to others.

Fortunately, finding people is easy on Twitter. In the case of personal "family and friends" accounts, Twitter makes it easy to invite people that you are already connected to via e-mail and other media. In the case of businesses, the goal is to start your community with the people you are already doing business with, but to add others you don't know as quickly as possible.

For businesses and crowdfunders, the open nature of the Twitterverse makes searching for people and their Twitter streams a piece of cake. In fact, the challenge you will find is not actually "finding people"; it's trying to determine which of all the people you find are worth following! Here are several techniques that you can use to find people start your Twitter community:

- Use the "Find Friends'" link on the Twitter site to find people you know through your various Gmail, AOL, MSN, Hotmail and Yahoo! accounts.
- Use the "Browse Categories" link on the Twitter site to find people according to categories of interests.
- Search Twitter profiles. Registered Twitter users have the option to post bio information on their accounts. This is a great way to discover information about people and their interests and possibly follow them. Twitter itself has a profile search tool called Twitter Bio Search. You may also want to consider some of the third-party applications that are available. The most popular third-party applications include Tweepz, Followerwonk, LocaFollow, and Twiangulate.

Connecting Websites to Twitter

You have undoubtedly seen the little blue Twitter bird icons on webpages. You can click on the icon and be taken right to Twitter. After you sign in, your profile page will load. Most business sites and crowdfunding platforms offer the little blue Twitter bird "Tweet" icon as part of their designs. Twitter also offers a variety of other Twitter widgets. Here are a few on the Twitter website:

- The **Profile** widget shows a miniature real-time version of the timeline on your profile page.
- The **Search** widget is a real-time version of a search window with a search term that you determine.
- The **Faves** widget is a customizable, real-time version of a "faves" timeline.
- The **List** widget displays all the tweets that you have assigned to a list.
- The **Facebook** widget displays all your tweets in your Facebook page.

Best Practices for Businesses

The Twitter platform can be used with great success to enhance your business and crowdfunding efforts, but not by simply establishing an account and starting to tweet. You should spend some time researching what others are doing and see if you can identify the practices that seem to define the most robust communities. As you start to use Twitter more, think about how you wish the personality of your community to evolve and ways that you can foster growth in that direction. Following are several suggestions to consider when you want to build engaging, interesting Twitter communities.

Give Your Business Account a Personality

Twitter business communities are not a place for you to be stiff and formal, spouting product specifications and company policies. The best practice with a business Twitter account, and certainly one used for crowdfunding, is to make it more folksy. Not slapstick, mind you, but your Twitter business communications should provide a nice balance of formal business stuff, informal chat, and other material.

Establish a Voice

Regardless of whether you are the only person involved with your Twitter account or there are others, make it a little personal. The days of the company talking down to its customers are gone. The exchange is more level now, and it's fully interactive. Customers want to deal with real people, not customer service reps reading boilerplate copy off of monitors. So make it a little personal; sprinkle your tweets with opinions, thoughts, a little slang, and things like that. Strike a balance between being a person on your customer's level yet running a business.

> **ALERT**
>
> It's common for a company to fail to listen to what people are saying about its business, its brand, its products, and even its mission. Companies often get caught up in customer acquisition and forget that dealing with existing customers and their concerns can be just as powerful as acquiring new customers. Regularly monitor comments about your business and your brand.

Make Your Tweets Short

Believe it or not, 140 characters can be too long for many tweets. The whole point of Twitter is to communicate chunks of information succinctly. Remember that many of those receiving your tweets are very busy people, and they need to grasp the gist of your tweet in a second or two. Also, many people receive their tweets on Twitter on scrolling feeds and you have just a moment of exposure on those, too.

Share Inside Information

Share behind-the-scenes info, photos, and scoops about your business. Even better, give a glimpse of developing projects and events. This is not only an invaluable way to generate interest in what you do; you will find the "scoop tweets" get retweeted a lot. It's hard to get better promotion than that.

Use Hashtags on Your Campaign or Project

Make sure that you use hashtags on words and phrases related to your business. You want everyone who searches for your keywords to find you! This is especially true for your crowdfunding campaign. Think of it this way: Most people searching Twitter are not looking for your campaign, but as soon as an unrelated Twitter search pulls it up, they will see it. This is a very powerful method to promote your campaign, cause, or project.

Ask for Recommendations and Opinions

Your Twitter community is a wonderful research asset for you to use. As members of the community, people love to be engaged in discussions and research. Many of them will be glad to help you out. Want to know what people prefer for a color of a new product? You couldn't ask for a better group to survey. Need some outsourcing done? Ask your Twitter community for suggestions. In the case of crowdfunding, you will find that many members of your Twitter community are strong advocates of your project or your cause.

Respond Quickly

Twitter is not like e-mail and other social media where discussions occur over a period of time. Twitter is more like real-time communication. A very good practice to adopt is to respond to queries and questions rapidly. This is the nature of Twitter. Rapid response is the norm and is expected by many users.

Champion Your Community

Be actively involved in the flow of tweets within your community. Reply publicly to great tweets posted by your followers and customers. This will go a very long way.

> **ESSENTIAL**
>
> Some companies build Twitter communities quickly by offering special deals via Twitter. They encourage customers to follow their companies not only on Twitter but on other social media. These specials could be special offers, discounts, or deals on remnants. The draw here is that people love to get discounts and special treatment and gladly sign up to receive them.

Spread Out Your Tweets

Rather than hammering out lots of tweets first thing in the morning, spread them out during the day. Also, don't tweet too often, particularly with redundant content. In the case of business accounts and crowdfunding, too much tweeting looks like spam, which will kill all your good intentions. A few tweets a day containing useful, interesting data is all that is necessary to keep your community engaged.

Encourage Retweeting

Ask your followers to retweet you if they like your tweet. Getting your tweets retweeted brings you into new Twitter account communities and broadens your base. Also, when people do retweet you, thank them. You will find this goes a very long way.

Educate Followers

Twitter is a perfect platform for demonstrating industry leadership and know-how. Reference articles and links about subject material as it relates to your business. Occasionally tweet tips and techniques. Encourage readers to retweet them if they find them useful.

Final Thoughts for Crowdfunders

One of the most important parts of a crowdfunding campaign is your promotional plan. A promotional plan is a document that outlines the methods by which you intend on promoting your crowdfunding project, not just during the campaign but before and after the campaign. Smart crowdfunders put quite a bit of thought into this because they know that promotional plans can make or break a campaign. Many a failed campaign had no promotional plan at all.

A good promotional plan should start with prepromotional efforts. Remember you can visualize the Twitterverse as a collection of millions of small communities and it shouldn't be hard to find some of these that have an interest in your crowdfunding project and your mission. By all means, communicate with these groups and let them know what you are thinking of doing before you launch your campaign. Ask for their opinions and ask them to spread the word. This sort of effort primes the pump so that when you start your campaign, you can make an announcement and get some traffic quickly.

During the campaign, Twitter should be one method that you use to stay in touch with your backers. Most of the crowdfunding platforms give you the ability to send updates via e-mail but doing so via Twitter should be done also. The key is to keep your backers and others who are interested engaged in the entire campaign process from start to finish.

CHAPTER 11

Promoting Your Project on Facebook

Although launched just nine years ago, Facebook is arguably the most important social media platform on the web today. The latest statistics about Facebook show that as of mid-2012, Facebook had over 900 million registered users. This is one out of every eight people on earth. Regardless of whether you are involved with a small business or a crowdfunding campaign, you should have Facebook involved in your outreach strategy. Most of your customers or potential donors are already there. To be successful, you should be there, too.

The History of Facebook

Mark Zuckerberg was just twenty-three when he founded Facebook at Harvard University in 2004. Zuckerberg was a gifted computer programmer and had already developed a number of other early social networking sites while at the school. One was called CourseMatch, which allowed users to connect with people in the same degree program. Another was Facemash, a site where you could view students' pictures and rate their attractiveness.

In February, Zuckerberg launched a platform called "The Facebook." The name came from a printed document that was distributed to all incoming Harvard freshmen that profiled students and staff. "The Facebook" was quite popular, and within a month over 50 percent of the undergraduate population had signed up and created a profile page.

Zuckerberg immediately realized that the popularity of Facebook would extend far beyond the confines of just Harvard University and soon extended it to other Boston universities and eventually all U.S. universities. In 2005, the service was renamed to just "Facebook" and the service was extended to all U.S. high schools. In 2006, Facebook was further extended to anyone with a valid e-mail address, and the business went supernova.

Facebook, Inc., held an initial public offering on May 17, 2012, with a share price of $38, valuing the company at $104 billion, the largest valuation to date for any newly listed public company.

FACT

If you think that the creation and ascendancy of Facebook would make a great screenplay, you aren't alone. The movie *The Social Network* premiered in October 2010 to much critical acclaim. The movie concentrates on the human drama behind the rise of Facebook, with a focus on conflicts involving ownership of the Facebook concept. Although criticized by Mark Zuckerberg for inaccuracies, the movie grossed over $200 million in its first year and received eight Academy Award nominations.

Who Is on Facebook?

For those that have left their younger years behind, it is easy to think of Facebook as being just a hangout for teenagers, but that assumption is far from true. Today Facebook is used widely by all generations. The statistics (2011 data from Facebook), in fact, look something like this:

- Users aged 13–17: 20.6 percent
- Users aged 18–25: 25.8 percent
- Users aged 26–34: 26.6 percent
- Users aged 35–44: 14.8 percent
- Users aged 45–54: 7.4 percent
- Users aged 55–64: 4.2 percent

As you can see, Facebook usage is hardly skewed toward teenagers; over 50 percent of the users are age twenty-six and above. Furthermore, as Facebook matures, one would expect that the proportional size of the older age distributions will grow larger because, in the future, the platform will offer more resources for those age groups.

QUESTION

Which country has the most Facebook users?
As of mid-2012, Europe had the most users. Here are the global statistics: Europe, 223,376,640; Asia, 183,963,780; North America, 174,586,680; Latin America, 141,612,220; Africa, 37,739,380; Oceania/Australia, 13,353,420; the Caribbean, 6,218,960.

What Do People Do on Facebook?

So how do people use Facebook? The answer to that, of course, is different for every user, but the metrics below, from *Social Media Today*, illustrate a few statistics concerning things that people do on Facebook:

- The average user has 130 friends on the site and sends out eight friend requests per month
- The average user spends an average of fifteen hours and thirty-three minutes on Facebook per month
- The average user visits the site forty times per month and spends twenty-three minutes on each visit

- The average user is connected to eighty community pages, groups, and events and creates ninety pieces of content each month
- 200 million people access Facebook via a mobile device each day
- Facebook generates a staggering 770 billion page views per month

With statistics such as these, there should be little doubt that Facebook needs to be part of your social media strategy. It is especially smart to start a Facebook page for your crowdfunding campaign before you launch your campaign. This will build up a base of interested fans who can provide momentum to your campaign when it launches.

Nine Reasons Why Your Business Needs to Be on Facebook

Your business, and certainly your crowdfunding campaign, should be tied to a Facebook fan or business page. It's the world's largest social media site, and you just can't afford not to be there. The following are some of the most important things that Facebook offers you and your business.

It's a Direct Connection to Your Customers

Connection is king. Your customers want to connect not only with you, but with each other. Even if they don't think they want to right now, they will soon. The days of a company being an unapproachable fortress raining decree down on customers are essentially gone. With Facebook you can establish relationships with your customers, and this can translate into high customer loyalty and significantly increased sales.

It's a Connection Between Online and Offline Marketing

You can tie your offline marketing efforts, such as offers in newspapers, magazines, direct mail, and signage, directly to your Facebook page. Once people go there, they can discover a whole lot more about your company and what you do. Not long ago, the object of print and signage offers was to drive customers into your store. While that may still be true for some brick-and-mortar stores, today's offers often drive people to a Facebook page.

Once at your page, customers can experience what you and your business are all about, which then drives them to both your online and brick-and-mortar store.

It's a Way to Promote Your Brand

Your Facebook page is a wonderful place to promote your brand. By visiting, customers will find interesting brand-related content that can help convert them into fans and customers.

A Way to Get Immediate Feedback

Facebook is a wonderful way to gather customer feedback on your products, services, promotions, and just about anything else. If you have an existing customer support mechanism at your business, Facebook won't replace it, but it may make it much more effective.

Facebook offers a free analytical tool called Facebook Insights that will allow you to see who is visiting your Facebook pages and what they are doing there. This is a fantastic way to analyze what content people find interesting. You can use this information to help plan future content and even help guide product planning and strategy. You will find more information about this tool later in the chapter.

It Can Direct Customers to You

Properly built and optimized Facebook pages can perform well in search results and can lead potential customers to your Facebook page when they click on your link. Also, Facebook's new internal search tool is being used a tremendous amount, and these searches can lead customers to your page.

It Can Boost Your Sales

Facebook offers its own paid site advertising, which may work very well for you. It is "self-serve," like Google AdWords, so you can try it out and see how well it works. The advantage is that the pool of potential customers is so large, the Facebook advertising may end up being an affordable way to capture customers that you may not easily find any other way.

Your Competition Is Probably There

Your competition is most likely already on Facebook. If you're not on Facebook, you're behind in the race, and that's not a great spot to be in a competitive business environment.

It Doesn't Cost Anything

Well, this really isn't completely true; it does take resources (meaning someone's time) to create a Facebook page, and resources can cost money. However, the actual process of setting up a business or fan page is free on Facebook.

Your Website Might Be Boring

Many business websites are rather old school. They function like fancy brochures that just happen to be on the web. Facebook pages, on the other hand, are dynamic, interesting . . . and dare we say, fun? Today, some small businesses are actually opting to have a presence just on Facebook because customers often like Facebook more than standard websites and it saves the businesses money.

Some Facebook Terminology

If you are already a Facebook user this list may be somewhat redundant, but if you are new to the platform you need to learn some of the basic vocabulary used on the site. Don't be too concerned if some of these words don't make perfect sense right now. Much of Facebook makes a great deal more sense when experienced in context during interaction on the site itself.

- **Fan:** A user who chooses to "Like" a page. The pages that a user Likes show up in the user's news feed.
- **Friends:** People who can post on your wall and have certain other privileges.
- **Group:** A collection of Facebook users with a common interest. Any Facebook user can create or join a Facebook group.
- **Homepage:** A user's main Facebook page.

- **Like:** A button you click on to show that you're a fan of a page or that you like a post.
- **News Feed:** An aggregation of the wall posts of a user's Facebook friends, published on the homepage.
- **Page:** When used in the context of homepages, a business homepage.
- **Profile:** When used in the context of homepages, a personal homepage.
- **Wall:** The core of a profile or page that aggregates new content, including posted items (e.g., status updates) and recent actions (e.g., becoming a fan of a page).

A Page or a Profile for Your Business?

Facebook allows you to create two types of homepages: *pages* and *profiles*. In the past there was some confusion as to which type was best used for businesses, because there are some significant differences in the way the two pages behave.

Since Facebook's last redesign in December 2011, the situation is much clearer. Facebook now makes a clear distinction between the two page types. The bottom line is that "profiles" are now only for individuals to use, and "pages" are only for businesses. The following section is taken from Facebook's official policy on this matter:

> *"Facebook profiles are meant to represent a single individual. Organizations of any type are not permitted to maintain an account under the name of their organization. We have created Facebook Pages to allow organizations to have a presence on Facebook. These Pages are distinct presences, separate from user profiles, and optimized for an organization's needs to communicate, distribute information/content, engage their fans, and capture new audiences virally through their fan's recommendations to their friends. Facebook Pages are designed to be a media rich, valuable presence for any artist, business or brand."*

For further clarity, here are some of the differentiating characteristics between pages and profiles:

- Pages allow anyone to become fans, but access to the profiles is limited.
- Pages do not allow the ability to invite friends. In fact, pages cannot maintain a friends list; they can only maintain a fan list.
- Pages do allow you to update your status as well as profiles. Pages also allow pictures, videos, discussion boards, wall posts, groups, and other business-related elements.

As an administrator of your business page, your name and profile will not be visible on the page. Likewise, when you post information or respond, it will appear that the posting is generated by your company. This is different from a profile page, where postings come from you, the page administrator. On a business page, you can also designate multiple administrators, all with anonymity, who can help you with your page maintenance.

Setting Up a Business Page

Facebook does a very good job of helping you set up a page on its site. Here is the procedure for setting up a Facebook Page:

1. The first order of business is to establish a Facebook account so you can sign in and begin using Facebook.
2. Go to the Create a Page page, located at *www.facebook.com/pages/create.php*. Click on the category that best suits your project.
3. Facebook will ask you to choose a classification for your new page. This is an important decision, as it will affect how you are ranked in searches.
4. Choose a name and a category for your page. This should be your company name, brand, or product name. If you elect to classify your business as a local business, you will be asked for additional information here. This local data is important for searches.
5. Enter your business information. This is an opportunity for you to upload your company or brand logo and also suggest your new page to people that you know to generate fans.
6. Add business features. Facebook offers a number of free add-ons for your business page, such as discussion boards.

Chapter 11: Promoting Your Project on Facebook

On a Facebook business page you are an administrator, but you also want to become a fan. Click the "Like" button anywhere on your page and you become a fan of your own page. This will get you listed among all the other fans of your page, and all the other pages you are a fan of will show up in your profile. All of this helps to give your business more visibility.

How to Promote Your Page

After you have constructed your business page, you can pause for ten minutes or so, get another cup of coffee, and then settle into page promotion. One of the goals of having a presence on Facebook is to start building a nice community. Here are a few ideas to think about to start building your community quickly.

Create an Engaging Page

The most important thing you have to do is create a place that people want to visit. There could be no better way to promote your business, your brand, and your products. You need to have a site that offers engaging content with images, videos, and other graphic elements. Facebook also offers you plenty of features that you can add to your pages, such as discussion boards and iFrames (boxes that contain content, such as video, from other sources).

Enlist Your Existing Customers

As soon as you have your page up and running, be sure to invite those who are customers now. This may be through e-mail addresses or other links. The importance is to get a group of known people to jump in and start interacting with your new page as quickly as possible so the pump gets primed and momentum begins to build.

Make Your Page Searchable

You certainly want your page to be searchable by Google and the other search engines. If your page isn't "seen" by the major search engines, you are invisible to a good part of the Internet. By default, Facebook allows your page to be visible, but you might want to double-check that you have set it to be publicly indexed. Here's how: Go to "Edit Page," click "Manage Permissions," and make sure the "Page Visibility" box is unchecked.

ESSENTIAL

> One of the most valuable features of Facebook is the News Feed. This is a central part of someone's profile page, showing not only what they are up to but what their friends are up to. For example, when someone becomes a fan of your page or posts a comment, that activity also is published on all of that person's news feeds. This is significant because a single event potentially may be shared with a large number of people, giving your business tremendous visibility and credibility.

Use Facebook Ads for Promotion

Facebook ads allow you to advertise internal sections on Facebook such as Pages, Groups, and Events in addition to external websites. Facebook ads are set up similar to Google AdWords and are easy to try out. Like Google AdWords, there is some experimentation and optimization involved to get the best results but if you set up an ad campaign properly, you may acquire new customers at low cost.

How to Use Facebook Ads

If you look on the right side of virtually all Facebook pages you will see a column that says "Sponsored," with a number of ads directly below it. These are Facebook ads. Facebook ads are a great way for you to capture targeted users and present them offers. You can use them for many things. You can direct users to content you manage on Facebook, such as your homepage, a group, or an event. You can also use them to direct users off of Facebook to webpages, landing pages, crowdfunding campaigns, and other destinations.

If you are familiar with the Google AdWords advertising platform, you'll see that Facebook's ad creation and management tools are very similar. The instructions on how to create and manage Facebook Ads on the Facebook website are extensive. Here is a quick overview of creating Facebook ads:

- Visit your homepage. On the right-hand border you will see ads with the word "Sponsored" above them. Click on the Sponsored link and you will be taken to the Facebook advertising page. At the bottom of that page will be links to direct you to the advertising section.

- Choose your destination: the page that your ad will link to. It can be on Facebook itself or it can link to an external location, like the website of your crowdfunding campaign.
- Write a title that grabs attention.
- Create your ad copy. The copy in the body of your ad is important. You quickly want to state why a reader should feel compelled to click on the ad's link.
- Choose an image that will appeal to your audience.
- Take a good look at your ad and see if it meets the objectives that you have established. Is it appealing enough that someone will look at it? Is it compelling enough that they will click on the link to learn more?
- Choose the audience demographics you would like to target. Facebook gives you many demographic choices. You can also target people by likes/interests and connections on Facebook. Advanced options include relationship status, languages, education, and workplaces.
- Specify precise interests of your ad's target audience, or define their interests more broadly. You may want to start with an exact match in a particular demographic—for example, an age range—and see how your ad campaign works out. If your click-through rates are low, you can switch to a broad match later on.
- Select a payment type and a budget for your ad campaign. After you have established your Facebook ad program, it is very important to monitor the results daily. Especially when one is learning the craft of pay per click, there is much trial and error involved before optimum results are obtained. The key is to try different variations of the content, placement, and demographics and monitor the results.

Best Practices for Using Facebook

Once you establish a Facebook page for your business or crowdfunding campaign, you need to be sure it is interesting and engaging. Social media platforms like Facebook give you an opportunity to build a place that people want to visit and build a community around. Here are a few tips to help you make your page a great place to visit:

- **Welcome newcomers.** You want to maximize the percentage of people who visit your page and click the "Like" button. Have a statement that welcomes newcomers and tells them why you are glad they are there.
- **Be helpful and have a little fun.** When people visit your Facebook page, they are looking for some kind of interaction. Have interesting content and things to read and do.
- **Create a connection between Facebook and your business.** Whether your business is brick-and-mortar or purely online, you need to make this connection. Your Facebook page does not have to be an island, nor should it be. It should have links back and forth to your other web properties.
- **Embed videos on your page.** Facebook makes it very easy to embed videos in your page. Videos are highly engaging content. Many Facebook page owners do not use this ability enough.
- **Create contests.** This is a wonderful way to get people to visit your Facebook page. Contests, which can be advertised offline or online, are especially powerful ways to generate new fans.
- **Introduce products on Facebook first.** Facebook fans love receiving advance information about new products and services. This is a sure-fire way to get lots of "Like" clicks when you announce things.
- **"Like" other Facebook pages,** especially those that are associated with your business in some way, such as vendors or customers. This connects their community with yours and leverages marketing efforts.

In general, you want to make your Facebook page an interesting place to visit. You want a community of people to assemble that are interested in your business and what you do. Definitely be creative and give your visitors and fans lots of interesting content and you will establish a loyal following.

How to Analyze Your Facebook Presence

There are many tools that you can use to measure traffic, leads, and customers on the Internet. Fortunately Facebook offers you its own analytics package absolutely free. Called Facebook Insights, this package allows page administrators to answer questions like "Who is engaging with us?" "Is my page working well?" "Does our content strategy work?"

The Facebook Insights dashboard will help you answer many of these questions. As stated by Facebook, "Insights provides Facebook Page owners with metrics around their content. By understanding and analyzing trends within user growth and demographics, consumption of content, and creation of content, Page owners are better equipped to improve their business with Facebook."

There are two general groups of insights of Facebook Insights. User Insights give you statistics on total page Likes, or a number of fans, daily active users, new Likes/Unlikes, Like sources, demographics, page views and unique page views, tab views, external referrers, and media consumption. In Interactions Insights, you'll find numbers for daily story feedback (post Likes, post comments, per-post impressions), and daily page activity (mentions, discussions, reviews, wall posts, and video posts).

Because this tool offers so much data, you need to sort through it and identify which information is meaningful and will help you make decisions about your engagement and content strategy. If the data you want is not readily available, you might want to do some manual calculations to derive the numbers you're looking for. Ekaterina Walter, a social media strategist at Intel, suggests the following Insights metrics be followed:

- **Monthly fan size growth:** Record the number of fans (or "Likes") you have on the first of every month to see what your growth looks like. If you see something like 10 to 12 percent monthly growth, you are doing extremely well.
- **The average number of Likes or comments:** These are your basic engagement measures. If you know the average number of times fans interacted with you for every single post, you will be able to identify which discussions are of more interest to your fans.
- **Unlikes and attrition rate:** You will always have some unlikes every month, but you would like to keep that number to a minimum. Pay particular attention if you see a spike in that number, because that will mean there is some objectionable content on your site.
- **Demographics:** Demographic data, such as the ages of your fans, their gender, and where they came from, is always useful to look over.
- **Page views:** This metric can help you identify the number of returned fans. If you take the number of page views and subtract the number

of unique page views, you will see how many of your fans are actually coming back to your page.
- **Mentions:** This is the number of times people tagged you in their posts. This metric is important because it is the easiest way for your fans' friends to click through to your page. Every time someone tags you, the name of your page appears as a link. It is much easier for someone to click on that link and learn more than it is to search for your page manually. One of your goals should be to increase the number of mentions by your fans.
- **Tab views:** If you have multiple tabs on your page, Facebook will tell you the percentage of traffic each tab receives. This metric will help you decide whether you want to keep or possibly get rid of some of your tabs. Because you can only have six tabs visible on your page at one time, this data is especially helpful for prioritizing them.
- **Referrers:** This metric tells you where the traffic to your page comes from. You want to increase exposure to your page on the sites that bring you the most traffic.
- **Impressions:** If your page has more than 10,000 fans, you will see the number of times your post was viewed (impressions). This metric is not exact, since every time someone's page refreshes, it counts as an impression. This number is usually a little overblown, but can show you how many times your post has been seen.

Some of these metrics require constant manual tracking and analysis, which is a big downside. However, they will help you make decisions about your engagement and content strategy in order to allow more effective interactions with your customers.

When you see a spike in any of the Insights metrics, you should do more research to find out what caused it. Sometimes a single mention somewhere else on the Internet can have a dramatic impact on your Facebook visits. If you think that might be the case, play detective and go find out where that happened so you can decide if it is a place to include in your future promotional strategy.

CHAPTER 12

Using YouTube

YouTube is the largest video site on the Internet. While most of the videos on YouTube are homemade, it isn't the videos themselves that make YouTube such a significant place; it's the communities that exist there. Businesses large and small are now using YouTube because they can easily tap into these communities and develop their own. YouTube should play a key role in the marketing outreach plan for your crowdfunding campaign.

The Beginnings

YouTube was formed by three former PayPal employees: Jawed Karim, Steven Chen, and Chad Hurley. After they left PayPal, the three were exploring new opportunities and realized that there was a significant need for a site that would allow people to host and share videos. This was the beginning of the YouTube phenomenon.

Launched in 2005, YouTube proved immensely popular right away. Site traffic the first month was over 3 million visitors and reached a staggering 38 million visitors by the end of its first year. This made YouTube one of the fastest-growing sites in Internet history. In October 2006, just a year after YouTube was launched, Google acquired the business for $1.65 billion from the original founders.

Today YouTube is a key property in the Google empire but operates more or less independently. In fact, the look and feel of YouTube is relatively unchanged from the early days. Undoubtedly this comes from a decision to not tinker with something that works.

YouTube Today

According to Alexa, a major Internet infometrics company, the YouTube website receives the second-highest amount of traffic globally, with an estimated 60 million unique visitors per month. In the United States, it ranks fourth in Internet traffic.

FACT

> A recent article in *Time* magazine stated that, "For every minute that passes in real time, sixty hours of video are uploaded to YouTube." Think about that for a moment. That's ten years' worth of video uploaded every day. *Time* goes on to state that, "More video is uploaded to YouTube every month than has been broadcast by the three big TV networks in the past sixty years. And the pace is accelerating."

Today, YouTube is far more than just a site to park your videos. It is so popular that it is fast replacing traditional television viewing. According to Google, the average YouTube viewer spends 153 minutes watching videos every day. This is in contrast to just 130 minutes a day of standard television. The age distribution of YouTube viewers is heavily based in the eighteen to thirty-four age range, which represents approximately 37 percent of all viewers. In terms of gender distribution, viewership is approximately 55 percent male, 45 percent female.

While most people watch YouTube on their desktop computers, more and more are using other devices. In particular, many people use their smartphones for viewing YouTube videos. This used to be difficult to do, but with large-bandwidth mobile networks like 3G and 4G becoming common, streaming video is easy to view on mobile devices. In fact, one of the most popular iPhone apps is just for YouTube viewing. Other devices include the new wave of Internet-enabled flat-screen TVs, which are designed to easily access YouTube content.

YouTube Communities

YouTube is a site teaming with diverse communities. This is an important concept to grasp because in order to gain marketing traction on YouTube, you need to actively participate in these communities. Think of this process as being a two-way street: By paying attention to others in the YouTube microcosm, you are drawing attention to yourself. This is how social marketing works. Keep this up and you will soon have your own community.

> **ESSENTIAL**
>
> Most video marketing approaches you are exposed to today on standard television are very direct. The point is to grab your attention quickly and then present a hard offer. Think Billy Mays selling OxiClean, or just about any video of someone selling used automobiles. YouTube marketing is very different. Extensive research illustrates that users simply won't watch hard pitches; they prefer informative, educational approaches.

For those of you who are local retailers or provide a local service, here's an example of how you might participate on YouTube. Let's assume you have a car repair business. You will find that YouTube has many videos concerning automobile repair and automotive culture. Join the channels that involve those topics and post a video of your shop and what you do there. Choose a topic that seems to be of concern to your automotive customers and offer a solution. For example, you might post a video about "Why tire rotation is so important on all-wheel drive cars." This sort of thing can be immensely powerful because it establishes your business as a source for solutions as well as a good corporate citizen by offering "free" advice.

If you are promoting a crowdfunding campaign with global appeal, your campaign can be even more powerful because your efforts aren't tied to a specific location. You can use your videos to spread the excitement of your project and your campaign to the whole world. Imagine, for example, that you have a social entrepreneurial campaign on StartSomeGood.com that is involved with global warming. You will find communities on YouTube that are directly concerned with this topic, and many others whose interests intersect. Post your campaign video and invite others to view it. It may generate a tremendous buzz that travels through YouTube communities and draws a great number of people to your crowdfunding campaign.

Channeling

Every person with an account on YouTube has his or her own channel. This is really just a profile page in YouTube-speak. As soon as you upload a video, YouTube creates a channel for you.

Once you have a channel, people can subscribe to your content just as they do with other social media. On Facebook, people can subscribe to your Facebook page; on Twitter, they can receive your tweets; on YouTube, they subscribe to your channel. As with other social media, people can receive messages when your content is updated, which on YouTube generally means when new videos are posted.

After you upload your first video and establish your first YouTube channel, you will discover that your channel page is highly customizable. Here are the major items you can edit on your YouTube channel page:

- Channel title
- Channel type
- Channel visibility (Yes/No)
- Channel tags
- Discoverable (via e-mail)
- Channel themes
- Channel colors
- Channel background
- Channel content modules

With the ability to modify your channel with elements such as these, you can customize it in very unique ways. To get some ideas of the possibilities, visit other users' channels and see what you like. Some users have done some very creative things with their channel pages.

YouTube also offers a special kind of channel called a *brand channel*. Brand channels allow an even higher degree of customization than standard channels do and are very popular with companies that want to form a community around their brand and associated videos. Visit YouTube and you will find many brand channels for major companies.

What distinguishes a brand channel from standard YouTube channels are the following characteristics:

- A 960 × 150 pixel banner at the top of the page that can be linked (made clickable)
- A 300 × 250 pixel image on the left side of the channel page that can be made clickable
- The main video of the channel can be configured to play as soon as the page loads
- Two self-hosted gadgets to add additional functionality to the channel
- A custom thumbnail image can be supplied by the user
- The ability to use demographics to restrict access to the channel (example: display language)

Unlike standard YouTube video channels, brand channels are not free. In order to establish a brand channel account, you must have an AdWords account and be willing to spend a great deal of money on pay-per-click (PPC) advertising. Rates vary, but commitments of over $100,000 per year are expected. Brand channels are clearly not an option for smaller businesses.

Your Comments Please

When you put your videos up on YouTube, you can allow people to post comments underneath them. Allowing people to tell others what they think of your video is an important part of the social media experience. Nevertheless, it can be a double-edged sword. On one hand you would like lots of positive, fun comments on your videos, but that isn't always what you get.

The anonymity of the Internet allows people to express themselves quite frankly. The result is that you will occasionally find some negative comments and, in some cases, downright rude ones.

Thankfully, YouTube gives you some control over this process. At any time, you can set your account preferences to allow, disallow, and allow-with-approval comments that people would like to post. And this can be customized for individual situations; for example, you can set comment preferences differently for each of your videos.

> **ALERT**
>
> Some extremely effective videos are not really videos at all; they are video slide shows. Making a video requires a camcorder and a moderate amount of experience. In many cases, you can get your point across, certainly for a crowdfunding campaign, just as well with a video slide show. Most of the video editing programs allow you to take still photographs and add titles, music, and voice-over to create wonderful video slide shows. Look around YouTube and you will find some excellent examples.

A common question involves how to approach the comments issue. Is it best to protect yourself by simply disallowing comments, or should you just allow them and remove the negative ones? The answer to this, of course, is up to you, but there are two considerations. First, if you disallow all comments, or if you carve out all the negative ones, the "commentary" will seem somewhat artificial. It will look like you are controlling the process, and this may cause some viewers to form conclusions not only about your video, but also about the integrity of your business. Second, if you are going to allow full commenting, you need to monitor the process often to respond to the comments and possibly remove the ones you don't like. This may require additional resources that you haven't budgeted for.

YouTube also allows people to upload "response videos," instead of commenting via text. You have control over response videos, too. The same three options apply: You can allow them, disallow them, or allow them after approval. Viewers can also rate videos with the familiar thumbs-up and thumbs-down "voting" icon, and you should decide on a policy for that.

Let YouTube Do the Hosting

Recognizing that one of YouTube's strengths is to host video content, the folks at YouTube give you a wide variety of options for embedding videos or linking them to other sites on the web. This can be a tremendous advantage for you, especially if you have a large number of videos that you would like to use. There are a number of ways to utilize the videos that YouTube hosts for you:

Linking

The simplest way to use YouTube's video hosting capabilities is to provide a URL link back to the YouTube site. You can paste the link in its entirety into any textual communication, or you can attach it to the underlying HTML code. The best way to obtain a video's full URL address is to go to YouTube and click on the "Share" button under the video. From there you can cut and paste it wherever you would like. Note that you can provide links back to your YouTube channel page too; they don't have to go just to your individual videos.

Embedding

A very cool way to display YouTube videos is by embedding them in webpages. Embedding means that you generate HTML code that inserts the YouTube video directly into a webpage. The effect looks professional and you can customize the insertion for your webpage. You can even customize an embedded video in several ways:

- YouTube's default embedded player is borderless. You have the option to add a border if you like.
- You can override the standard gray color scheme with the color scheme control. This provides you an opportunity to match the embedded player more closely to a website's color scheme.
- You can specify the size of the video player that you want embedded on a webpage. This allows you to match the size of the player with the other graphic elements on the page.
- When someone views a YouTube video, YouTube stores a cookie on the user's computer. This is technically to enhance the user's experience by storing the video player preferences, but you may be sensitive to your visitors' privacy and wish not to store data on their computers. YouTube allows you to override cookies with a checkbox option.

- If you have uploaded your video in a high-definition format (HD), you can instruct the YouTube video player to play in HD.
- You have the option to choose an iframe code for playback on mobile devices. This typically uses either HTML5 or Flash format depending on the type of mobile device being used.

Have you looked at a YouTube video and seen a banner across the bottom with text and a website link? These are Call-to-Action Overlays, and they are a paid service that YouTube offers. Each overlay has a headline, two lines of text, and a website URL. Clicking on these banners will take the user to a URL of the advertiser's choice. This is the only option that YouTube offers advertisers to link away from the YouTube website.

Search Optimization

When people search for information online they use keywords, or keyword phrases, typed into search query fields. When they do so, they are presented with a ranked list of items that the search engine feels is the best match for the keywords entered. You probably know that this is how Google works and may know that YouTube operates the same way.

As the owner of videos on YouTube, you should know how to optimize the system so that your videos appear when target customers type in the appropriate keywords. This is called search engine optimization, or SEO. Search engine optimization needs to be part of your social marketing plan. If people can't find your videos when they search, it doesn't matter how good your video is; no one is ever going to see it. YouTube gives you three ways to describe your videos: tags, the title, and the video description. You should know how to optimize all three for best results.

ESSENTIAL

The optimum aspect ratio for YouTube videos is 16:9. This refers to the ratio of the width of the video image to the height. Standard video has an aspect ratio of 4:3 and this can be displayed on a YouTube video player but it will have black bars on the right and left sides of the image. Most of today's camcorders will record in either aspect ratio but 16:9 is recommended.

Tags

YouTube tags are basically keywords. Back in 2005, when YouTube first went live, this was the term the site used, and it has stuck since then. Tags can be individual words or keyword phrases. Each video you host on YouTube has a Tags field where you can fill in the words that you feel describe the video the best. Experts say the Tags field is the most important of the three descriptors to optimize, because this is where YouTube's search programs look first. The secret is to try to think like the person who is looking for something and guess the tags that she would use. In most cases, this isn't difficult, but experts say there is a real art to guessing what other people type into search engines. It's easy to think that they will type in what you would, but this often isn't the case.

Title

YouTube also looks at your video's title when it is matching videos to viewers' queries. Optimizing a title is a lot more challenging because titles are shorter—no more than 100 characters—and shouldn't be a list of keywords (it should look like a title!). If you spend a little time thinking about it, though, you can usually develop a good, keyword-rich title that will be both descriptive for your viewers and be recognized by search engines.

Video Description

Optimizing the descriptive text on your video is much easier than optimizing your title. You have a lot of room to work with and you can use keywords that may not be powerful enough for the title. An important point to keep in mind the first time you craft the description of your video is to do so naturally. If you stuff your video's description with keywords to intentionally steer traffic, YouTube will penalize you with lower rankings.

While not under your direct control, there are a few other things that will make your videos more appealing to YouTube's search algorithms. The first, and most obvious, is the number of views that your videos receive. If you have made a video about your crowdfunding campaign and it generates thousands of views, this is pretty good evidence that you have something of broad appeal to offer. YouTube naturally will rank that higher than less appealing videos.

The other thing that will help your video to rank higher is the number of people who have embedded your video into their webpages. The same logic applies here: The more people who embed, the more attractive your video must be.

Tracking

No matter what marketing function you are performing online, you should monitor it. There are two reasons for doing so. First, on the Internet, this is easy to do; second, you can optimize any marketing campaign rapidly when you fine-tune things and track your results. Stories of people doubling their response rates in just a few weeks are common.

Fortunately, the folks at YouTube give you access to some wonderful analytical features, in particular their Analytics tool. The Analytics tool breaks down the metrics of every video in your channels into four groups of statistics:

- **Performance:** The total number of views and subscribers over time in numerical and graph form.
- **Engagement:** The total number of likes/dislikes, comments, shares, and favorites added/removed.
- **Demographics:** The geographies where viewers come from and their gender.
- **Discovery:** Statistics on where viewers' requests for videos originate, and top traffic sources.

These four groups of statistics can be used to gauge the performance of your YouTube videos and your channel. Armed with statistics you can optimize engagement for the specific audiences that you wish to reach.

CHAPTER 13

Making Your Campaign Video

The statistics aren't subtle. Crowdfunding campaigns that have videos are over 100 percent more successful than those that don't. Consider it a given that you want to promote your campaign with a video in which you introduce yourself, explain your project, and generate some excitement about what you are doing. Don't be too concerned about the "professional" aspect of your video. Many crowdfunding videos are well produced, but more homespun videos made by the project creators themselves can be equally effective.

First Impressions

When you check out a crowdfunding campaign, the first thing you see is the introductory image or the campaign video. You should think of these as being the "first impression" of you and your project. As your mother always said, "You never get another chance to make a first impression," and this certainly holds true for your introductory image or video. It is the first thing visitors see and it has to be engaging; you have just a few moments to hook the viewer and lead him deeper into your campaign. Fortunately, with a little preparation and research, making an effective campaign video isn't difficult to do.

Crowdfunding campaigns utilizing campaign videos collect 122 percent more funds than those that don't. This particular statistic was provided by the crowdfunding site Indiegogo, but other sites report similar numbers. Bottom line? You need a video to introduce your crowdfunding campaign, or you are destined to underperform those that do.

Do Your Research

The first thing you need to do is learn what others are doing in their videos. You should spend an evening or two looking at other campaigns and their videos. Watch each a few times and take notes. Note the things that seemed to catch your eye; things that you like, things you didn't like, and general impressions of each one overall. Do this for a number of campaigns that met their funding goals and also with ones that didn't. Ask yourself if you can identify some of the characteristics that may have helped the successful campaigns do well and hindered the unsuccessful ones.

Here are a few items to look for while researching:

- Who is behind the project, and how do they present themselves?
- What is the project they propose? Is it easy to understand?
- Are they generating enthusiasm for their campaign and project?
- What is the call to action that they propose?
- What is the target audience for the campaign? Is it being addressed well?
- Does it seem like the goal is reasonable? Is it too high or too low?
- What does the project creator intend to do with the funds?

- What kind of rewards do they offer, and are they attractive?
- How long will this project take, and how long will it take to receive the rewards?
- What seems to be missing from the presentation? Are there any unanswered questions?

As you look over these other campaigns, remember that the success of a campaign is due to quite a number of factors. Don't feel that you are going to copy the look and feel of the videos attached to the highly successful campaigns you find. While they are probably great examples of the video craft, your video can be just as good, yet distinctly your own style.

It may be helpful to think about this research phase as assembling your "campaign video tool kit." As you look at other videos, you are going to form a lot of conclusions about the various techniques that other crowdfunders use. Collect this information for your tool kit and use the good stuff when designing and producing your own campaign video.

Develop Your Pitch

After you have assembled your video tool kit, you need to work on crafting your pitch. It is important to remember that the object of your presentation is to motivate someone to pledge your campaign. This requires you to have a carefully thought-through argument as to why they should.

When crafting your pitch, the first item on the agenda is to grab your viewers' attention right away; within the first five to ten seconds of the video is smart. Just as with a good book, you want to "set the hook" quickly and then move into brisk, engaging content. This is simply good storytelling, which is really what you are doing with your campaign video: You are telling a compelling story.

Incidentally, there are two things that you want to introduce right away in your video: yourself and your project. There isn't a correct order for doing this; you may want to lead with the excitement of your project, or you may want to begin the video by welcoming your viewers. Either method will grab attention and draw viewers in.

ALERT: Be very careful of utilizing images and audio clips that you find on the Internet. They are likely copyrighted and are the property of those who created them. The smartest thing to do is to use your own images and audio when you can. It is also fine to utilize royalty-free media. There are many websites that specialize in this and they can be found by simply searching for "royalty-free media"; iStockPhoto is one of the larger sites.

Over the course of the video, you want to elaborate on your project and express how important it is to you. For example, if you want to deliver food staples to a remote village in Tibet, by all means show the audience images of the village and its inhabitants, and show how you intend on delivering the food to them. Second—and it is hard to overstate this—show your enthusiasm for your project and your mission! Essentially what you are trying to do is tap into the altruism of others, and that extends not just to the subject of your project but to you, too! As you learned earlier in this book, you will find that there are many people out there who are peers and share your passion. Once they find out more about you, many will want to help you succeed. This is one of the truly exciting parts of crowdfunding.

Your Pitch Checklist

Now that you have the fundamentals of how to develop a good pitch, here are some of things you may want to include. The key is to place yourself in your viewers' position and think like they do. Remember, you are telling them a story; a story about you, your campaign, and your project. The better you tell this story, the more funds you will raise.

The audience for your campaign is likely to have questions like these:

- Who are you?
- What is your campaign about?
- What background do you have that is relevant to your campaign?
- How long will your project take to complete?
- How much funding do you need?

- What will my money be used for?
- What are the rewards that you are offering?
- What plans do you have after the project is completed?

Be sure that your campaign video addresses all these things, or are at least included in the written text on your campaign page. You don't want your potential pledgers to have to chase you for information you left out; they may simply leave and find another project that interests them.

Recording Your Video

Today there are a lot of devices that you can use to capture video, and most of them can be used to record the video for your crowdfunding presentation. The one you choose depends, essentially, on how professional you want your presentation video to be.

As a rough rule of thumb, the more money you wish to raise, the more professional your video should look. More polished videos impart a professionalism that ripples through an entire campaign, which usually translates into higher pledging. However, this is a rough rule of thumb. Not all highly successful campaigns have professional videos. Some are far less polished but make up for it with wonderful, engaging content; material that is compelling enough to get pledgers excited about the campaign.

Professional Camcorders

The best way to capture high-quality video is to use devices that are designed solely for this purpose. High-performance camcorders, such as professional and semiprofessional models, have ultrasharp lenses, high-resolution imaging elements, and great codecs (chips that process video). Camera technology like this can deliver "broadcast quality" video that can be used by virtually all media channels. The downside, of course, is that professional camcorders are expensive and rarely worth the investment just for a crowdfunding campaign. A far better option, if you decide you want to use professional-quality gear, is to borrow or rent it. Since presentation videos should be just two to three minutes in length, the amount of time you will be using the camcorder will probably be short.

Consumer Video Camcorders

The next tier down would include consumer camcorders and less expensive devices like flip video recorders and the like. Keep in mind that the video you are recording for a crowdfunding campaign is not destined to be blown up for display on HDTV screens; it is for distribution and display on smaller computer monitors. This means the resolution and quality of the video does not have to be big-bucks broadcast quality. Frankly, inexpensive camcorders and flip video recorders may be just fine for capturing the video that you intend to use in your campaign. If you are in doubt, make some test shots with the gear you have, upload it to YouTube, and see what it looks like.

> **ESSENTIAL**
>
> As is the case with most professional video productions, you may find that your indoor scenes need a little additional lighting. You can achieve this inexpensively with clamp lights, which are available at most hardware and home supply stores. Most are under $10, and with a 100-watt bulb installed they can throw a lot of light around. Experiment with placing clamp lights in different locations to remove the dark areas of your video scenes.

Cell Phone Cameras

You may find that the video you can capture from your smartphone or cell phone is perfectly adequate for web distribution, and thus for a crowdfunding presentation. In fact, most of the current generation of cell phones and smartphones can capture competent video; some of them in 720 and 1080 HD formats. Both of these high-resolution formats are superior to standard-resolution video and will yield images of greater sharpness and clarity. The disadvantage of using cell phones for video is really just the physical size of the phone and the physical limits of the technology. For example, a cell phone may be simply too difficult to hold steady, and the small lenses that cell phones have don't capture as much light as larger camcorders do (which means they're not as good for low-light situations). Despite those limitations, many crowdfunding campaign videos are shot on cell phones, and the video quality is adequate. Again, if you are in doubt, make some test shots, upload them to YouTube, and see what they look like.

Recording Audio

With today's camcorders and other video recording devices, you generally don't have to worry about capturing the audio that accompanies your video shots. All of these devices have decent built-in microphones to record audio. However, there are a few things you should know about the quality of the audio being captured; some of these devices are better than others and may be more flexible, too.

Dedicated camcorders generally capture sounds better than smartphones and flip video recorders because they have larger, more sensitive microphones. Camcorders also allow you to record multichannel sound (sound with left, right, and surround-sound channels) but this is not really necessary for crowdfunding videos—at least not yet. Dedicated camcorders also often allow you to connect higher-end separate microphones for special applications.

If you are filming outside or your actors are a distance from your video recorder, you may wish to "mic 'em up." This refers to placing external wireless microphones on each of the actors and recording what they say by attaching the wireless microphone receivers to the external microphone inputs on your camcorder. This is a technique that works quite well and is commonly used in professional video productions.

Editing Software

Back in the 16 and 35mm film days, most editing took place on big mechanical editing tables, the most famous of which were the Steenbeck and Moviola machines. On these mechanically complex devices editors physically handled film stock and performed editing tasks by cutting and splicing the film by hand. This style of editing was called "linear editing" because the editing was done in sequence. You couldn't jump around and edit different sections of the film without unwinding hundreds of feet of film stock to get to the section you wanted. Conceptually, linear editing is still done today. For example, when you are recording an event on video and you pause your camcorder (think of recording a sporting event and pausing during half time), you are performing "in-camera linear editing."

By contrast, today virtually all computer-based video editing programs perform non-linear editing (NLE). This is a far more flexible way of editing that allows you to import and assemble all of your video clips on a "timeline" and move them around like puzzle pieces to create all sorts of sequences. Add to that capability a huge range of production tools, such as titling, transitions, and special effects, and you have at your fingertips an amazingly powerful movie creation device.

Chances are that you already have some experience with the NLE editing programs bundled with your computer's operating system. This includes products such as Microsoft's Movie Maker (bundled with Windows OS) and Apple's iMovie (bundled with Apple OS). If not, don't be overly concerned; most of the consumer video editing programs available today are easy to learn and use.

> **ALERT**
>
> Be especially careful about downloading free video editing software packages and/or video conversion software from unfamiliar sources on the Net. Many of these packages contain spyware and malware and are difficult to remove. Unless you like having lots of silly menu bars that will slow down your computer and spy on your web habits, it is best to skip them entirely and stick with companies with reputable names.

Entry-Level Editing Software

You can get most entry-level editing software free. In addition to the bundled software already mentioned, there are quite a number of third-party freebies. Google's v-photo editor comes with basic video editing features and syncs with Picasa's online galleries. YouTube also offers its own YouTube Video Editor.

Enthusiast-Level Editing Software

Most crowdfunders will want to use the software in this category. These are very capable NLE video applications that range in price from $99 to $129. The range of complexity varies, but all are designed to appeal to the nonpro.

Spend some time researching these packages on the Net and pick the one that best suits your needs. Here are some suggestions:

- Cyberlink PowerDirector 10 Ultra ($99)
- Corel VideoStudio Pro X5 Ultimate ($99)
- Pinnacle Studio Ultimate v15 ($99)
- Adobe Premiere Elements 10 ($99)
- Avid Studio ($129)
- Vegas Movie Studio HD Platinum 11 Production Suite ($129)

Professional-Level Editing Software

Professional-level software is great stuff but more complex and more expensive than the first two categories. It is not necessary to have this level of software to make campaign videos, but it certainly won't hinder you either.

In the video editing high end, just as with photo software, there's a rivalry between Adobe and Apple. Apple's flagship is its Final Cut Pro X, which is a very capable NLE application that many editors swear by. It was recently upgraded to work with the 64-bit multicore machines and graphic hardware accelerators and is considered one of the most stable video editors available.

Adobe's flagship product is Premiere Pro CS5. Premiere Pro CS5 is also designed for 64-bit operation and supports a large variety of industry-standard input source formats. One of the advantages of Premiere Pro is that it is tightly integrated with other Adobe products, like After Effects, Audition, Photoshop, and others. This is a considerable advantage for the über-creative folks that live by Adobe Creative Suite products.

Others prefer Avid Media Composer. Avid Media Composer is an expensive product but many film and video professionals insist it is the standard to aspire to. Here's the roundup:

- Final Cut Pro X ($299)
- Adobe Premiere Pro CS5.5 ($799)
- Avid Media Composer 6 ($1,999)

FACT

Try before you buy. Almost all the video editing programs allow you to download versions for a free trial. Most are time-limited, full programs that allow you to use all the features for thirty days before they lock you out. A few of the software packages allow you to use the applications themselves, but some key features are disabled until you purchase the product. This is an excellent way to try out editing software. In many cases you may be able to finish your campaign video within the trial period.

Action!

So now that you have your camcorder fully charged, your video editing software fully installed, and your mind filled with ideas for the ultimate campaign video, it's time to start filming. The problem is, you aren't sure where to start.

Here are a few tips to help you conceptualize and plan your campaign video. The first is the basic film school technique of using master shots and cutaways, and the second is the nearly ubiquitous planning tool called storyboarding.

Master Shots and Cutaways

The foundation of most films and videos involves master shots and cutaways. Here's how it works: Imagine that you are making a music video for a famous band. One of the easiest ways to do this is to shoot an entire song while the whole band is performing. The shot encompassing the whole band for a four-minute song is pretty boring, so you shoot "cutaways." You ask the band to play again, and this time you shoot close-ups of the band members, the audience mosh pit, girls fainting, and other such things.

Later, back at your computer, you fire up your editing software, and import the master shot and audio onto your timeline. Then you import the cutaways and overlay them on top of the master shot without affecting the original audio. This technique works very well to break up the visual monotony of the wide shot and can be performed by virtually all the software editing packages. The resultant video is far more interesting and was pretty easy for the filmmaker to shoot.

Chapter 13: Making Your Campaign Video

> **ESSENTIAL**
>
> In the video and film industry, the "cutaway shots" are called B-roll. B-roll shots are the close-ups and filler that is occurring presumably when the A-roll (the main video) is being shot. You will want some B-roll in your campaign video. It will be things like pictures of people working on the project, external shots of your location, product shots at different angles, and other things tied to the content on the A-roll in some way.

Think about the master and cutaways concept when you are shooting your campaign video. Keep the camera rolling for the master shots and then grab some interesting cutaways later on. If you revisit some of your favorite campaign videos, you will see this technique used over and over.

Storyboarding

Need a little more planning? Professionals often use storyboards. A storyboard is a series of illustrations detailing the sequence of shots, actions, and effects that make up a film or video project. Storyboards can be hand drawn or composed digitally. For standard crowdfunding, hand-drawn storyboards are just fine (extra points for drawing them on the back of a napkin, by the way).

In 1928, Disney Studios created storyboards for the first Mickey Mouse cartoons. Storyboards have been used ever since then by filmmakers the world over. Alfred Hitchcock used them in all of his films and claimed that once he had one, he never needed to touch a camera during filming. He could simply point to the storyboard and tell an assistant, "Do this." That's the power of storyboards.

Making a storyboard for your crowdfunding campaign video should be pretty easy. Don't worry about your talent as an artist. Draw stick figures if you need to. Just get your thoughts onto paper and start to visualize how you will record and edit your video.

ALERT — You will find that your NLE application has many special effects. Most of them are fun to look at but are not recommended for your campaign video. Here's why: These fancy transitions do not really add any value to the presentation that you are making. In fact, a lot of them look sort of goofy and may detract from your message.

Final Checklist

Now that you have assembled your campaign video and you are about to publish it (convert it to a video format that is web friendly), go through the following checklist to be sure you haven't left out anything critical. You may find that some items can be corrected via editing, but others may require shooting more video. The important part is that they're caught now before you "go live."

Did You Grab Your Viewers' Attention Right Away?

Make sure that in the first ten to fifteen seconds you have shown or said something that grabs your audience. If you don't, chances are they won't come back. It's like reading a magazine. You open up to an article, read a few sentences, and if nothing great seems to be there, you are off to other articles in the magazine. Opportunity lost.

Is Your Video Short and Message Clear?

As soon as you have your viewers' attention, get right to the core points you are trying to make. Subsequent commentary and imagery should be designed to reinforce your core points. If you have any material that is repetitious and weak, it is best to take it out. The goal of your campaign video is to motivate viewers to donate to your project. It is easy to think that a little additional entertainment may help your video, but in many cases it may hinder it. Keep it short and sweet.

Did You Sell Yourself?

Many people find that selling themselves is the hardest part of crowdfunding. The fact is that your audience wants to get to know you and what you are all about. It's critical that you illustrate the human interest story behind your crowdfunding campaign. Otherwise, it just becomes a pitch from a faceless somebody somewhere. Appear in your video right away and introduce yourself. Explain your passion for your project and tell them why it is so exciting for them, too. This is the stuff that motivates people to pledge. They want to feel like they are members of your community and that you are a peer to them.

Did You Demonstrate Value Creation?

You want your viewers to get an immediate feeling on how you are creating value in some way. They will be interested in helping you out if you have a strong value creation mechanism illustrated. If you are making something, show your audience what it is and how they will benefit from it. If your project is socially oriented, show how their contribution will help others and help change the world. If your goal is to build a business, show your viewers how the products or services of this business will benefit them directly. Creating value, directly or indirectly, is what motivates a great deal of what people do.

Did You Issue a Call to Action?

Any video can reinforce the brand you are creating, but you want much more than this. You want to generate an audience reaction that leads to actionable steps. This call to action can take the form of a simple request ("Donate now so we can reach our goal").

Spread the Word

Your campaign video is something that you design specifically to introduce and draw people into your project. If you craft a great video, one that really engages your audience, you definitely have fulfilled your mission by creating a portal into your campaign. However, you may have created something equally powerful: a video-based asset that can make it on its own out on the Internet.

Think of it this way: Your video probably contains most of your pitch and lots of exciting, engaging content. It is a capsule of your entire project, and it can be sent out on the Internet to help you promote your crowdfunding campaign. Your job now is to give it a nice sendoff party.

The first thing to do is post it to the video sharing sites like YouTube, Vimeo, Viddler, and others. These websites will generate "embed tags" that allow others to embed your video on their webpages and blogs.

Next, get Google interested. Video is considered a higher form of engagement than just articles and blogs, and Google will usually place it higher in search engine rankings. You definitely want Google to take notice of your video by describing it well in the title tags you attach to it. Here is a list of five "must dos" to get the word out.

- Post your video on YouTube, Vimeo, and other video networking sites.
- E-mail the URL to mailing lists of people you know and ask them to share it with their friends.
- Post your video on Facebook, Twitter, LinkedIn, and other social networking sites.
- Make sure you have a call to action in the descriptive text where viewers are asked to share it with others.
- Write a press release, link it to your video, and share it with prominent newsletter sites.

It is important to realize that there is a multiplier effect at work here. The more people watch your video, the higher your rank on Google and the more exposure you will receive. When the search algorithms at Google and the other search engines see a large number of people linking to a video within a twenty-four-hour period, it views that video as hot stuff and moves it up quickly in the rankings. This is what you want to happen!

CHAPTER 14

Protecting Your Idea

Once your idea is posted on a crowdfunding site it is available for the whole world to see. This, of course, means that it may be copied or used in some way without your permission. While the likelihood of someone copying your idea is remote, you need to be aware that there are many ways entrepreneurs and artists can protect their intellectual property in case this occurs. This chapter will survey the various methods of protecting your ideas and concepts.

Intellectual Property

Intellectual property is a broad term that refers to the legal rights that can be given to "creations of the mind." These rights, which are similar to those most often associated with real or tangible property, are granted by a combination of federal and state statutory laws in the United States.

Intellectual property, often referred to as "IP," can be divided into two general categories: *industrial property*, which includes patents, trademarks, and designs; and *copyrights*, which include written and artistic works. Both of these two groups are broadly considered intellectual property, but are different in significant ways, as you will learn later in this chapter.

> **eV FACT**
>
> Even though intellectual property refers to "creations of the mind," it is important to realize that this does not refer to the "ideas" themselves. The idea for a device, product, or process is not patentable. What can be patented is the realization of the idea, something that can successfully be built and have a useful purpose.

The reason that societies establish laws to protect intellectual property is to spur innovation. If one's ideas could be easily copied and exploited by others, there would be little incentive for creative individuals to follow through with developing them. For example, suppose you have an idea for a new invention involving home safety. If a competitor could simply steal your idea after you release it, you might never bother to develop it in the first place. The results of this action would be that you, the inventor, would lose the potential to profit from your invention, and society as a whole might never benefit from your idea. Thankfully, the possibility of scenarios such as this was recognized by lawmakers long ago, and intellectual property protection laws have been established by the governments of most countries.

For entrepreneurs there is yet another reason to consider intellectual property protection: to build value in your business. If the basis of a new business is generated directly from your idea and you anticipate needing financing or someday selling the business, you will be much more likely to interest investors if you clearly show that your idea IP is an asset that is owned by the business. This makes the company more valuable.

Protecting Your Intellectual Property

Should you really be concerned about your idea being stolen? The answer is Yes. Although actual incidences of ideas being stolen are quite rare, the possibility does exist. You need to know what you can do to protect yourself so that if someone does decide to use your intellectual property without your permission, you will have some recourse.

Document Everything

The most important concept is to document your ideas and concepts as you develop them. This means things like keeping a written log of your ideas and related thoughts, along with dates and signatures attached. Many inventors are compulsive about this and do it using standard lab notebooks.

ESSENTIAL

> When you document your thoughts in a lab notebook or journal don't just sign the pages and contents yourself; have them signed by a witness. This can be as casual as having a friend or neighbor act as your witness, as long as it's someone who can verify not only your idea but the fact that he or she witnessed you signing the document on the day and time that you actually did.

It is especially important to document any times that you shared your idea, either in person or via other means. Keep a log of who you spoke with, along with where and when. The reason for this documentation is that in the unlikely event that someone does steal your idea and successfully gets a patent or other protection, you stand a good chance of getting it invalidated in a court of law.

And, of course, there are formal legal methods of protecting ideas and concepts using legal instruments such as patents, trademarks, and copyrights.

Patents

When the U.S. Patent and Trademark Office (USPTO) issues a patent, it is granting intellectual property rights to a person who invents or develops a tangible idea or process. This legal protection was established in the United States by the founding fathers and is included in the Constitution. Article One, Section 8, Clause 8 of that document states that "The Congress shall have power . . . to promote the progress of science and useful arts, by securing for limited times to authors and inventors the exclusive right to their respective writings and discoveries." Historians note that this concept was entirely unique at the time; for the first time in world history, the intrinsic right of an inventor to profit from his intellectual property was recognized by law.

While the patent process is thoroughly entrenched in U.S. commerce today, most people still misunderstand what rights a patent really grants. Specifically, a patent does not grant the right to make, produce, or import something; *it grants the right to prevent others from doing so*. In the language of the statute itself, patents grant "the right to exclude others from making, using, offering for sale, or selling" the invention in the United States or importing the invention into the United States. What is important here is the phrase "the right to exclude others." This means that if someone is exploiting what the patent system has deemed your intellectual property, you can pursue legal means to stop that person from doing so. This, of course, is a very powerful right to which you are entitled as a result of being granted a patent.

Prior to 1995, United States utility patents had durations of seventeen years from the date that the patent was issued. Today, however, that duration has been extended to twenty years, with the clock starting from the date that the patent application was actually filed. In some cases, five-year extensions can be granted to utility patent grants, but this is rare. Design patents have shorter periods of protection; they are granted a fourteen-year term that begins with the date of issue.

Types of Patents

In the United States, the patent office recognizes three types of patents: utility, design, and plant patents. Here is a brief examination of each of the three types.

Utility Patents

Anyone who invents or develops items or processes that are useful may be granted utility patents. These encompass machines, devices, processes, manufactured objects, new substances, and many other items. It is important to note that utility patents can also be obtained on new and useful improvements on existing products, processes, and the like.

Design Patents

Original ornamental designs for manufactured items may be granted a design patent. Design patents can be described as protecting the "form" of an item while having little concern with the "function." A good example of a design patent might be the shape of the original glass Coca-Cola bottles. These fluted, curvilinear bottles are strongly indicative of the Coca-Cola brand and were originally protected via a design patent (today the shape is protected by trademark rights, which are explained later in this chapter). Design patents carry shorter terms than those of utility patents in the United States: just fourteen years from date of filing.

Historically design patents have been considered relatively weak methods of protecting the form and shape of objects. In other words, it is not difficult for a competitor to make minor changes in an object's shape and claim it constitutes a new ornamental form.

Plant Patents

Plant patents may be assigned to anyone who invents, asexually reproduces, or discovers a new variety of plant. Plant patents are especially important in the pharmaceutical and agriculture industries because so many of their products originate from unique varieties of plants.

Patentability

In order for a particular concept to be granted a United States patent, the patent office requires that it meet three specific criteria: it must be "novel," "useful," and "nonobvious." If you are considering patent protection for your idea or concept, you should take a good look to see if it meets these criteria:

- **The concept must be novel.** The term "novel" has a strictly defined definition according to patent law. For an idea or concept to be "novel," it must be a fresh, new idea. In other words, it was not known or used prior, it was not described in any printed publication, and it certainly isn't covered by another patent. The prior existence of an idea is often referred to as "prior art." In other words, a patentable

idea cannot be shown in any publication or any previous patent. This would constitute "prior art" and invalidate its novelty because it obviously isn't a completely new idea.
- **The concept must be useful.** For an object or idea to be "useful" means that it fulfills a useful purpose. For example, in the case of a machine, it means that it must operate and perform its intended purpose. In the case of a process, the process must actually work as intended, not just as described.
- **The concept must be nonobvious.** The concept of being "nonobvious" is often described as "having a sufficient difference from what has been used or described before that a person having ordinary skill in the area of technology related to the invention would not find it obvious to make the change." In other words, the concept must be unique enough so someone who routinely works in the subject field would not consider it a routine difference or change in what they frequently do.

Provisional Patent Applications

Filing a formal utility patent application is a substantial process that takes a lot of time and can be expensive. Thankfully the USPTO developed a form of protection in 1995 called the "Provisional Patent Application" that allows you to obtain a degree of protection quickly without filing a full-blown utility patent application.

Provisional Patent Applications are very different from standard patent applications. The most important of the differences is that you submit provisional patents to the USPTO like standard patents, but they are *not* examined for content and they do *not* mature into a standard utility patent like a utility application can. In fact, Provisional Design Applications are automatically abandoned twelve months from their filing date.

QUESTION

Should you bother with a provisional application?
It depends. If you are convinced that you have a great new idea that is a sure winner, you may want to go right for the utility patent. If you are still fleshing out your idea, consider a provisional application, which will allow you to take your time doing research as well as to fine-tune your idea and perhaps form an organization to bring it to fruition.

Don't feel you are alone if you are wondering what good provisional applications actually are. They are misunderstood by many people. Provisional applications are designed to simply identify the subject matter involved for a utility patent application, to be submitted later and to establish an official filing date. Basically, you can envision them as a placeholder that gives you one year to develop your concept, gather financing, and arrange other things before you submit your actual formal utility patent. Those who do file a provisional patent application can legally use the phrase "Patent Pending" in all documentation and correspondence. In this context, "Provisionals" are quite popular among inventors and others.

Trademarks

A trademark is a distinctive indicator using a word, name, symbol, or combination of these elements to represent a unique good or goods. It is generally a mark used in commercial trade to identify the source of goods and distinguish them from the others. A service mark is similar except that it identifies and distinguishes the source of a service instead of an actual product or goods. "Roto-Rooter," for example, is a service mark that represents a specific company that performs drain cleaning.

It is important to realize that trademark rights are significant and can be used to prevent others from using "confusingly similar marks"; however, they cannot be used to stop others from making or selling the same goods or services. For example, H. J. Heinz Company can stop anyone who tries to sell products that use packaging and logos similar to those used by Heinz, but it cannot stop other companies from selling ketchup!

eV FACT

> Types of trademarks can be identified by the following symbols: ™ indicates an unregistered trademark, and is a mark used to promote goods; ℠ indicates an unregistered trademark, and is a mark used to promote services; and ® indicates a trademark registered with the USPTO.

Trademarks that are used in interstate and foreign commerce are generally registered with the USPTO, but not always. If you are making goods or performing services, you can use a trademark without federal registration and have some protection. Such unregistered trademarks may still be considered legally valid because they are covered by common law rights, which are rights that exist simply because of usage. However, it should be noted that unregistered trademarks are not nearly as robust as registered ones, and you may only be able to protect them within the geographical area in which you use them. If you are considering national or international distribution of your product or service, you are strongly advised to consider a federally registered trademark.

Copyrights

A copyright is a form of protection for original works of authorship such as literary, musical, and artistic works, both published and unpublished. Copyrights are registered in the United States by the U.S. Copyright Office, a part of the Library of Congress, for the life of the author plus seventy years. They grant the owner of a copyright the exclusive right to reproduce and profit from his or her intellectual property, or to transfer those rights to other people or organizations.

It should be noted that a copyright protects the form of the expression rather than the subject involved. For example, a painting of a vase of flowers could be copyrighted, but not the subject. It is the way the artist portrays the vase of flowers that is unique, and that is what can be considered intellectual property.

Control of Your Name

When you crowdfund, you present more than just your idea for the world to see; you present yourself, too. You do this on the actual crowdfunding site itself and certainly on all the associated social media, blogs, and other public forums involved. In fact, this is a highly desirable thing, because those who tend to pledge crowdfunded projects are especially interested in the people and stories behind the scenes. However, just because you have made yourself more visible so people can see who is behind the crowdfunded project doesn't mean that your name and identity can be used in ways you disapprove.

The law involved here is called "The Right of Publicity." Any unauthorized use of your name, nickname, stage name, picture, or video can be considered infringing on your right of publicity, and you can ask the perpetrator to cease and desist from doing so. Although this situation is almost unheard of, it is good to know that an actual law can be used to prevent someone from doing this.

The First to File Rule

Just recently a major overhaul was made in the United States patent system. The United States previously had what was considered a "first to invent" system with regard to its patent approval process. This meant that the first person, or group, who conceived an invention or process, and reduced it to practice, was considered first in line for patent approval. This means that if you are the first person who came up with an idea and proved it could work then you have the legitimate rights to call it your own. Meanwhile, virtually all the rest of the world uses a "first to file" system, which means that the first person who actually *files* the application for a patent is considered the first in line. This may not be the person who first came up with the idea.

On September 16, 2011, the America Invents Act was signed into law by President Barack Obama. This unprecedented act changed the American patent law process so it now aligns with the rest of the world. The United States patent process is now officially a "first to file" system. The reasoning behind this radical change in patent law is that it streamlines the severely backlogged American patent process (1.2 million backlogged, early 2012) because it eliminates a great deal of the research that the patent examiners have to do. As a result, this potentially accelerates American innovation.

However, the first to file rule doesn't mean true "first inventors" are left out in the cold; it means that the burden of proof has shifted. If you invent something "first" but don't file it, you may still have rights to the idea but you would have to appeal to the USPTO to determine who was the first inventor, and thereby who is entitled to the patent. Essentially, the game now goes to those who file first.

Obtaining Patents and Trademarks

There are two ways to obtain patents and trademarks. You can do it yourself or hire an attorney or other third party to do it. As you might imagine, there are advantages and disadvantages to each method.

Thousands of inventors have successfully filed for patents and trademarks on their own. The USPTO website has extensive resources to guide you if you decide to do this yourself. In fact, federal law requires patent examiners at the U.S. Patent and Trademark Office to help individual inventors who apply for patents without a lawyer's help. There are also many web-based resources and books that can assist you. With some study and determination, filing for patents and trademarks is not difficult to do.

> **ALERT**
>
> Beware of little-known organizations that offer to help inventors with patent and trademark assistance. There are many of these companies on the Internet, and they are quick to take your money and simply file your paperwork with little oversight. If you need help, seek a local, or known, professional patent attorney to give you a hand.

In many cases, depending on parameters such as available finances, time frame, and the anticipated value of what is being patented, you may want to hire an attorney to file the paperwork for your patent or trademark. For many people this is a wise decision because there are many pitfalls that a professional patent attorney can help you avoid. The downside, of course, is cost. It is rare that professional attorneys earn less than $150 per hour, and many earn considerably more. As you would for many services that professionals provide, you should shop around and get quotes from lawyers that specialize in patent law. In most cases, working with a local patent attorney is a good idea because you can physically meet with him or her during the process.

Determining Whether Your Idea Is Already Patented

Before you start the patenting process, you should know whether your idea has been developed or published by someone else. If you intend to seek patent protection yourself, any prior art will quickly invalidate the process. Second, you should be aware of infringement. If you intend to sell, use, make, or import something involving someone else's idea, you are liable for infringement on *their* patent.

Today, however, avoiding trouble by identifying the uniqueness of ideas is easier than ever. Not only does the USPTO have an extensive search engine for all U.S. patents filed since 1790; so do many other organizations. Here are a few you might consider when searching for patents and trademarks:

- U.S. Patent and Trademark Office: (*www.uspto.gov/patft*) Covers U.S. patents issued from 1790 to the most recent weekly issue date. The USPTO also has considerable resources for the neophyte inventor to use.
- Google Patents: (*www.google.com/patents*) Google has designed a remarkably simple yet powerful patent search engine. Over 7 million patents are catalogued, all with full images.
- Free Patents Online (FPO): (*www.freepatentsonline.com*) Covers patents and applications from USPTO, EPO, WIPO, and JPL abstracts.
- European Patent Office: (*www.epo.org/searching/free/espacenet.html*) The EPO offers this excellent search engine for European, U.S., Patent Cooperation Treaty, Japanese, and other worldwide patents.
- Japan Patent Office: (*www.jpo.go.jp*) A searchable database of Japanese patent abstracts, which includes the patent number, title, inventor, company, and abstract of the patent.
- CIPO (Canadian Intellectual Property Office): (*http://patents1.ic.gc.ca/intro-e.html*) This is a Canadian patent database with data from 1989 to the present, including the patent number, classification, and title of patents.

CHAPTER 15

The Campaign's Finished

When you run a crowdfunding campaign, it seems like the campaign itself is a marathon, especially during the last few days when the pledging gets frenetic. However, after the campaign is finished you are really just halfway through, and for many campaigns the second half is when the real work begins. Now you have to deliver those rewards you promised and deal with all those backers who are going to expect frequent updates on the whole process. No question this can be a challenging time in your crowdfunding life, but this chapter will give you lots of tips to make it go as easily as possible.

The End of a Campaign

The end of a crowdfunding campaign can be pretty exciting. As it gets closer to the time the campaign formally ends, additional pledges will usually come flowing in. In the case of a really successful campaign, they may absolutely flood in. Frankly, there's nothing more satisfying to see than your total pledge count increase every time you click on the refresh button on your browser.

If you have had a successful campaign and hit your funding goal (or blew right by it), you deserve to be congratulated for a job well done. Honestly, this is the time to pause and enjoy the moment. It's time for a little celebration. You have earned well-deserved congratulations.

> **ESSENTIAL**
>
> After your campaign ends you will probably be surprised with how many of your backers send you personal messages congratulating you and asking all sorts of questions about the campaign and the rewards. This is not just because they are acting impulsively and want their "stuff," but more because they feel a part of your campaign and a connectedness to your project.

What's Next?

Once the campaign has closed, you enter into a very different phase. You now have many backers who are eager for information and are waiting for their rewards. If you properly set expectations during your campaign and told the crowd that delivery won't occur for a while, you'll be okay. However, you should know that many people who pledge crowdfunding campaigns tend to confuse the project with standard retail business models. In other words, they will expect to get their rewards quite soon.

The bottom line is that expectations for rapid reward delivery are going to occur no matter how well you explain what a crowdfunding campaign is all about. In other words, now that the campaign has ended, you, the project creator, have to go off and hand-make all those rewards. Even if you go out of your way and emphasize how excited you are to build all the rewards, and how much work it is going to be, some backers will want them right away anyway. Just expect it and when they start asking "how much longer," politely answer that you are working as hard as you can and they will be available "soon."

The First Update after the Campaign Ends

All the major crowdfunding sites allow you to send updates to those who have pledged your campaign. Hopefully, you did this many times during the campaign to spread information as it developed and to rally the troops. If not, you will need to do this quite a bit now that the campaign has ended, because your backers will expect it. In fact, some will soon demand it.

If your campaign was successful, you should send out your first update to everyone as soon as your campaign ends—if possible, within the hour. Here's what you should address:

- Announce that the campaign has ended, what the goal was, and how much was raised
- Thank everyone for pledging and for spreading the word to their social networks
- Reiterate how excited you are that your project will now begin
- Explain that you will be updating them as often as possible
- Reiterate the time frame for the project and the steps involved
- State a date or time frame within which you expect to ship the rewards

Even if your campaign wasn't successful, it's important to send out an update. Since there is a chance that you may run your campaign once again with a lower pledge goal or other modifications, this is a good time to keep the troops rallied. Thank them all for their participation and convey any thoughts that you may have about the campaign and why it was a positive experience for everyone involved. If you think you may be running a followup campaign, tell everyone that may occur.

The Next Day

The day after your crowdfunding campaign ends, log in to your website as an administrator. When you do, you will see some new things on your dashboard page. With a Kickstarter campaign, you will find all the final campaign statistics filled in, along with contact information for your backers. There will also be a graph that shows pledge activity over the course of the campaign, a pie chart showing where backers were referred from, a bar chart showing reward popularity, and several other informational items.

ALERT

> People may contact you after your project closes and ask if they can still pledge. The answer to this is up to you, of course, but they won't be able to go through the standard crowdfunding channels for payments that the others did. Your best option would be to have them send you the funds directly to your PayPal account or just have them mail it to you. Just be sure to keep track of these "add-ons" because their data will not be included with the backer's reports that the crowdfunding site prepares for you.

The other thing you will see is a tab labeled "Backers Reports." Click on this tab and you will see a spot that will become very familiar to you in the coming months: the Backers' Report Page. This is a listing of all of your backers and all the data that was collected by the crowdfunding site from them. On Kickstarter, the list includes:

- Backer's name (this may be a screen name or nickname)
- Backer's e-mail address
- Date of the pledge
- Amount of the pledge
- Status of the pledge (whether the backer's credit card was successfully charged)
- Responses to survey (filled in after you send a survey out)
- Notes to self (a text field where you can enter notes)
- A private message link to the backer

You will also find a link on the backers' page that takes you directly to your Amazon Payments account, as well as a large blue button that connects you to a page to create custom backer surveys.

Chapter 15: The Campaign's Finished

Survey Says!

Most of the major crowdfunding sites allow you to send an online survey to all those who backed your project. This is a very valuable tool and can save you a great deal of work in collecting information from your backers. Dealing with your backers via any other method, especially via standard e-mail, will increase your workload tenfold. This is especially true if you have a very large number of backers to deal with.

QUESTION

When should I send out the survey to my backers?
There is no hard and fast rule about this but there are two schools of thought. One says that it is best to capture all of your backers' information soon after your campaign closes so you can start getting the data ready for use, such as product preferences and shipping arrangements. The alternative is to wait until you are ready to deliver the rewards and then you will get the most up-to-date information from your backers, particularly any address changes. Either way works but if you are going to hold off on the backers' survey, make sure your backers know when they can expect it and give them an estimated date.

The survey forms that are provided to you by the major crowdfunding sites are configurable. In other words, you are allowed to design the form so that all the information you need from your backers can be captured. Fortunately, this is easy to do.

Most of the major crowdfunding sites allow you to send a survey form to your backers only once (this is an important detail!) so make sure that you ask your backers for all the information you need. At minimum, you should consider asking for these items:

- Backer's "pledged" name (this may be a screen name or nickname)
- Backer's e-mail address
- Backer's real name (first and last)
- Backer's full address
- Backer's phone number
- Product options (things like color, size, etc., if applicable)
- Comments

Many of the survey forms that the crowdfunding sites allow you to send have a built-in requirement that you should know about: The forms are coded so that the backer must fill in *all* the fields or the survey form won't submit. In other words, if you leave a field blank, you can't click the "Submit" button. Why is this important to know? Because it may confuse your backers when their form won't submit, even when text is displayed that says "all fields must be completed." To avoid confusion like this, make sure that in the directions you leave for your backers you mention that all fields must be filled in. Let them know that they should write "N/A" in any blank field.

Keeping Records of Your Campaign

Most of the crowdfunding sites will allow you to download your backers' information in a file that you can import into most spreadsheet and text editing applications. Kickstarter, Indiegogo, and others give you all your backers' information in .csv (comma separated values) files. You can open .csv files with programs such as Microsoft Excel, Microsoft Office, Open Office, Notepad, and most text editors. It is not absolutely necessary to use the .csv files to view your backers' information, but it is very helpful with large populations of backers.

If you decide to use the .csv files, all you have to do is click on the file and your browser will download it. After you download the file, take a deep breath and open it. You will find that the data is all in there, technically organized in the proper fields but will probably look like a mess. This is because the file was imported using the default settings for the .csv data. You will probably find the text too large, columns too small, rows too short, and so on. If you have some experience with spreadsheets you may know that this is a common situation, and within minutes you can adjust the spreadsheet formatting so the data is more usable. If you don't have spreadsheet experience, this may be a time to have a friend help you out.

ESSENTIAL

If you aren't a spreadsheet guru, but are determined to wrestle your downloaded .csv backers' data files into a manageable form by yourself, don't despair. There are many free sites on the web that will step you through the basics of Microsoft Excel, Open Office, and other spreadsheet applications.

Chapter 15: The Campaign's Finished

How Do You Get Your Money?

On all the major crowdfunding sites, the money that is collected from the backers is processed by a third-party financial company. Kickstarter uses Amazon Payments, and most of the others use PayPal. While the pledging experience for these two companies is different for your backers, for you the crowdfunder, it is similar. Your funds are simply collected from your backers and placed in your account. The financial firm typically charges 4–5 percent for processing the funds, and the crowdfunding site also will collect fees, typically 5 percent or more.

In case you are unsure of the sequence of events, this is how backers' pledges are typically processed. First, assuming a campaign is successful (the final goal has been reached), all the backers' credit cards are processed at once, at the end of the campaign. The money collected is posted to your Amazon or PayPal account, where it is generally held for several days. (Not long ago Amazon Payments held crowdfunded funds for fourteen days, but this has been shortened to just a few days now.) After Amazon Payments and PayPal release the funds, the money sits in your account until you transfer it to your personal or business bank account.

Shipping Your Product

Shipping is like the roughage in a crowdfunder's diet. During the campaign nobody wants to talk about it, but after the campaign closes, you have to talk about it daily. If you have a digital product, you don't have to worry much about shipping details; you can e-mail it to backers, send it via Dropbox, or ship it in a small mailing envelope. If you have a tangible product, and it's something large, you'll need to figure out how to ship it.

When you ship things to backers, you have numerous options to consider. Shipping can be very expensive, especially if you are shipping internationally. It makes sense to do a lot of research before you arrange for shipping. If you have many items to ship, you can save a lot of money by picking an optimum service.

Fortunately, the Internet makes things much easier than they were in the old days. All the major shipping services like the U.S. Postal Service (USPS), FedEx, UPS, and DHL explain their services and quote rates on their websites. There are also many websites that will help you compare the shipping rates among the various carriers so you don't have to visit each carrier's website. A few goods ones are: ShipGooder.com, PackBuddy.com, and ShippingSidekick.com.

ALERT

> If you are going to be shipping a lot of items as a result of your crowdfunding campaign and you believe there may be significant sales volume afterward, you may want to call the sales rep in your area for FedEx, UPS, DHL, or other carriers. When you deal directly with a sales rep you can usually negotiate shipping rates that may save you money.

Packaging and Packing

The cost of packaging and packing materials can add up pretty quickly when you need to ship a lot of items. If you don't often deal with packaging materials, you will probably be surprised at how expensive they can be. Plan on spending as much time choosing the packing materials you are going to use as choosing the shipping service. You will find in most cases that the extra time you spend on these steps will pay off immensely.

To obtain packaging, you basically have two choices: You can get it free—or at least at no extra cost—from some carriers, or you can simply pay for it outright. Let's start with the free stuff.

First of all, free shipping materials aren't really free; their price is built into the cost of the shipping service. For example, when you visit your local post office, you will see a wide selection of boxes, sleeves, and envelopes for shipping things via the USPS Express Mail and Priority Mail services. Even though these two services are "premium" services, when you factor in the cost of the packaging, you may end up paying no more than you would for first class with your own packaging. To determine whether this is the case, simply take one of your rewards to the post office, package it up in various ways using your own materials, and ask the postal clerk which way is cheapest. Pretty simple. The private carriers such as FedEx, UPS, DHL, and others also offer free packaging in their shipping depot centers. As with the USPS, try out the various shipping services and see which is the most affordable to use.

The second way to obtain packaging is to buy it. You can buy packaging at office supply stores, but you will find it is very expensive at those locations. Unless you are shipping just a few items, you need to buy your packaging for a commercial packaging company. Two large companies that offer excellent prices are Uline and PackagingPrice.

> **FACT**
>
> Even though the pricing for small quantities of shipping materials is very high at office supply stores, you may want to talk to them about setting up a commercial account. Pricing for larger packaging orders with a commercial discount will be much more affordable.

Ongoing Updates

During your crowdfunding campaign you likely sent out a number of updates to your backers answering questions, announcing changes you were considering, and further promoting your project. After the campaign is over, the frequency should increase quite a bit. The reason for this is that your backers will pepper you with questions, and when you get the same question several times in a row, it's often easier to answer the question by sending out an update to everyone. Also, regardless of how often and in how many places you explain the process and timeline involved in making and delivering the rewards, you will still have a constant stream of questions about these issues.

Most of the major crowdfunding sites allow you to send a text-only message in addition to images, audio, and video. Most crowdfunders simply send updates containing text and images, which is fine for the vast majority of communications. However, sending video- and audio-only updates will seem a little more personal and may be more effective in some cases. In particular, if part of your reward creation process involves something that can be captured on video, say a scene for your documentary, showing this raw footage to your donors will keep your nervous donors ("When's it going to be done?") at bay.

Believe it or not, some of your backers will complain that you send out too many updates, and some will ask for more. You can't please everyone. Most crowdfunders report that sending two updates per week is just about right. By the way, backers who do not wish to receive updates can opt out of the ones that are sent from most platforms. The opt-out is in the form of a link at the bottom of update e-mails.

CHAPTER 16

Five Successful Campaigns

One of the most productive things you can do as you get ready for your crowdfunding campaign is to take a look at what others before you have done. Fortunately, all the crowdfunding sites archive their past campaigns for anyone to view and analyze. This chapter will look at some of the great ones and some of the average ones. Studying the many common threads that run through these campaigns will provide you with guidance and examples of how to do it right.

TikTok+LunaTik Multi-Touch Watch Kits

- **Platform:** Kickstarter
- **Creator:** Scott Wilson and MINIMAL Studios
- **Backers:** 13,512
- **Original Goal:** $15,000
- **Amount Pledged:** $942,578

No examination of crowdfunding campaigns would be complete without looking at the TikTok+LunaTik watch campaigns that finished on Kickstarter December 16, 2010. This campaign created a buzz that went viral on the Internet because of the magnitude of the total pledges. Although the TikTok+LunaTik project has been surpassed by several crowdfunding campaigns to date, this one was the first to just about glance the $1 million mark.

The TikTok+LunaTik watch kit campaign was for a custom-made case designed to enclose the then-new iPod nano. Because the iPod nano had a clock function, there was a lot of talk that it would make a wonderful watch if there was some sort of way to mount it on your wrist. This observation did not slip by Scott Wilson and his MINIMAL Design Studios. He designed two models and crowdfunded them on Kickstarter.

When looking at the TikTok+LunaTik campaign, one of the first things you see are striking images of the two watch models. The photography is excellent and there are many views shown. The text describing the watches points out that MINIMAL Studios designs products for major brands, but their dream is to make their own products. Kickstarter, as they explain, "is a great way for us to realize many of the ideas that we have in our small studio that we know people will love but big companies are scared to do."

eV FACT

One of the major reasons that the TikTok+LunaTik campaign was such a success had to do with the tightly networked nature of "the Apple nation." Apple fans are a very passionate and loyal group and have hundreds of active communities across the web. When the TikTok+LunaTik campaign initially hit, news quickly spread outside Kickstarter's borders and Apple fans quickly linked back to the campaign and pledged.

The video for the TikTok+LunaTik campaign opens with Wilson introducing himself and his company. It then goes into a series of shots showing design drawings and early renderings of an electronic watch. Wilson goes on to elaborate on the quality of the work that his firm produces and his vision for the TikTok+LunaTik watches. The video does a very good job of combining a heartfelt appeal with a feeling of considerable product expertise.

The rewards offered by Wilson hit the $25 and $50 sweet spots perfectly. For $1, pledgers received a thank you; for $25, a preorder of the $34.95 retail TikTok model; for $50, a preorder of the $69.95 retail LunaTik model; for $70, a preorder of both models; for $150, a red-anodized, signed LunaTik model; for $500, a red-anodized model plus ten TikTok and LunaTik watches (only 100 available).

Mosquita y Mari

- **Platform:** Kickstarter
- **Creator:** Aurora Guerrero
- **Backers:** 888
- **Original Goal:** $80,000
- **Amount Pledged:** $82,468

There can be little argument that crowdfunding is one the largest disruptive forces to ever descend upon the independent filmmaking community. True, the advent of affordable, broadcast-quality camcorders was a major watershed, but the availability to fund productions via the crowd is huge. There has never been a more exciting time to be a filmmaker.

Writer/Director Aurora Guerrero is a talented filmmaker living in Oakland, CA. Her Kickstarter project *Mosquita y Mari* is a coming-of-age story that focuses on the relationship between two young Chicano girls growing up in Huntington Park, Los Angeles. The characters, Yolanda and Mari, are two fifteen-year-olds growing up in immigrant households. Both are expected to put family first in their lives, and this is a source of conflict as they become closer and closer friends. This semiautobiographical movie was awarded partial funding by the Latino Public Broadcast Association, and Guerrero created a Kickstarter campaign to collect the additional funding needed to finish the production.

The tag line of Guerrero's film is especially intriguing: "A new voice in independent filmmaking." That combined with the curious Hispanic title *Mosquita y Mari* (Mosquito and Mari) is an engaging combination that pulled many backers in. Once on the campaign page itself, potential backers found a few images, the campaign video, and text that explains the story line behind *Mosquita y Mari*. Guerrero does an excellent job of breaking her campaign text into the sections for the reader:

- **Introduction and Welcome:** Explains that she obtained partial funding for the movie and invites the audience to help her finish it
- **What's the Story?:** The story line behind her movie
- **What Inspired *Mosquita y Mari*:** Explains how the film is semi-autobiographical and the passionate emotions that drove her to create this screenplay
- **Where Will the Funds Go?:** Excellent section in which Guerrero explains exactly where backers' money will be used. A great quote from her is "Every cent of your donated money will make its way into every shot of the film."
- **What Are the Plans for the Film?:** Thoughts on the distribution of the film after its completion
- **Who's Involved?:** A list of the talented team that she has assembled to help craft *Mosquita y Mari*

The 3:23-minute campaign video opens with Aurora Guerrero introducing herself and then explaining the narrative behind her *Mosquita y Mari* film. This is interspersed with lively shots of street life in the Huntington Beach area complete with background music. The last half of the video shows what appear to be random production shots and provides a preview of the original musical score.

ESSENTIAL

It is very common for one of the rewards of a film or video campaign to be a DVD of the finished product. Interestingly, this is not one of the rewards in Aurora Guerrero's *Mosquita y Mari* project. This illustrates the willingness of the crowd to simply back what they believe in for the sake of helping the project succeed. The backers seem to understand that the most important thing is to empower Aurora Guerrero with funding so she can actually craft her vision.

These are a few of the rewards for *Mosquita y Mari*: for $1, an honorary shout-out on the *Mosquita y Mari* Facebook page; for $10, an honorary shout-out and a bumper sticker; for $25, a supporter listing, special coffee cup, and a download of the original score; for $50, a behind-the-scenes docu-special and original score; for $100, a collection of Guerrero's earlier films; for $2,500, a day on the film set (and maybe an appearance on film); and for $5,000, an associate producer credit.

Natural Resources

- **Platform:** Indiegogo
- **Creator:** Cara Vidano and team
- **Backers:** 831
- **Original Goal:** $45,000
- **Amount Pledged:** $48,412

Natural Resources is a San Francisco retail store and resource center. Established more than twenty-five years ago, Natural Resources offers extensive products and support for women who are pregnant and those who are in their early parenting stages. The present owner, Cara Vidano, purchased Natural Resources from the original owners several years ago and expanded the operation. Originally in a 900-square-foot store offering a few classes, today Natural Resources is in a 2,500-square-foot store and offers dozens of classes covering subjects such as childbirth preparation, newborn parenting, breastfeeding, mother/baby support groups, father support groups, infant massage, and introducing solid foods. Natural Resources isn't just a store; it's a community, and is considered a venerable institution within the area in which it operates.

However, the recession has not been kind to the business. Although it was still surviving, Cara Vidano needed help last year to keep Natural Resources going. The problem was primarily inventory. As any business owner can attest, keeping inventory is expensive, but without it, sales and profits suffer quickly. After much research and thought, Vidano decided to ask the community for help to keep Natural Resources open.

ALERT

> Indiegogo and other sites do not host your video on their site as Kickstarter does. When you want to use video on a Kickstarter campaign, you upload it to the site. This has an advantage because Kickstarter allows you to choose the first "thumbnail" image when you set up your campaign. Indiegogo and other sites embed videos hosted by YouTube, Vimeo, and other video sharing services. Some of these services do not allow you to choose a custom thumbnail or the opening image that you would like.

When you first visit the Natural Resources campaign, you are greeted with a fresh, clean look. The Natural Resources logo is in the upper left corner and the first image on the video shows a busy store in action. Scrolling down reveals a text format that resembles a letter to those reading. It starts off with "Dear Friends" and ends with "Cara Vidano and the Natural Resources Family." In the body of the text, Vidano explains:

- What the Natural Resources store represents
- The history of Natural Resources
- Her purchase of the company
- The downturn in the economy and the effect on Natural Resources
- The need for additional funding
- What she intends to do with the funding to restore healthy operations

The video on the Natural Resources campaign is filmed in an interview style. It opens with Vidano introducing herself and then has various employees and customers discussing what Natural Resources is like as a store and as a community resource for child birthing and raising. The video does not contain the pitch for funding. That is concentrated in the campaign site.

Some of the rewards (perks, as Indiegogo refers to them) offered on the campaign are the following: for $10, a thank-you and a name displayed at Natural Resources; for $40, a Comfy Cozie wrap; for $50, 50 percent off any membership and a name displayed; for $100, a three-year extended membership; for $500, a three-year extended membership and 15 percent off all products; and for $5,000, a lifetime membership and 30 percent off all merchandise permanently.

She and the Sun

- **Platform:** RocketHub
- **Creator:** Melissa Ahern and Andy Stack
- **Backers:** 20
- **Original Goal:** $5,000
- **Amount Pledged:** $6,080

She and the Sun are the brother/sister musical duo of Melissa Ahern and Andy Stack. Originally hailing from Buffalo, New York, the two grew up in a family that encouraged music in the house and singing in the church choir. Andy, the older sibling, departed for New York City several years before Melissa and forged a career as a session musician on guitar and vocals. Later, Melissa joined him in the city when she arrived to study studio composition at SUNY Purchase, and the two joined forces as a serious musical endeavor.

The brother-and-sister duo wished to record their first album and needed the resources to hire additional musicians and the services of a professional mixing and mastering engineer. They wanted to professionally produce a CD with professional graphics and duplication.

The small profile view of Stack and Ahern's RocketHub campaign shows a black-and-white image of the two musicians with a bold white title underneath that states "Support the release of our first album!" The description of the campaign explains that they are the brother-and-sister musical duo called She and the Sun and they are looking for funding to professionally produce their musical tracks.

Clicking through to their full campaign reveals a video and text that resembles a personal letter to potential backers. The text begins with "Hello friends, fans, and others that fall into their own category," and continues on to explain how the brother and sister grew up, moved to NYC, and are now looking for funding for their first professional album.

The campaign video is a well-produced music video of the two musicians singing in Central Park. Delivered in montage style with the musicians' singing interspersed with cutaway shots, the video is nicely done. There is no pitch or other discussion in the video.

Stack and Ahern crafted some great reward tiers for their campaign. Here are some of the most popular ones: for $10, a digital download of the album;

for $15, a digital download of the album and a CD; for $20, a signed CD; for $75, a signed CD with a personal note and handwritten lyrics; for $250, a signed CD with a personal note and handwritten lyrics and a signed guitar; for $1,000, a live duo performance; for $5,000, a live performance of the entire band.

Flint and Tinder

- **Platform:** Kickstarter
- **Creator:** Jake Bronstein
- **Backers:** 5,578
- **Original Goal:** $30,000
- **Amount Pledged:** $291,493

Flint and Tinder is a recently finished campaign that did very well on Kickstarter. Launched by Jake Bronstein, the creator of popular magnetic Buckyballs, Flint and Tinder is a project that endeavors to make a brand of men's underwear that offers superior comfort and durability, and is completely made in America.

The Flint and Tinder Underwear story starts with the observation that virtually all men's underwear is made offshore and is constructed of materials that are acceptable, but certainly nothing terribly strong or durable. It would appear that the marketplace has driven this product category to a certain level of price and construction quality; "It's being made good enough." This is the market opportunity that Bronstein sees. Partnering up with a solar-powered, family-owned clothing manufacturer here in the United States, Bronstein leverages the existing manufacturing facility, which is known for producing high-quality T-shirts, and is using that company's expertise to make his underwear. One of the distinguishing characteristics that Bronstein points out is that his underwear is made only of 100 percent Supima cotton, which is a soft, durable variety not used by other brands.

Chapter 16: Five Successful Campaigns

FACT

> The story of the Flint and Tinder name is interesting. After Bronstein had made a lengthy presentation to a venture capital firm regarding his plans to "reignite American clothing manufacturing by offering higher-quality products at competitive prices," one of the venture capitalists in the room stated that "the only way to reignite American manufacturing is with a flint and tinder." Thus, the Flint and Tinder brand was born.

When you first look at the Flint and Tinder campaign, you are struck with the unusual name and the headline "Premium Men's Underwear." This is a decent draw. The images on the campaign are acceptable, showing models posing with various versions of the underwear and a chart of the different colors available. The text is more engaging and points out the features of the brand. This quote is from the campaign text: "Flint and Tinder [offers] highest quality ingredients for SUPERIOR COMFORT and DURABILITY, 100 percent made in America — SUPPORTS USA ECONOMY and is fairly priced." Down further in the text, the difference between pima cotton and Supima cotton is explained.

The real clincher on the Flint and Tinder site is the video. Bronstein himself hosts the presentation and within twenty-eight seconds delivers his opening pitch for making high-quality, American-made underwear. The rest of the video illustrates the great production facility with which he has partnered, with many shots of workers making garments. At the end of the video, Bronstein asks for your help with the statement "Make this your next set of underwear." He ends the video with "Don't you think it's time we did better?"

The rewards for the Flint and Tinder campaign fit the optimum funding sweet spots nicely. A sampling of their rewards: for $5, a set of three boxes of Flint and Tinder matches; for $15, one pair of briefs, boxers, or boxer-briefs; for $36, three pairs of briefs, boxers, or boxer-briefs; for $75, two T-shirts and three pairs of briefs, boxers, or boxer-briefs; for $125, a twelve-pack of briefs, boxers, or boxer-briefs; and for $3,600, 365 pairs of underwear.

CHAPTER 17

Local Investing

There are some profound advantages to investing in local businesses and enterprises. Some of the advantages are so compelling that you may wonder why there was ever a shift away from local investment at all. This chapter will look at examples of local investing from the past, explain how early attempts are working today, and help you as you consider how you might want to get involved in this exciting new business area via crowdfunding.

The Definition of Investing

Definitions of investing generally involve phrases like "something one does in expectation of future returns." This usually involves the purchase and ownership of assets that can be expected to grow in value. Most people think of investments in contemporary financial terms, things like bank accounts, stocks, bonds, mutual funds, and other financial instruments. However, "investing" covers a far wider gamut of concepts.

To put the concept into complete context for you, it is useful to explore the means by which people invested in the past. What we will see is that investing was not just for future returns, as many conceive it today. Investing was also done for the higher good; to improve one's community and to help the people one knew and lived among.

It Was a Wonderful Life

A great example of local investing involves America's savings and loans institutions. As famously portrayed in the 1946 Frank Capra film *It's a Wonderful Life*, savings and loans were part of the backbone of American mortgage lending in the early twentieth century. The effect they had on America cannot be overstated; these uniquely American institutions were instrumental in the development of thousands of towns and cities across the entire country.

FACT

> A tongue-in-cheek rule called the "3-6-3" rule used to be attributed to the "good life" that savings and loan owners allegedly led. It referred to the fact that banks would deliver 3 percent interest on depositors' accounts, lend the depositors money at 6 percent, and then be out playing golf at 3 P.M.!

However, not many people realize how most savings and loans actually came into existence. In many cases they were arranged by prominent local business leaders for the specific purpose of promoting homeownership among local citizens. These local leaders were not bankers. They were local stakeholders who believed that the mission of savings and loans was part of a broader social agenda, not just to earn a profit for the owners, but to also build a community. They felt that mortgage lending not only allowed citizens to establish roots where they lived, but also taught the habits of consistent savings and mutual cooperation; concepts that strengthened personal integrity.

Korean Kyes

Another example of local investing is practically clandestine. It involves the ancient Kye (pronounced KAY) lending practice that flourishes in South Korea and has been brought to the United States by Korean immigrants. Kyes are very common in the United States today and represent a major way that Korean communities finance their own fledgling businesses.

A dozen or so family members, friends, and/or associates gather monthly and discuss which members of the group may need financial assistance. After that identification, each member of the Kye group then donates a specific sum to a common pot that is presented to the needy member. It is agreed that this sum will be paid back with interest to each donating member of the Kye within a certain period of time. Mutual trust among members is what makes Kyes work.

Kyes are especially important for new immigrants because they often are the only way that those who lack credit history and assets to secure loans can obtain startup capital. Although there are no statistics on Kyes, there is no question that they are one of the reasons that thousands of Koreans have prospered operating grocery stores, liquor stores, dry cleaners, and other small businesses in cities across the United States.

A Shift in Attitudes

Michael Shuman, a lawyer, economist, and expert on local investing, believes that Americans are undergoing a shift in attitude concerning investment options, and this shift has to do with the big, multinational financial firms.

Consider that over the last several years, we have been treated to a continuous detailing of egregious behavior on behalf of these companies. In 2008 alone, for example, there was the $700 billion federal Troubled Asset Relief Program (TARP) bank bailout, the collapse of AIG, and the Lehman Brothers bankruptcy, to name just a few. With unsavory details emerging, such as eight-figure CEO pay, shell games involving exotic financial products, and the hoarding of bailout funds provided by the taxpayers, many Americans have simply lost faith in big financial institutions. The result, argues Mr. Shuman, is that Americans no longer believe that Wall Street, once considered the center of financial stability and fiduciary responsibility, is the safest place to put their money. Americans are now looking elsewhere.

> **FACT**
>
> Hyper-local is a term you will encounter a great deal when reading about local crowdfunding. The term is a modifier that connotes the character of being oriented around a well-defined community. Generally you can think of hyper-local as defining a street, neighborhood, or community.

Amy Cortese, a prominent business writer and author of *Locavesting: The Revolution in Local Investing and How to Profit from It*, says that "elsewhere" may be in our own communities. The problem isn't just a mistrust of Wall Street; it's the realization that little of what Wall Street does actually benefits the local community.

Take the following statistic into account: "A dollar spent at a local independent business, on average, generates three times more local economic benefit than a dollar spent at a corporate-owned chain." This quote from Ms. Cortese's website evokes the concept of "economic multipliers." Economic multipliers are the turbocharging factors that occur when certain actions are taken. The concept is simple if you think of it this way: When money stays local it benefits local businesses, local people, and the community, and has a much greater value than when distant companies pull it out of the loop. This is because there is a multiplier effect when local money stays local.

By the way, this is not what large corporations desire at all, as Ms. Cortese points out. The job of large, distant organizations is not to build local communities into great places for people to live. The job of any corporation is to increase shareholder value, and this effectively means shunting as much local money away from the region and into shareholders' pockets as possible. There is nothing wrong with this, of course. This is simply the way capitalism often works. It is the job of educated citizens to realize these consequences and to take appropriate actions if they feel it isn't in their, or their community's, best interest.

Chapter 17: Local Investing

FACT

There is a lot of talk about the unfair advantages that other countries have when producing goods for sale in the United States. It is true that many other nations can produce goods very economically, but there is a secret neutralizer that few recognize—energy prices. As the price of transportation fuels increases, the more competitive local producers are. Thankfully, this is especially true for America's farmers.

Local Crowdfunding Websites

A number of companies and websites have recently been established that focus specifically on crowdfunding local enterprises. As you know, the Internet is rapidly evolving and the trends that may lead to long-term business success are constantly changing. Thankfully, a number of pioneers have jumped in and are assisting local enterprises right now.

Lucky Ant

Lucky Ant (*www.luckyant.com*) is a hyper-local crowdfunding site that has an interesting business model. In contrast to other crowdfunding sites with page after page of active projects, it features just one neighborhood business a week for communities to support and fund. Lucky Ant is currently operating just in New York City, but plans to expand into other cities around the United States in 2013.

The way this works is that retail businesses in need of funding can submit proposals on the Lucky Ant website. There is no submission fee. In addition to the business name and contact information, the folks at Lucky Ant want to know what the money will be used for and the amount needed.

QUESTION

Where did the name Lucky Ant come from?
Many Internet properties have really odd names for a reason. Phrases that are unique are often granted trademark status quickly because there can be no confusion with existing trademarks. The folks at Lucky Ant, however, chose their company name not for its whimsical, unique character but because it referred to the social, cooperative nature of ants working together to build better communities.

Once a proposal is submitted, it undergoes a screening process. If the business is selected for participation, it is featured on the front page of the website. The duration of each project is just one week, and as is the case with some of the crowdfunding websites mentioned earlier in the book, the funding is all or nothing. In other words, if the financial goal is reached, the credit cards of those who pledged will be charged and the featured business receives the funding. Lucky Ant receives a 5 percent fee for managing the process. If the goal is not reached, no credit cards are charged and no money changes hands.

Interestingly, not only can local businesses approach Lucky Ant with proposals, people can nominate local businesses that they would like to support. As the Lucky Ant website explains, "Your favorite spots are a part of your life, and now you can be a part of theirs, too."

Cofolio

Cofolio (*www.mycofolio.com*) is a website whose mission is stated as "Connecting Small Businesses with Local Investors." The business model at Cofolio is more collaborative than simply a spot on the web for transactions to occur. The site is actively involved in directing client businesses to the resources necessary to successfully raise funds.

Here's how the Cofolio process works: The first step is for a business that needs capital to create a business profile that explains the business opportunity and the amount of funds it would like to obtain. Cofolio then sends a marketing kit to the business that outlines the most effective ways to advertise the investment opportunity to the local community. After that, those who receive the marketing materials and wish to invest in the featured business are directed back to the Cofolio website, where contact information and refundable deposits are collected.

What is interesting about the Cofolio model is that it operates on a fixed pricing schedule rather than collecting a percentage of investment funds. As of mid-2012 it charges $50 per month for a regular business listing and states that premium listings will be available "down the road." Cofolio also seems to be gearing up for the transition to equity crowdfunding, as the site states that assistance with this type of crowdfunding investment instrument will be offered in the future.

Chapter 17: Local Investing

> **QUESTION**
>
> **What is the difference between a flash mob and a cash mob?**
> Flash mobs are groups of free-spirited individuals that assemble at specific places to engage in performance art. Cash mobs have a different purpose. They consist of groups of people that assemble at places with the common goal of helping out struggling businesses. Cash mobs typically organize via social media and then descend on the target business to purchase its goods and services. The show of support and resultant cash flow is a wonderful thing for any struggling entrepreneur to experience, and may even save the business. Cash mobs are unlikely to be a major fundraising trend, but they are a lot of fun and demonstrate people's altruism.

Three Revolutions

Three Revolutions (*www.threerevolutions.com*) bills itself as the world's first crowdfunding platform for food ventures. The slogan on its website gets right to the point: "Put your money where your mouth is." While not being an organization that limits itself to exclusively local investing, local investing is a major part of what it does.

According to the website, the mission of the folks at Three Revolutions is to help catalyze a "re-connection to our food sources." This involves engaging farmers, farm suppliers, chefs, retail outlets, and anyone else involved in local food supply chains with the enthusiastic consumers of their food products. The way they do this, as you may imagine, is via crowdfunding.

Three Revolutions cites a 2010 Carrot Project study that found that over 40 percent of farmers who sought bank loans for their businesses were turned down. Fortunately, crowdfunding can change that. Crowdfunding is a way for communities to decide what ventures they would like to see succeed and be able to do something about it.

Smallknot

Smallknot (*www.smallknot.com*) is a New York City organization that connects shoppers with local mom-and-pop businesses in need of modest loans. The formation of Smallknot is yet another story of how active, forward-thinking citizens can take action to improve their communities.

The story is inspiring. Smallknot was founded by three Wall Street lawyers who got fed up with their favorite East Village small businesses closing up shop due to recessionary pressures. Knowing that traditional banks were unlikely to help out these eclectic little businesses, they founded Smallknot to help out. Their impetus was simply to improve the hyper-local area that they live in for everyone involved.

> **eV FACT**
>
> Social lending is another technique being used to help local businesses. The key to social lending is that it represents an authentic loan, not a trade for perks. The way it works is that multiple donors loan small amounts of money to a small business and the multiple loans are all eventually paid back. In effect, this "crowd banking" spreads the risk over multiple donors that all have the same goal of helping out a small business.

Smallknot collects money on behalf of those donors who wish to assist a local business and essentially arranges a business loan. The small business then agrees to pay back the loan over a mutually agreed-upon time frame, and then it receives the funding directly from Smallknot.

It is interesting to note that this concept opens the door to some unusual marketing techniques for the businesses. In order to entice donors, for example, they can sweeten the deal by giving out perks similar to what reward-based crowdfunding sites do. Things like free baked goods, private dinners, customized experiences, and unique products are all wonderful methods to attract support from potential donors.

Community Crowdfunding Ventures

With interesting similarities to the ethics that drove local leaders to establish savings and loans almost a century ago, some communities are forming their own crowdfunding ventures to spur local investment. What distinguishes these efforts is that while they are full-service crowdfunding organizations, they limit their operations to a specific geographical area. This is a significant concept. The limited scope not only taps into the powerful sense of community that local and hyper-local areas exhibit, but may actually help foster it due to the presence of the organization and its website.

Fund St. Louis

The slogan on the Fund St. Louis website (*www.fundstlouis.org*) says it all: "Community Crowdfunding for a Dynamic St. Louis." Being dedicated to the crowdfunding efforts of a limited geography—the city of St. Louis and its surrounding communities—the organization exemplifies the local investing ethic.

The website that Fund St. Louis has created is remarkable. The site is not overly complex yet offers many resources to support local crowdfunding initiatives. Not only that, it is a visually pleasing site composed of soothing blues and greens with professional-looking graphics and intuitive page layout.

Like many start-up companies, there is an interesting story behind Fund St. Louis. The founder of the site and his wife were parents of young children and enjoyed living close to extended family in the St. Louis area. However, they were struggling with a common dilemma: They love St. Louis but recognized many of the best career opportunities lay outside the area. In their own words, "Does one settle for mediocrity but be close to family" or "leave and chase the big career?" Tough decision. One day, a solution presented itself. As the Fund St. Louis site states: "Why not become a catalyst to create a more vibrant, entrepreneurial environment in the St. Louis area?" Thus began the Fund St. Louis story. It will be interesting to see how it grows.

The National Crowdfunding Association Gets Local

In March 2012, the National Crowdfunding Association (NLCFA) was formed. This crowdfunding advocacy group is comprised of a wide array of companies, firms, and individuals, all of whom have an interest in the success of equity crowdfunding. The NLCFA is one of the first such trade groups to form.

In April 2012 (just five weeks after its founding) the NLCFA announced its CrowdFund Local initiative. CrowdFund Local is being promoted as a packaged service for municipalities through which they can tap their local leadership to establish a crowdfunding platform for local businesses.

The NLCFA promotes an interesting vision for the role of local banks on the local crowdfunding scene. As the organization notes, it is common knowledge that community banks are risk averse and entrepreneurs suffer because they can't get loans. With local crowdfunding, however, a new small business lending model may emerge, a sort of partnership between the "crowd" and local banks, which would mitigate the banks' risk. The combination of funds raised from the crowd and funds loaned by a bank in a risk-sharing arrangement would be a win-win for all parties: the crowd, the bank, and the entrepreneur. It would seem that there are great possibilities here.

The NLCFA admits that the CrowdFund Local initiative is still a work in progress. The organization is in a strong "listening period," during which the particular crowdfunding needs, techniques, and limitations will all soon come into view. This is a wise position because the expansion of crowdfunding into local markets is really just beginning, and many changes and shifts are sure to surface.

A Perfect Opportunity

If you are interested in getting involved in local crowdfunding to obtain funding, provide funding, or participate in virtually any other aspect of this effort, a perfect storm may be brewing for you. It can be stated with some certainty that crowdfunding on the local level will offer significant business opportunities very soon. Consider these points:

- Local investing engages a multiplier effect that allows communities to become vibrant and prosper. Americans are beginning to understand that where they buy and invest has a direct impact on the communities in which they live and work.
- Crowdfunding is getting a lot of press. Recent high-concept projects on Kickstarter and other sites in particular have received great press online and in the standard print and television media. The concept of crowdfunding is becoming mainstream.

- There is no question that there is a strong anti–Wall Street bias developing in the United States. People are beginning to think that their hard-earned investment funds were not treated with fiduciary care and frankly, were used imprudently for the personal gain of a select few Wall Street executives.
- The passage of the Jump Start Our Business Startups Act on January 3, 2012, officially made the selling of equity via crowdfunding intermediaries legal for the first time since 1933. This allows small businesses to offer ownership in their companies and will likely become a major investment activity toward the end of 2012, when SEC crowdfunding regulations are expected to be promulgated.

Your Opportunity

So, what does this mean for you? It can be summed up in one word: opportunity. As general crowdfunding makes its way from early platforms, like Kickstarter and others, to a multitude of local crowdfunding sites, a world of opportunities opens for anyone who wants to get involved. Local crowdfunding is new and a rapidly evolving target, so educate yourself fully on the marketplace before you jump in. Chances are that you will be able to identify quite a number of opportunities in your local market. You might want to consider combining forces with other local entrepreneurs to form a group that identifies potential local investment opportunities and pursues them.

CHAPTER 18

Crowdfunding for Social Good

Crowdfunding is changing the landscape of fundraising for nonprofits, social enterprises, and other organizations whose mission is the social good. Not long ago social change was driven primarily by large organizations that functioned as intermediaries between donors and those needing assistance. Today things are different. Springing up all around these larger enterprises are far smaller groups, in some cases just individuals, who are driving social change via direct funding methods such as crowdfunding. If being a "change maker" interests you, there couldn't be a better time to get involved.

The Social Enterprise Movement

Before going into the details of crowdfunding and fundraising for organizations involved with social change, it's important to first take a look at the different types of groups that exist. There's actually a broad spectrum of types of organizations that pursue socially positive initiatives, but for the sake of discussion this chapter will distill them into a few manageable categories.

The first type of social-good organization that most people think of is nonprofits. The business model that nonprofits employ involves funding via charitable contributions and fundraising drives. Today, the social enterprise movement also encompasses a large population of for-profit businesses and many hybrid entities. The commonality shared among these groups is not organizational structure, but the mission to drive social change.

In fact, the actual form of the business entity really isn't important at all when effecting social change. It is really just a strategic question: What organizational form best advances the social mission involved? What type of organization is most effective? For purposes of understanding and discussion, though, it is convenient to break social enterprises into two broad groups: the *nonprofits*, which are organizations that are not allowed to distribute profits, and the *social enterprises*, which are organizations that are allowed to distribute profits to members.

Nonprofits

Nonprofit organizations are very common in the United States and play a vital role in society. However, the term *nonprofit* is somewhat generic, and its breadth is poorly understood.

A short definition of a nonprofit organization could be *an organization that exists for the purpose of serving a public or mutual benefit rather than the pursuit or accumulation of profits for owners or investors*. Just a few examples of nonprofit organizations in the United States are universities, religious organizations, political parties, foundations, advocacy groups, art museums, youth recreation associations, trade associations, and some medical centers and hospitals.

Stricter definitions of nonprofit organizations would include references to the Internal Revenue Code (IRC), also known as the U.S. federal tax code. This is because, although there is no one central federal organization that oversees nonprofit organizations, the primary regulator, in a functional sense, is the Internal Revenue Service. Although there is some oversight on the individual state level, it is basically the federal government—the IRS—that determines whether or not an organization is a legitimate tax-exempt entity.

It is common for people to refer to nonprofits as 501(c)(3) organizations. This refers to the section of the U.S. tax code that deals with charitable organizations. It is important to realize that while charitable organizations make up the bulk of nonprofit organizations in the United States, they represent just one of thirty-two tax-exempt organizations recognized by the IRS.

Today, some 1.5 million organizations are registered with the IRS as being nonprofit or tax-exempt organizations. In addition, there are millions of smaller associations that do not register with the IRS. This is because they are smaller, informal organizations with revenues of less than $5,000 per year and thus are exempt from IRS oversight. Nonprofit organizations in America have combined revenues of approximately $621.4 billion, which represents 6.2 percent of the nation's economy. Some 10.2 million people are employed in the nonprofit sector.

FACT

> If you want a good example of a profitable activity that directly benefits a nonprofit organization, think cookies. Specifically, Girl Scout cookies. In 2012, 2.3 million Girl Scouts sold $656 million worth of cookies, with 50 percent going to state and national council operations and 10 percent going to local operations. Cookie sales are the major fundraising method utilized by the Girl Scouts of America.

Charitable nonprofit organizations generally fund their operations via donations. Because of this, the process of soliciting donors and collecting funds becomes a critical part of a nonprofit's internal operations. Indeed, the success or failure of an organization's fundraising efforts will directly dictate how effective the group is. The lifeblood of any organization is cash flow, and nonprofits are no different. They must have cash flow to continue to operate, and this occurs primarily through donations.

There are three ways that nonprofits obtain donations: directly from individuals, from grants, and from philanthropic organizations. Understanding how funding is best solicited among these three channels can be complex.

Thankfully there are many private and online resources that allow nonprofits to learn about the "best practices" for doing so. These resources can easily be found on the web. The open sharing of this fundraising information is unique; it is a function of the altruism of those involved and the collaborative nature of the pro-social organizations.

Many of those who are engaged with nonprofits comment that an especially engaging part of the nonprofit process occurs among the members of the organizations themselves. Because citizens actively participate, these organizations can bring together people with divergent opinions and backgrounds and allow them to work together. This is a valuable benefit because it teaches mutual cooperation and harnesses altruism that may not be expressed in ordinary daily life. Nonprofits, as such, can be powerful generators of positive societal values.

Social Enterprises

Social enterprises, in contrast to nonprofit organizations, exist to create a profit but do so to advance a specific social agenda. They use standard business and commerce techniques to advance their social, environmental, and human justice agendas. The tools that they employ are the organization's products, services, and sometimes even employment, such as that offered to workers who are disadvantaged in the business workplace.

ESSENTIAL

> Some of the most powerful social enterprises involve missions that engage America's youth. If you want to enable change that is long lasting and transformative, teach the future leaders and citizens of your community about issues you are passionate about. You may not only be a catalyst for larger-scale change; you may actually change the life of a youth. There are few things with more impact than that.

The spectrum of social enterprises is relatively broad and somewhat difficult to categorize. Here are a few categories that you may recognize:

- Theater companies that produce professional performances and also teach the actor's craft through workshops and internships

- Food kitchens that produce food products for sale but also provide workforce development and employment for the disadvantaged
- Housing development corporations that build and manage properties with a focus on low-income housing and teaching construction skills to at-risk youth
- Retail thrift shops that sell clothing and other household items, using profits to fund social work and social programs

The common thread through all these organizations is that they engage in a commercial activity but use profits to promote their social or environmental agenda. The pursuit of the common good is the primary purpose, literally woven into the organization's DNA. Sometimes this mission is so seamless that it isn't obvious. Chances are you already do business with some social enterprises without even realizing that they are such!

Why Are Social Enterprises Necessary?

Have you ever wondered why there are so many people in need? Why don't people respect the environment more? Why don't people seem to care more about the plight of others? And, frankly, why do we desperately need more organizations to promote social good?

Understanding the driving forces that create society's problems may help you put a sharper focus on social entrepreneurship, and should you decide you want to get involved, may help you conceptualize your mission.

Market Failure

Some argue that there are significant holes in every type of economic system. Whether you are talking capitalism, socialism, planned economies (communism), or variations in between, it's the nature of the beast. While a given economic system may do most things to the advantage of its people, there are always blind spots where the system fails, sometimes very badly. Take Wall Street, for example. In the last several years we have seen some egregious behavior among Wall Street firms. Some of the things that Wall Street investment firms have done have worked out to a terrible disadvantage for their investors. Is this because Wall Street is packed with terrible, immoral people? No, Wall Street firms are staffed with people who believe that capitalism is driven by the pursuit of personal gain and that's what they did. They felt they were operating within the rules (although there are many people who disagree with that, sometimes violently).

Government Failure

Regardless of the type of government involved, some things are done well and some are done poorly. This is inevitable whenever a society has a central government. The reasons why governments do things poorly are myriad and often hard to fathom. It could be that there is a lack of knowledge about issues, or too much cost involved to do anything about an issue, or simply political obstinacy. There also is the common feeling that even when governments do get involved in social issues, they often don't do it well because there is too much bureaucracy and red tape. Again, it is the nature of the beast.

Historical Precedents

Communities are usually formed well before formal governments are instituted. In the early, formative years of any community, citizens commonly come together to address issues and work together to form solutions. Even when communities grow and governments are developed, citizens continue with formal and informal groups to develop solutions for the problems that are identified. It is within this sort of historical framework that we can see how social enterprises make perfect sense today. Social enterprises are literally formed by local citizens with the intention of creating value for their communities. This is the power of social entrepreneurship.

Social Entrepreneurs

Technically anyone who starts an organization with a mission to effect social change is a social entrepreneur, but the term has taken on a special meaning today. It seems to be directed more toward those who pursue for-profit social strategies than those that are nonprofit. This is undoubtedly because the realities of today's financial climate make it challenging to operate as a nonprofit. Donations via fundraising drives, grants, and other charitable methods have declined significantly because people, groups, and institutions just don't have the money to give the way they do during better times. The result? For-profit organizations in many cases are having an easier time generating cash flow, and a lot of social entrepreneurs are opting for that strategy.

Most of the today's social entrepreneurs are business people first who recognize the profit potential of enterprises but have social causes in mind. They envision commercially viable organizations, like their solely profit-minded brethren, but their prime motivation, often behind the scenes, is to build a better society and to help solve social problems. You might envision a successful social entrepreneur as a business person with two "bottom lines," one financial and one social. Both must be driven "into the black" or the dual mission of the social organization isn't achieved.

Before the advent of crowdfunding, becoming a social entrepreneur required superhuman efforts. One had to actually build an organization, a "thriving company" so that enough cash flow was thrown off from operations to invest in the social mission planned. Thankfully, the situation is not as intimidating today. Crowdfunding has brought social entrepreneurship to the masses. Now anyone with a passion for social change and the drive to make it happen can put his idea up on a crowdfunding site and get involved quickly.

Crowdfunding Social Change

The crowdfunding revolution has changed some areas of enterprise profoundly and permanently. Consider, for example, independent filmmaking. It certainly can be said that the entire business of independent filmmaking is vastly different today than it was just a few years ago.

Consider what filmmakers had to go through before the crowdfunding revolution. First, the actual creative vision, the "movie" the filmmaker wanted to make, was just a facet of the process. Sure, it had to be a good story, even brilliant, but there would be no way that it would ever see the light of day unless money was obtained to create it. So, back in the "old days" filmmakers had to be just as skilled at pitching studios and financing films as they were at understanding Arriflex camera apertures and montage sequences. For the first-time filmmaker, it was especially difficult because without a track record, few studios or other production facilities wanted to take a chance on "unknowns."

Today, it's very different. Let's say you have an idea for a great documentary that you would like to shoot about the plight of tarsiers (tiny, tree-dwelling primates) in Borneo. This is how you might go about it. First, you would research the topic and outline the documentary you would like to make. Then you would create a great three-minute pitch video and put it on Kickstarter with compelling copy that explains why you are going to create this high-concept documentary and why you need funding. For compensation (rewards) you offer your pledgers (backers) a copy of the film in DVD form. If you execute this crowdfunding campaign well, you may find yourself on an aircraft to Borneo in just a few months, fully funded and ready to go.

It's the same story for those who wish to effect social change. It starts with a vision of what you want to do, who you would like to assist, and what situation you would like to bring attention to. This becomes the mission of your project or crowdfunding campaign. Your next job is to articulate it and make a pitch on a crowdfunding site for financing. If you do it well, you may be successful and will be off making a difference in the world sooner than you think.

Before You Start Your Social Change Campaign

Chances are that you have been thinking about your concept for social change for a while, perhaps even several years. And now that you have discovered the power of crowdfunding, you are eager to design a crowdfunding campaign and get it rolling. Is this when you should jump in? Well, not yet. Spend a little more time reflecting on a game plan before you start designing your campaign.

ESSENTIAL

> Fundraising can seem awkward for first-timers. It seems almost like begging. You might think it feels like a one-way street, where you are pulling money from a donor's pockets with little to offer in return. But in reality it is a wonderful two-way exchange in which you provide the vision and the opportunity to change something significant and donors provide the resources to help it happen.

Identify a Need and a Goal

Before you begin your campaign, you need to specifically state what your project is. This is not a statement about your social mission and the change you wish to create in the world. It is more pragmatic. What set of activities are you going to execute with the money that you raise? For example, if you are raising money for a new well in an African village, your project is just that. You may want to identify the overall situation in the village, such as years of drought and its effects on the village children, but the project is the well you want to build.

How much money do you want to raise? This question is trickier than you may think. In the case of the well in the African village, there is not only the cost of the well itself but many other items that you must account for when determining the amount of money you need to raise. For instance, you cannot forget issues like transportation to the village for both the well components and the people who are going to install it. If the installation will take many days, the cost of things like lodging and food must be included. You may also need to provide some training so that when problems occur after you leave, local citizens can take care of it themselves. You may want to think of this whole package as being the "total well cost," which may be several times more than just the cost of the well and associated plumbing.

Outreach

If there is anything that is going to hobble your project, it is failing to realize that you need to attract potential donors to your campaign. Tom Dawkins, a prominent social entrepreneur and cofounder of StartSomeGood, explains this as the "build it and they will come" fallacy. He explains that many people think crowdfunding sites are unique places on the Internet that are packed with people who just love to fund projects. This is not true at all. Although it is true that there are lots of people who find sites like Kickstarter fascinating places to look for cool things, few go there to just throw money around. What really happens with successful campaigns is that they include an outreach plan that was designed to point people to the crowdfunding effort. These plans utilize things like social media, press releases, white papers, and other techniques to generate and spread enthusiasm for a crowdfunding campaign.

Rewarding and Communicating with Pledgers

The selection of rewards that you offer to those who fund your campaign is very important. The object of your campaign is to collect funds for a socially beneficial project, and you need to offer rewards that fit well into that context. A standard reward is "swag" or items with the project logo on them. This might include things like hats, T-shirts, and bumper stickers. For a socially beneficial project, you may want to have the donors' names immortalized on your website or at a particular project site. People love to see their names attached to causes they believe in. For those who pledge high amounts, you may want to offer a really high-concept reward, like a private trip with you or a personal appearance by a member of your staff somewhere; some sort of "custom experience" that is unusual and personal.

Think about how you will stay in touch with your pledgers. Unlike a lot of standard crowdfunding campaigns, where the object of the project is to make something and deliver it, campaigns for the social good may represent just a starting point. Your donors' funds may help you complete a particular part of the project, but there may be second phases, third phases, and more. The question you need to ask yourself is, How am I going to stay in touch with my pledgers? Then tell them! You don't need to overthink this. Best methods of staying in touch are via dedicated websites, e-mail newsletters, Twitter, Facebook, and other social media sites, as discussed in Chapter 8. Remember that by staying in touch with your donors you continue their engagement, and they may wish to contribute to further phases and projects that you execute.

Fundraising Is Storytelling

One of the first things to understand about fundraising is that it involves storytelling—really good storytelling. When you tell a good story, you draw your audience into your vision and many will want to participate. Stories are absolutely key to raising money.

However, many people go through life without fully understanding what "storytelling" really is. Most see a good story as mere entertainment, but not a lot more than that. However, the concept of a "story" and what it represents is far deeper than many people think.

For thousands of years, storytelling was a key way to convey a society's culture, values, and history to others. Teachers of all types have used stories as instructional tools, conveying important information in the form of legends, myths, and fables. They realize that a story represents far more than just the words it contains; a story is like an "information capsule" that can deliver meaning at many different levels.

> **ESSENTIAL**
>
> Scientists believe that people are hard-wired to communicate and process information as stories, just as they are hard-wired to learn and process verbal language. No wonder you can remember with virtual photographic memory the fairy tales of your youth. You are cognitively wired to do so.

Telling Your Story

No matter what the intended purpose, being able to tell a good story is essential. There are those who can recite information and then there are those who can weave it all together into a great, engaging narrative. Guess which approach is the one that people enjoy the best and remember long-term?

You may think that storytelling is an inborn talent. After all, aren't some people simply better at it than others, just as some people are born with natural artistic talent? While it is true that some have a knack for storytelling, it is not something everyone is simply born with. You can easily learn the basics of telling a good story.

Think of a situation or event that you have been involved with and craft a narrative about it. Then tell it to some people. As you might imagine, you can't ask for objective advice about your storytelling, especially from friends; they are going to say you are great. The best thing to do is just observe and notice when they react when you are speaking. If you get positive reactions, if people seemed really interested, if their eyes are right on you and engaged, then you probably are doing a good job. If not, read on.

There is an instructional exercise called "string of pearls" that may prove helpful to novice storytellers. It is a simple, step-by-step method of telling a story by hitting the salient parts in the right order. This may be a good exercise for you to use when you are crafting the story of the project that you are crowdfunding. The idea of the "string of pearls" exercise is to break your narrative into six parts and cover each one, in sequential order:

1. Who is involved? Was it you alone, someone else, or a number of people? If others, who are they and how are they related to you?
2. What happened? Explain the action—or in the case of a crowdfunding story, what you wish to happen. Without going into extraneous details, make sure you explain the entire event. Explain how you feel about it.
3. Where did it happen? If you can establish a location that's familiar to your audience, your job is easier because they will have visual and emotional images to reference. If not, paint your location with words that evoke vivid images and emotions.
4. Describe the conflict. This is the bulk of the narrative. What is the importance of this story? What happened, or in the case of your crowdfunding campaign, what would you like to happen? Why is this so important to you and to your audience? Here you can use a lot of emotional language to draw your audience in.
5. What is the resolution? What did you do, or what do you suggest to solve the conflict? This may be a simple action, although in the case of most crowdfunding projects it may be more complex. This is where specific details are likely to be necessary.
6. What is the conclusion? Here you describe how things are different after the resolution, or will be different, and how you or others feel about that.

The Top Four Lessons

Tom Dawkins lectures widely on social entrepreneurship and is an expert on fundraising methods, in particular crowdfunding. Mr. Dawkins suggests that you keep in mind the following top four "lessons" for campaign fundraising success.

It's Not a Crowd, It's Peers

Tom is very emphatic about this definition. He insists that you establish a mindset right away regarding the people who will fund your campaign. It is misleading, he believes, to characterize those who are going to fund your project as random people from the crowd. This is, of course, how some people will discover your project, but the majority of donors are not those that just stumble in. It is more appropriate to consider your backers as your peers and, in fact, the entire process as "peerbacking." Peers, he explains, are people who identify with what you are doing and care about your project. In fact, they care so much about it that they want to give you funds to see it succeed.

Prime the Pump

Tom also suggests that you line up your first five donors and get them to pledge as soon as your project goes live. There is a little crowd psychology here. You don't want to have your project "empty" in the early days. People draw conclusions when they see projects that are void of pledges. This is human nature. Questions may arise in the back of a pledger's mind if no one else has pledged. *Is there something they know that I don't know?* Doubt like this is a terrible thing. The chances are that someone who is in doubt will quickly leave the site and may never visit your campaign again.

You Have to Ask, and Then Ask Again

You have to ask people to pledge money to your project. You can't just be polite and ask them to "check out" your campaign. You have to use active language and ask for support. This is a key part of fundraising. Remember that you are not asking for charity; you are inviting donors to become a part of your exciting project, and the only way to do so is to contribute funding.

Establish a Time Limitation

People respond to deadlines. Establish the fact that not only is the window for funding your project limited (typically thirty to sixty days), but so is the opportunity to complete the project. Going back to the example of the African well, you would need to let your audience know that this is a village in critical need of fresh water. With fresh water, children and adults can bathe, which leads to better hygiene; the villagers can raise crops, which leads to village self-sufficiency; and they can properly cook their food, which leads to better nutrition. All of these results are desperately needed right away to make this small patch of humanity a better place for its inhabitants—and your donors can help make this happen if they act soon.

CHAPTER 19

Equity-based Crowdfunding

Until now, crowdfunding in the United States has meant that a company looking for capital received either donation-based, lending-based, or reward-based funding instead of actually selling ownership (equity) in the business. That changed on July 5, 2012, when the Jumpstart Our Business Startups (JOBS) Act was signed into law. The law is expected to take effect in early 2013. In order to prepare for what is going to be somewhat chaotic in the beginning, it's important to examine the issues involved as well as precedents to the JOBS Act.

Equity

Simply put, equity is the value of a property or company, minus any debts or liabilities incurred by the company. In the accounting world, investing in a company's equity means owning a share of the business, generally in the form of stock certificates or other ownership documents. In the investment world, equity means actual ownership in a company and the right to future profits and value growth. That could mean receiving periodic dividends, or an increase in the value of stock shares as the company prospers. Owning equity is considered a way of building wealth.

> **ALERT**
>
> One of the principal reasons that owning stocks (equity) in companies is a way of building wealth is that there are organized markets where stocks are bought and sold. These markets are the New York Stock Exchange (NYSE), National Association of Securities Dealers Automated Quotations (NASDAQ), and regional exchanges such as the Chicago Board of Trade (CBT). It should be noted that equity-based crowdfunding is not likely to include this kind of trading, although exchanges involving crowdfunded equities may develop as the practice grows.

The sale of equity-based securities is tightly monitored by various government agencies, most notably the Securities Exchange Commission (SEC) and state regulatory agencies. By understanding the evolution of government oversight of securities in the United States, the rollout of equity-based crowdfunding comes into historical context.

The Roaring Twenties

From 1921 through most of 1929, America reveled in a great period of peace and economic prosperity. The "Roaring Twenties" was an exciting time fueled by new technologies, industrialization, and cultural change. The Dow Jones Industrial Average, indexed on the New York Stock Exchange, rocketed from 63.90 to 381.17 and the new national pastime was buying

Chapter 19: Equity-based Crowdfunding

and selling stocks. Shares of Ford, Standard Oil, and Radio Corporation of America (RCA) grew in value every single day, creating a horde of wealthy investors.

FACT

The Dow Jones Industrial Average was created by Dow Jones Co. cofounder Charles Dow and statistician Edward Jones on May 26, 1896, to provide an indication of the overall health of the stock market and America's economy. Originally composed of twelve companies, today the number is at thirty. Only about twenty, however, are manufacturers of industrial and consumer goods. The others are in financial services, entertainment, and information technology.

The bad part was that few people actually studied the finances and fundamental businesses of the companies in which they were investing their life's savings. As long as you were "in the market," it was "the cat's pajamas." After all, for almost a decade it seemed the stock market always went up.

Unfortunately, whenever vast sums of money are involved, it doesn't take long for crooks to come out of the woodwork, and during the 1920s thousands of fraudulent companies swindled millions of naive investors.

FACT

When the Stock Market Crash of 1929 happened there were no real protections to prevent it. Today, safeguards are in place to stop the market from declining too fast. If the Dow Jones Industrial Average drops more than 10 percent before 2 P.M., the New York Stock Exchange closes for one hour. If it drops more than 20 percent, it closes for two hours. A drop of 30 percent may shut down the market for the remainder of the day.

Another major factor that contributed to the crash was the then-new concept of buying on margin, which gives the buyer the right to purchase shares at an agreed-upon price without having to pay for them in full. That means for every dollar invested, a margin investor could "borrow" nine dollars' worth of stock from a broker. In financial terms, this is called being "leveraged." For just one dollar, the investor can control, or leverage, nine additional shares. The power of this concept is that if the stock increases in value just 1 percent, the investor would make a 10 percent profit. Unfortunately, if the stock drops that 1 percent instead of rising, a margin holder would lose the one dollar investment plus owe the broker the other 9 percent. Multiplied by thousands of shares, investing on margin created a very risky environment.

Adding to the risk was the fact that 40 percent of all bank loans were being used to purchase stocks, because the Roaring Twenties were all about getting rich on stocks. And then the bubble burst.

The Stock Market Crash of 1929

Because America's economy was superheated throughout most of 1929, the Federal Reserve raised interest rates several times in an attempt to cool things down. However, by October, a powerful bear market correction began. On Thursday, October 24, panicked investors traded a record 12,894,650 shares because they sensed that an overinflated speculative bubble was about to burst.

QUESTION

What is a bear market?
When the stock market, and the DJIA in particular, fall by more than 20 percent over an extended period of time, it's considered a bear market, which indicates a lack of confidence. Conversely, in a bull market, the number of shares traded is high, and sometimes more companies enter the stock market. Technically, though, in a bull market the overall value of the market rises at least 20 percent.

J. P. Morgan and a few other influential bankers poured some of their own money into the market to try to stabilize matters, and it appeared over the weekend that the crisis might have peaked.

That optimism only lasted until the opening bell on the following Monday. By the time the market closed, the Dow had fallen by more than 22 percent, to 260.64, setting the stage for catastrophe. On Black Tuesday the market opened at 252.6. More than 16 million shares were traded in a matter of hours, and the market lost $14 billion, closing at 230.7. By July 8, 1932, the Dow had sunk to 41.22 and tens of thousands of millionaire margin investors were bankrupt.

> **FACT**
>
> The term "irrational exuberance" is often used when describing the tendency of financial markets to periodically overinflate in value and then settle back to normal. Attributed to Alan Greenspan, who served as chairman of the Federal Reserve from 1987 to 2006, the term was actually used to describe the overinflated Japanese economy in the mid-1990s. Nevertheless, it became the catchphrase for the dot-com boom.

The Crash of 1929, although exacerbated by unprecedented drought that devastated the nation's farms, generally is considered the catalyst that brought on America's Great Depression, which fostered mass poverty and shanty-towns filled with unemployed Americans. Businessmen who had been millionaires were reduced to selling apples on street corners, and one-third of Americans were living below the poverty line. Although the Great Depression lasted eleven years, the Dow Jones Industrial Average didn't surpass its 1929 high of 381.17 until November 23, 1954, a full twenty-five years later.

The Securities Act of 1933

The Securities Act of 1933, also known as the "Truth in Securities Act," was the first law that imposed regulations on the United States securities industry. Passed as part of President Franklin Delano Roosevelt's "New Deal," it was designed to restore faith in the U.S. banking and capital market system and stimulate the stagnant economy by protecting investors from fraud and giving them access to accurate financial information.

> **FACT**
>
> "New Deal" referred to a series of economic programs, such as the National Recovery Administration (NRA), Works Progress Administration (WPA), and Civilian Conservation Corps (CCC), which were initiated by President Roosevelt and his team of advisers between 1933 and 1936 in order to put Americans back to work and end the Great Depression. The backbone of the New Deal focused on the "3 Rs": Relief for the unemployed, Recovery of the economy, and Reform of the country's financial system.

Public Disclosure of Financial Information

The Securities Act of 1933 requires companies offering stock to the public to disclose financial information when they register their securities with the Securities and Exchange Commission (SEC). The information is then made available to the public in order for investors to make informed decisions. As further assurance of the validity of the information, the SEC has the power to penalize companies for inaccuracies and fraud.

Investors Have the Right to Sue

A key part of the Securities Act of 1933 prohibits misrepresentation in the financial disclosures. If investors who purchase securities suffer losses because they were intentionally misled by fraudulent financial data, they can sue the company involved to recover their losses.

State Securities Laws

While the Federal Securities and Exchange Commission is the main enforcer of the nation's securities laws, individual states have their own regulatory bodies. These bodies are headed up by state securities regulators, and they have most of their impact in the area of registration of securities brokers and dealers and investment adviser representatives.

Every state also has specific "Blue Sky Laws," designed to protect individual investors against fraudulent securities sales and practices. While they vary from state to state, most require companies making securities offerings to the public to register their offerings with the state before they can be sold. The reason they are referred to as Blue Sky Laws is that they are state laws designed to protect small investors from those selling securities offering returns on their investments "that can be as high as the blue sky."

Rise of Equity Crowdfunding

As soon as the concept of crowdfunding began to gain steam in the early part of 2000, talk began about the possibility of selling equity shares in start-up businesses over the Internet. The concept was already allowed in certain European countries and it was working out quite well. The problem with this concept in the United States, however, was that the regulations put into place by the Securities Act of 1933 essentially made it too difficult and too expensive for small businesses to comply with the Securities Act in order to offer equity shares to the general public.

However, it wasn't long before people started to question whether this was prudent financial policy. After all, the Securities Act of 1933 was drafted in an era when there were no computers, and the transparency of data that people enjoy today wasn't even imagined. When the issue of investor protection arose, equity-crowdfunding advocates were quick to point out that the decision to risk money on a small business should rest with the investor, not with the seller. After all, if the government acknowledges that individuals are capable of spending money at a casino or on lottery tickets without being required to engage a professional counselor, why should they not be able to spend their money supporting local businesses?

The House Proposes H.R. 2930

In February 2011, a group of entrepreneurs banded together and formed a group called the Startup Exemption. The goal was to lobby decision-makers in Washington to update the U.S. Security Laws and allow entrepreneurs and small business owners to raise a limited amount of funding via equity-based sales through crowdfunding.

With the assistance of Small Business and Entrepreneurship Council (SBEC), a 70,000-member, nonprofit, small business advocacy organization, members of the Startup Exemption participated in two hearings on Capitol Hill. As a result, the Entrepreneur Access to Capital Act (H.R. 2930) was introduced by Rep. Patrick McHenry (R-NC) on September 14, 2011.

> **FACT**
>
> On November 3, 2011, the U.S. House of Representatives passed H.R. 2930 with a vote of 407–17 in an extraordinary display of bipartisan support. It loosened restrictions on the Securities Act of 1933, and allows issuers of equity to raise up to $2 million if they supply investors with audited financial statements, and $1 million without those statements. In addition, individual investments through crowdfunding are capped at $10,000 (or 10 percent of their annual income), whichever is less.

The Senate Proposes S. 1791

After H.R. 2930 was introduced in the House, many members of the Senate were immediately concerned that certain aspects of the bill should be modified. As a result, they drafted similar legislation proposing additional protections for investors. On November 2, 2011, Senator Scott Brown (R-MA) sponsored the Democratizing Access to Capital Act (S. 1791). The Senate bill was substantially the same as H.R. 2930, although it lowered caps on both the amount of funding a small business could raise and how much any individual investor could invest. On December 8, 2011, both H.R. 2930 and S. 1791 were referred to the Banking Committee, which met several times that month to discuss the many bills that had been raised in the Senate and House regarding capital formation for small and mid-sized businesses. There also were concerns about providing enough investor protection from unscrupulous and fraudulent players, the role that state securities regulators would play in the process, and that a patchwork of differing state regulations would impede the intent of the proposed legislation.

Single Bill H.R. 3606 Is Formed

After the Christmas recess, the Senate Banking Committee continued debate for several months. Sensing a loss of momentum, equity-based crowdfunding advocates mobilized again to lobby the Senate Banking Committee to act, and on March 6, 2012, a further hearing was held.

> **FACT**
>
> The investment caps for individual investors vary according to their gross income. Individuals earning $40,000 or less would be permitted to invest up to 2 percent of gross income, while individuals earning $40,000–$100,000 would be permitted to invest up to 5 percent of gross income. Those earning more than $100,000 would be permitted to invest 10 percent of their gross income up to a maximum of $100,000.

Around the same time, the House packaged seven of its earlier crowdfunding capital formation bills into a single bill, H.R. 3606. This bill, also referred to as the JOBS Act, contained the equity-crowdfunding portions of bill H.R. 2930 and integrated bills already in the House and Senate. H.R. 3606 passed the House on March 8, 2012. In mid-March Senator Jeff Merkley (D-OR) released bill S. 2190, which contained parts of early Senate bills S. 1791 and S. 1970. It was added as an amendment to the JOBS Act bill, passed the Senate on March 22, 2012, and on April 5, 2012, President Barack Obama signed the JOBS Act into law.

So equity-based crowdfunding is now legal, but the regulatory rules aren't finished yet. H.R. 3606 requires the SEC, within 270 days of enactment, to issue such rules as are necessary for implementing equity crowdfunding transactions. Under that time frame, official SEC equity crowdfunding regulations were expected to go into effect in January 2013.

CHAPTER 20

Interpretations of the JOBS Act

On April 5, 2012, President Barack Obama signed H.R. 3606, the "Jumpstart Our Business Startups Act" (known as the JOBS Act) into law. An amalgam of several bills introduced and modified by both the United States House of Representatives and the U.S. Senate, it liberalizes the legal framework for the sale of securities in the United States. The intent is to give small and mid-size businesses access to capital through equity sales. This chapter will focus upon those parts of the JOBS Act that center on equity crowdfunding and its ramifications.

The JOBS Act

H.R. 3606, formally stated, is "An act to increase American job creation and economic growth by improving access to the public capital markets for emerging growth companies." Job creation is seen as a paramount issue by both Democratic and Republican lawmakers. The JOBS Act passed the Senate with a 73–26 vote and the House by 380–41. On April 5, 2012, the bill was signed into law by President Barack Obama in a ceremony held in the White House Rose Garden.

Rep. Scott Garrett (R-NJ), chairman of the Financial Services Subcommittee on Capital Markets and Government-Sponsored Enterprises, was a key backer of H.R. 3606. After attending the bill-signing ceremony, Garrett said, "Today was a good day for the U.S. economy and America's job creators. The JOBS Act will allow America's small businesses to unleash their entrepreneurial spirit on our economy by removing the heavy hand of government that has been standing in the way of economic growth. Free-flowing capital will foster competition, encourage innovation and provide the next generation of America's business leaders the financial tools they need to make their dreams a reality . . . this will create American jobs and shift our economic recovery into high gear."

> **ALERT**
>
> The JOBS Act represents legislation embodying a number of bills originating in both the House and Senate aimed at liberalizing access to capital. These original bills were discussed, modified, resubmitted, and eventually rolled into H.R. 3606. Although much of the business press has targeted the "Title III—Crowdfunding" section of H.R. 3606, it is important to realize that there are seven major sections, or Titles, within H.R. 3606, representing a hybrid of several bills introduced into the Senate and House. The actual bill appears in Appendix B.

- TITLE I—Reopening American Capital Markets to Emerging Growth Companies
- TITLE II—Access to Capital for Job Creators
- TITLE III—Crowdfunding

- TITLE IV—Small Company Capital Formation
- TITLE V—Private Company Flexibility and Growth
- TITLE VI—Capital Expansion
- TITLE VII—Outreach on Changes to the Law

Overview of the H.R. 3606 Titles

All the title sections in H.R. 3606 are designed to remove impediments to entrepreneurial growth in small to mid-size businesses in the United States.

Reopening American Capital Markets to Emerging Growth Companies

In the Title I section of H.R. 3606, a new category of securities issuers, Emerging Growth Companies (EGCs), is added to the Securities Act of 1933. EGCs are issuers that have total annual revenues of less than $1 billion. Along with that definition, there are also specific requirements in Title I relative to how the total annual revenue of an EGC is calculated in order to eliminate ambiguity. This section of H.R. 3606 also exempts EGCs from Section 951 of the Dodd-Frank Wall Street Reform and Consumer Protection Act, which requires publicly traded companies to hold a shareholder vote at least once every three years on executive compensation and on executive severance payments.

Title I also amends the Securities Act of 1933 to permit the publication of broker or dealer research reports about specific EGCs that are the subject of a proposed public offering, even if the broker or dealer is participating, or will participate, in the offering.

ESSENTIAL

> It is important to realize that the JOBS Act puts much of the analysis of risk in the hands of potential investors. The argument is that with the "transparency" of the Internet—meaning the ease with which data and background information are obtained—investors can now make informed decisions about investment opportunities by themselves.

Access to Capital for Job Creators

In the Title II section of H.R. 3606, the SEC is directed to eliminate the prohibition against general solicitation or advertising of sales of non–publicly traded securities, provided that all purchasers of the securities are "accredited investors." Under current regulations, "accredited investors" are defined as wealthy individuals, as defined by the JOBS Act, plus institutions such as banks, insurance companies, registered investment companies, corporations, and charitable organizations with more than $5 million in assets. The content of the Title II section of H.R. 3606 is based on proposed bill H.R. 2940, one of the several original bills rolled into the JOBS Act.

Entrepreneur Access to Capital

In the Title III section of H.R. 3606, securities laws are amended to provide for registration exemptions for certain crowdfunded securities. This Title, the core of the crowdfunding legislation, will be discussed in more detail in the following section.

Small Company Capital Formation

The Title IV section of H.R. 3606 allows the Securities and Exchange Commission (SEC) to exempt a certain class of securities from the Securities Act of 1933. These exemptions cover a wide variety of equity securities, debt securities, and debt securities-convertible that are involved in H.R. 3606 legislation.

ALERT

> The JOBS Act represents legislation voted into law, but it is important to understand that there is still much work to be done by various regulatory groups, such as the SEC, before many parts of the JOBS Act can be put into practice. For example, the first rulemaking deadline mandated under the JOBS Act was a ninety-day deadline for the implementation of changes to permit solicitation in private placements to accredited investors. This deadline was not met.

Private Company Flexibility and Growth

Based on the proposed bill now known as H.R. 2167, the Title V section of H.R. 3606 raises the allowable number of shareholders in private companies from 500 to 1,000 before mandatory registration under the Securities Exchange Act of 1934.

Capital Expansion

Based on the proposed bills now titled H.R. 4088 and H.R. 1925, the Title VI section of H.R. 3606 focuses on banks and bank holding companies. Under Title VI, banks and holding companies are now allowed 2,000 shareholders. It also changes the shareholder deregistration threshold from 300 to 1,200 shareholders, reduces regulatory burdens, and eliminates an impediment to raising equity capital from new shareholders.

Outreach on Changes to the Law

Title VII simply states that the Securities and Exchange Commission "shall provide online information and conduct outreach to inform small and medium-sized businesses, women-owned businesses, veteran-owned businesses, and minority-owned businesses of the changes made by this Act."

QUESTION

Will reward-based crowdfunding still be used for funding small businesses when equity-based funding becomes a reality?
One of the criticisms concerning H.R. 3606 is that a large number of potentially expensive documents need to be prepared for an equity-based crowdfunded offering. For example, preparing audited financial statements, a professional business plan, securities valuation, and other such documents will almost certainly require the services of financial professionals. Add to that the fees that the funding portals and potential intermediaries will charge and it is easy to see that reward-based crowdfunding is likely to continue as a way for smaller businesses to raise capital because of the low costs involved.

A Look at Title III: Crowdfunding

Title III of H.R. 3606 is titled "Crowdfunding" and is based on the H.R. 2930 legislation as submitted by Rep. Patrick T. McHenry (R-NC) in the House and S. 1791, submitted by Sen. Scott Brown (R-MA). Title III of H.R. 3606 covers the bulk of the liberalization of the Securities Act of 1933 with its attendant effects on equity-based crowdfunding. In particular, issuers launching a "crowdfunded" offering will need to meet requirements as specified by H.R. 3606 that include:

- **Issuer Requirements:** To qualify for the crowdfunding exemption under H.R. 3606, an issuer must be organized in the United States and not be a regulated investment company under the Investment Company Act of 1940.
- **Capitalization Limit:** The money raised by one issuer of equity may not exceed $1 million in any twelve-month period.
- **Investment Limit:** The total amount of equity or promissory securities sold to any investor by an issuer in any twelve-month period may not exceed:

  1. For investors with annual income or net worth of less than $100,000: the greater of $2,000 or 5 percent of the investor's annual income or net worth.
  2. For investors with annual income or net worth of more than $100,000: 10 percent of the investor's annual income or net worth, up to a maximum of $100,000.

- **Disclosure of Financial Information:** Issuers must provide potential investors with financial documents. The extent varies based on the size of the offering:

  1. For offerings up to $100,000: tax returns and financial statements certified by an executive officer of the issuer must be made available.
  2. For offerings up to $100,000 to $500,000: financial statements reviewed by an independent auditor must be made available.

3. For offerings up to $1,000,000: fully audited financial statements must be made available.

- **Formal Business Plan:** A complete business plan and intended use of proceeds from the offering must be available to prospective investors.
- **Funding Target:** The issuer must specify a target offering amount to be raised and a stated deadline for reaching the target offering amount.
- **Securities Valuation Method:** A description of the method that was used to price the securities is required prior to closing the offering.
- **Full Internal Disclosure:** Disclosure about the issuer's management and current ownership must be made available to all potential investors.
- **Annual Reporting:** After completion of the offering, the issuer will be required to file annual financial reports with the SEC.
- **Intermediary Restrictions:** The issuer may not compensate third parties for promoting the securities offering without meeting certain disclosure requirements to be defined by the SEC.
- **Advertising Restrictions:** The placement may not be advertised publicly, other than by posting notices directing prospective investors to the crowdfunding portal or intermediary.
- **Twelve-Month Sale Restriction:** Investors in crowdfunded offerings may not resell the purchased securities for a period of twelve months, other than to accredited investors or pursuant to a registered public offering in the business.

> **ALERT**
>
> The methods that will be used to price equity-based crowdfunded securities will be somewhat different from the traditional company valuation techniques used today. One of the principal differences is that equities from crowdfunded companies will initially lack marketplaces which are driven by the economics of supply and demand in which to trade shares. Valuation techniques will need to take that, and other financial factors, into account when establishing the sales price of crowdfunded shares.

Crowdfunding Intermediary Requirements

The crowdfunding model as envisioned by lawmakers will rely heavily on the emergence of crowdfunding portals, which may become the primary mechanism by which equity and promissory securities are offered to the public. These portals will be primarily web based, however, some may have physical locations similar to brokerages and other financial institutions today. An important part of H.R. 3606 is that crowdfunding portals are not required to register as broker/dealers so long as they comply with SEC requirements and those required of H.R. 3606 itself. These requirements include:

- **Investor Education:** Crowdfunding portals will be required to provide full disclosure and educational material to advise investors of investment risks.
- **Confirming Investor Understanding:** Crowdfunding portals will be required to implement mechanisms that ensure that investors review and confirm their understanding of the disclosures in the issuer's offering materials. This may be in the form of textual materials, webinars, e-learning modules, and other media that can be monitored and that allow reasonable verification of understanding.
- **Reducing Fraud:** The crowdfunding portals will be charged by the SEC to apply reasonable diligence to eliminate fraud on behalf of the issuers they represent. These measures are to be further defined by the SEC.
- **Escrow of Investors' Funds:** The crowdfunding portal will be charged with the receipt and holding of investor funds during the crowdfunding process. The funds will be released to the issuer only when the issuer's defined investment Funding Goal is met for the offering.
- **Verification of Investment Limitations:** The crowdfunding portals will be charged with ensuring that individual investors do not exceed the maximum investment limits as defined by H.R. 3606.
- **Elimination of Conflict of Interest:** The crowdfunding portals must bar their own officers, directors, and partners from holding any financial interest in an issuer.

ALERT: A popular option for today's reward-based crowdfunding campaigns is to establish a funding goal. In the case of Kickstarter, as explained earlier in the book, this is called "All or Nothing Funding"; if the funding goal is reached, the campaign is considered a success. If not, no money changes hands and the campaign ends. This paradigm will likely drive the bulk of equity-based crowdfunding. Most equity-based campaigns will have specific goals because the businesses involved will have specific cash needs in order to start or expand their operations.

H.R. 3606—Other Issues

There are several other issues involving the JOBS Act that, although not directly contained in the Title III section, still affect the implementation of equity-based crowdfunding.

State Securities Law Pre-emption

Individual states have oversight over the commerce of securities within their boundaries, with subtle differences from state to state concerning rules and regulations. Fortunately, the lawmakers involved with the JOBS Act foresaw this potential problem and limited the extent to which issuers in crowdfunded offerings and crowdfunding portals must comply with state securities registration requirements. Individual states are also pre-empted from charging filing fees in connection with crowdfunded offerings, with the sole exception of any state in which purchasers of 50 percent or more of the securities sold in an offering reside.

Alternative Liability Standards

One of the most significant sections of the Securities Act of 1933 was that shareholders could sue financial institutions or issuers that materially misrepresented details involved with the securities being offered, whether the misrepresentation was done purposefully or not. The JOBS Act is similar, but defines a different liability standard for claims brought by investors against issuers of crowdfunded offerings. The difference with crowdfunded securities is that the issuer may defend against such claims if it can show that company officers did not know, and could not have known "in the exercise of reasonable care" that there were material misstatements or omissions.

Implementation Timeline

While certain provisions of the JOBS Act took effect immediately after the legislation was signed into law by President Obama on April 5, 2012, many of the functional aspects of the act require further rulemaking from the SEC to take effect. For example, the SEC was required to release rules ninety days after enactment with respect to certain aspects of the legislation, including general solicitation rules for private offerings. In addition, the SEC has up to 270 days to release rules for other portions of the act, including the crowdfunding exemption and crowdfunding portal regulations. At the time of this writing, the SEC has been delayed on most of the time frames due to the research and work involved.

Waiting for Equity Crowdfunding

If you are thinking of starting a new business or expanding your existing business, you may be wondering how to move forward with crowdfunding at this time. With the right business concept, you may be able to start things right away with a well-designed crowdfunding campaign on Kickstarter or one of the other major sites. On the other hand, you may be interested in waiting for equity-based crowdfunding to become fully implemented, because you then will have the potential to raise larger sums of money.

ESSENTIAL

> Sometimes it seems that the SEC doesn't really want to liberalize capital formation to the extent allowed in H.R. 3606. However, the SEC has the dual duty to promote capital formation and to protect investors. From the beginning of discussions concerning crowdfunding, the possibility of "bad actors" scamming investors has provided a major point of opposition to parts of the JOBS Act.

How can you decide which approach is best? There are several considerations. First, reward-based crowdfunding is easy. If your new business idea is relatively simple and small in scope, such as recording a CD or making a film, reward-based funding is the way to go. It really doesn't make much sense to offer equity at such an early stage of an idea or business.

If you already have a small business or an ambitious startup, equity-based crowdfunding may be an avenue to consider, but it is likely to be much more expensive and difficult to do. Frankly, the experts say, many entrepreneurs lack the financial acumen, professional business plans, and basic tenacity they'll need to comply with the JOBS Act and possible further regulations from the SEC. They also may not have the cash to hire the accountants and lawyers they will need to meet the crowdfunding regulations. The bottom line is that you must do plenty of research, but you also should realize that traditional funding sources may be the most viable option for your business.

APPENDIX A

Glossary

Algorithms
In terms of search engines, the term "algorithms" refers to the math behind the way search engines work.

Adwords
Google's advertising system where "sponsored ads" are shown on search response pages.

Affliate Marketing
An Internet advertising and sales system where outsourced "sale affiliates" drive traffic to retailers' sites in exchange for commissions or royalties.

Amazon Payments
An online sales and credit card processing system hosted by Amazon Corporation. Amazon Payments is used by Kickstarter for the processing of backers' credit cards.

Auteur Theory
A creative theory where only one person is in charge of all creative decisions. The term *auteur* comes from the film world and refers to when some directors are in charge of all decisions that affect a film or video production.

Backer
The term used for those that donate or pledge to crowdfunding campaigns.

Blog
A website where content is generated by one or more people and becomes a destination for others to visit. Almost like an online magazine except that readers can comment and enter into discussions.

Blue Sky Laws
The state laws in the United States that regulate the offering and sale of securities to protect the public from fraud. Origins of the term are unknown but some say it comes from fraudulent promises that offer "Blue Sky" levels of returns.

Brand Marketing
A marketing method where the object is to build awareness in the brand name of a product or service. This can be contrasted to "direct marketing" whereby the object is to make a sale as soon as possible.

Broad Match
A selection of match criteria used by Google's search engine algorithms to choose keywords. Broad matches generally choose keywords or keyword phrases that are "similar" to specific keywords.

Call to Action
A "call to action" is a phrase often used in advertising to denote the "offer" and usually puts a time limit on the response period. A typical call to action might be to state that an offer is "good for just this weekend."

Campaign
Crowfunding sites usually refer to individual fundraising efforts as "projects" or "campaigns."

Channel
In terms of YouTube, a channel is a specific user's account page or homepage.

Crowdsourcing
Crowdsourcing is a method where a large group of people assemble to solve a problem.

Crowd Investing
Also referred to as "equity-based crowdfunding," crowd investing occurs when a group of people purchase equity or shares in a business.

Appendix A: Glossary

Crowdcasting
Crowdcasting occurs when a group of people drive a particular process. An example would be when a group of listeners choose the songs online that a radio station plays.

Crowdfunding
When a group of people fund a project, service, or activity.

Crowdpurchasing
When a group of people gather to purchase products or services, usually at discounted rates.

Crowdvoting
Crowdvoting occurs when a group of people gather to "vote" on a person or particular issue.

Curated
Curation in the context of crowdfunding occurs when a collection of projects or campaigns are gathered together in one location on the Internet. A group of campaigns executed by students of the University of New Hampshire could be curated into a single webpage for display.

Debt-based Crowdfunding
Crowdfunding where backers get their money paid back to them. Debt-based crowdfunding is also referred to as peer-to-peer lending.

Design Patent
A form of intellectual property granted by the U.S. Patent and Trademark Office for the cosmetic structure, or form, of an object.

Direct Marketing
Direct marketing refers to the process whereby products and services are sold directly to consumers or users.

Disruptive
Disruptive is a relatively new term that refers to a product or service that when introduced into a marketing channel "changes everything" often with better services, features and/or pricing. It "disrupts" the way business occurs and introduces change.

Donation-based Crowdfunding
When a group of people give money or donations to assist a cause. Donation-based crowdfunding is often referred to as "charity."

Embed
When used in terms of webpage design, embedding refers to the process when code is inserted into the HTML (or XHTML) text so that a function occurs when the page loads or is activated. Embedding sounds and videos into webpages is very common.

Emotional Intelligence
The psychological science where a person's emotional reactions can be judged.

Equity-based Crowdfunding
A crowdfunding process where backers purchase ownership or equity in companies and businesses.

Exact Match
A selection of match criteria used by Google to choose keywords. Exact matches generally choose keywords or keyword phrases that are "exact matches" to specific keywords; they literally are the same words.

Fan Page
When used in context with Facebook, a fan page is a company's "homepage." It is the page that companies use and those that visit can elect to become "fans of" and then receive updates from.

Friend
When used in context with Facebook, a "friend" is someone that you accept and allow to become a member of your personal community and receive updates from.

Funding Goal
When used in context to crowdfunding, the funding goal is the financial limit that project creators choose as the minimum that they would like to receive in order to start their projects.

Google+
Google+ is Google's new social media platform. It competes with other social media platforms, such as Facebook and Twitter but, in addition, offers many unique features.

267

Hashtag
A hashtag (#) is a convention used by Twitter users to denote a special topic that one can search for. For example, the hashtag "#Manhattanpizza" would allow a group on Twitter to find each other easily via search and then discuss, well, Manhattan pizza.

Homepage
In terms of the Internet, the homepage is usually the first page one is served when a website is visited. Homepages are sometimes referred to as the "main pages" and "index pages" in addition.

Hyper-local
A modifier that connotes the character of being oriented around a well-defined community. Generally you can think of hyper-local as defining a street, neighborhood, or small community.

IP
The shortened version of "Intellectual Property" and it refers to ownership of "creations of the mind." Rights to intellectual property are granted in the United States by the U.S. Patent and Trademark Office.

Korean Kye
Groups that form and provide private financing to internal members, often behind closed doors.

Like
In terms of social media, a "like" is a function that signifies that one approves of a particular webpage's content and connects him to the page involved.

Linear Editing
An older method of doing film editing was performed "Linearly." All of the creative modifications were performed in sequence starting at the beginning of the project and continuing until the end.

Locavesting
Locavesting is a term coined by Amy Cortese that refers to the movement to invest in local enterprises so that local funding stays in local communities.

Microwork
Many websites allow people to perform microwork, or small tasks, in exchange for money. Amazon's Mechanical Turk is one of the more popular microwork websites.

Mission Statement
A mission statement is a document where companies, or other entities, make a short statement concerning what they do and why they care. Mission statements are often parts of business plans.

Negative Match
In terms of keywords, a negative match refers to a keyword that does NOT identify a characteristic that you want. For example, if you are selling used cars, you want the keywords "used" and "cars", you do not want the keyword "junk" because that keyword does not identify someone who is searching for a good "used car." "Junk" would be a negative keyword for this search.

New Deal
The New Deal was a series of legal and economic reforms that occurred in the 1930s in the United States to spur the country out of the great recession.

Nonlinear Editing
Today sound and video editing is mostly done on computers and is done "out of sequence" or in a nonlinear fashion. Sounds and video clips can be cut and pasted like word processing documents to create finished songs and movies.

Nonprofit
Technically the term "nonprofit" refers to a specific classification with the Internal Revenue Service (IRS) that recognizes the way profits are allocated within certain organizations. The term is often used in a casual sense to denote charitable organizations.

Organic Search
Search engine pages usually have two types of search listings, sponsored (or paid) search and organic search. The organic search, usually on the left of a Google search

Appendix A: Glossary

page, is what is developed "free" by Google for anyone to use.

Outreach Plan
In terms of crowdfunding, an outreach plan is really just another term for one's overall promotional plan. The term refers to "reaching out" across the Internet to pull potential backers to one's crowdfunding campaign.

Outsourcing
Outsourcing refers to going outside one's business to obtain help. Many companies today outsource advertising, sales, creative, and other functions that may be obtained more affordably by employing specialized firms.

PayPal
One of the Internet's premier financial institutions and is used with many of the crowdfunding platforms as a method for backers to process donations.

Phrase Match
A selection of match criteria used by Google to choose keywords. Phrase matches are triggered when a keyword phrase (the phrase that is typed into a search field) contains certain keywords but not necessarily in a certain order.

Pitch
A pitch is an advertising and sales term that refers to the "offer" that is presented to someone along with terms and conditions. The goal of a good pitch is to make an offer that is compelling and is acted on quickly.

Platform
In Internet terms, platform often refers to a website and its methods. In terms of crowdfunding, Kickstarter, Indiegogo, and RocketHub are all three different crowdfunding "platforms."

Pledger
A pledger in fundraising terms is someone that commits to giving money under certain conditions. The term "backer" is also used for this.

PPC
Pay-per-click (PPC) is an advertising model used by many websites. The way it works is that ads are shown on search engine pages and if someone "clicks through" on the ad, the advertiser is charged for that click. Hence the term, "Pay-per-click."

Prohibited Content
In terms of crowdfunding websites, most have strict rules about what content they allow. Most do not allow pornographic or illegal items but many, such as Kickstarter, are very restrictive as to the type of campaigns they allow and exclude many more categories.

Project
In terms of crowdfunding, some websites refer to individual efforts to crowdfund as "projects" and some use the term "campaigns."

Provisional Patent
The U.S. Patent and Trade Office (USPTO) allows individuals to file a one year "provisional patent application." A provisional patent application is not evaluated by the USPTO but it establishes the date that potential IP has been submitted.

Quality Score
Google uses a concept called a quality score to assign ranking to sponsored adword campaigns. It reflects the quality of the sponsored ad and the website that it points to.

Reward-based Crowdfunding
Reward-based crowdfunding refers to projects that creators wish to complete and offer "rewards" or "perks" to those that back them.

Rewards
In crowdfunding terms, what you get when you pledge money to a campaign. Often the rewards are copies of the project itself, like a DVD or a wristwatch, but often they are other "perks" as defined by the project creator.

Search Engine
A search engine is a special webpage where you type in words of interest and websites that match that criteria are displayed. The three major search engines are Google, Yahoo!, and Bing.

Securities Act of 1933
As a result of egregious financial activity during the 1920s, the Securities Act was drafted by U.S. lawmakers to bring stability back into the market. It was part of the Roosevelt administration's "New Deal" and it was a great help to getting the United States back on track in the late 1930s.

SEO
Search Engine Optimization is a system that is used to make certain keyword searches rank high when keywords are entered into search engine fields. The object is to gain visibility so that most clicks that occur can be directed to targeted sites.

SMS Messaging
SMS messaging simply refers to standard text messaging. When you send a text on your cell phone to someone, you are using the Internet's SMS text protocol.

SERP
"Search Response Page," the page that is returned when you type keywords into a search engine field.

Social Enterprises
Organizations that perform missions for the social good. They are often nonprofits but some social enterprises have a for-profit component that is used to fund the social good mission that they perform.

Social Media
The web entities that allow groups of people to easily form groups and communities and interact. Facebook and Twitter are two of the major social media sites.

Split Testing
A technique where two different versions of content can be shown on the Internet and results can be tracked. For example, two different copies of an ad can be displayed to potential purchasers and one can see which ad copy "draws the best." Split testing is considered a very powerful mechanism by Internet advertisers to fine-tune campaigns.

Sponsored Search
The term used on websites for the paid ads. On Google webpages, it is the adword ads that are located on the right hand side of the page.

Survey
At the end of almost all crowdfunding campaigns, the platforms they occurred on usually allow you to "survey" the backers to get relevant information. This is often contact information, shipping addresses, and product preferences (color, size, etc.).

Tiers
In terms of crowdfunding, "tiers" refers to the lineup of rewards that backers are offered when they pledge to a crowdfunding campaign. Tiers are generally arranged from low cost to high cost on crowdfunding pages, hence the term "tiers."

Tweet
A sequence of 140 characters (maximum) that those that use Twitter communicate with.

Twitterverse
A whimsical term used to describe all the world's Twitter users. In some cases it refers to Twitter's public timeline that contains all the world's tweets.

Unsecured Loan
An unsecured loan is one that is granted to someone or a company on the basis of good credit. No attachment to physical goods, such as real estate or equipment, is involved.

Utility Patent
The standard patent issued by the U.S. Patent and Trademark Office is a utility patent. The term utility reflects that fact that the intellectual property covered by the patent has a distinct "utility" that is unique and usable.

APPENDIX B

Bill H.R. 3606

One Hundred Twelfth Congress of the United States of America

AT THE SECOND SESSION

Begun and held at the City of Washington on Tuesday, the third day of January, two thousand and twelve

An Act

To increase American job creation and economic growth by improving access to the public capital markets for emerging growth companies.

Be it enacted by the Senate and House of Representatives of the United States of America in Congress assembled,

SECTION 1. SHORT TITLE.

This Act may be cited as the "Jumpstart Our Business Startups Act".

SEC. 2. TABLE OF CONTENTS.

The table of contents of this Act is as follows:

Sec. 1. Short title.
Sec. 2. Table of contents.

TITLE I—REOPENING AMERICAN CAPITAL MARKETS TO EMERGING GROWTH COMPANIES

Sec. 101. Definitions.
Sec. 102. Disclosure obligations.
Sec. 103. Internal controls audit.
Sec. 104. Auditing standards.
Sec. 105. Availability of information about emerging growth companies.
Sec. 106. Other matters.
Sec. 107. Opt-in right for emerging growth companies.
Sec. 108. Review of Regulation S-K.

TITLE II—ACCESS TO CAPITAL FOR JOB CREATORS

Sec. 201. Modification of exemption.

TITLE III—CROWDFUNDING

Sec. 301. Short title.
Sec. 302. Crowdfunding exemption.
Sec. 303. Exclusion of crowdfunding investors from shareholder cap.
Sec. 304. Funding portal regulation.
Sec. 305. Relationship with State law.

TITLE IV—SMALL COMPANY CAPITAL FORMATION

Sec. 401. Authority to exempt certain securities.
Sec. 402. Study on the impact of State Blue Sky laws on Regulation A offerings.

TITLE V—PRIVATE COMPANY FLEXIBILITY AND GROWTH

Sec. 501. Threshold for registration.
Sec. 502. Employees.
Sec. 503. Commission rulemaking.
Sec. 504. Commission study of enforcement authority under Rule 12g5-1.

TITLE VI—CAPITAL EXPANSION

Sec. 601. Shareholder threshold for registration.
Sec. 602. Rulemaking.

TITLE VII—OUTREACH ON CHANGES TO THE LAW

Sec. 701. Outreach by the Commission.

H. R. 3606—2

TITLE I—REOPENING AMERICAN CAPITAL MARKETS TO EMERGING GROWTH COMPANIES

SEC. 101. DEFINITIONS.

(a) SECURITIES ACT OF 1933.—Section 2(a) of the Securities Act of 1933 (15 U.S.C. 77b(a)) is amended by adding at the end the following:

"(19) The term 'emerging growth company' means an issuer that had total annual gross revenues of less than $1,000,000,000 (as such amount is indexed for inflation every 5 years by the Commission to reflect the change in the Consumer Price Index for All Urban Consumers published by the Bureau of Labor Statistics, setting the threshold to the nearest 1,000,000) during its most recently completed fiscal year. An issuer that is an emerging growth company as of the first day of that fiscal year shall continue to be deemed an emerging growth company until the earliest of—

"(A) the last day of the fiscal year of the issuer during which it had total annual gross revenues of $1,000,000,000 (as such amount is indexed for inflation every 5 years by the Commission to reflect the change in the Consumer Price Index for All Urban Consumers published by the Bureau of Labor Statistics, setting the threshold to the nearest 1,000,000) or more;

"(B) the last day of the fiscal year of the issuer following the fifth anniversary of the date of the first sale of common equity securities of the issuer pursuant to an effective registration statement under this title;

"(C) the date on which such issuer has, during the previous 3-year period, issued more than $1,000,000,000 in non-convertible debt; or

"(D) the date on which such issuer is deemed to be a 'large accelerated filer', as defined in section 240.12b–2 of title 17, Code of Federal Regulations, or any successor thereto.".

(b) SECURITIES EXCHANGE ACT OF 1934.—Section 3(a) of the Securities Exchange Act of 1934 (15 U.S.C. 78c(a)) is amended—

(1) by redesignating paragraph (77), as added by section 941(a) of the Investor Protection and Securities Reform Act of 2010 (Public Law 111–203, 124 Stat. 1890), as paragraph (79); and

(2) by adding at the end the following:

"(80) EMERGING GROWTH COMPANY.—The term 'emerging growth company' means an issuer that had total annual gross revenues of less than $1,000,000,000 (as such amount is indexed for inflation every 5 years by the Commission to reflect the change in the Consumer Price Index for All Urban Consumers published by the Bureau of Labor Statistics, setting the threshold to the nearest 1,000,000) during its most recently completed fiscal year. An issuer that is an emerging growth company as of the first day of that fiscal year shall continue to be deemed an emerging growth company until the earliest of—

"(A) the last day of the fiscal year of the issuer during which it had total annual gross revenues of $1,000,000,000 (as such amount is indexed for inflation every 5 years by the Commission to reflect the change in the Consumer Price Index for All Urban Consumers published by the Bureau of Labor Statistics, setting the threshold to the nearest 1,000,000) or more;

"(B) the last day of the fiscal year of the issuer following the fifth anniversary of the date of the first sale of common equity securities of the issuer pursuant to an effective registration statement under the Securities Act of 1933;

"(C) the date on which such issuer has, during the previous 3-year period, issued more than $1,000,000,000 in non-convertible debt; or

"(D) the date on which such issuer is deemed to be a 'large accelerated filer', as defined in section 240.12b-2 of title 17, Code of Federal Regulations, or any successor thereto.".

(c) OTHER DEFINITIONS.—As used in this title, the following definitions shall apply:

(1) COMMISSION.—The term "Commission" means the Securities and Exchange Commission.

(2) INITIAL PUBLIC OFFERING DATE.—The term "initial public offering date" means the date of the first sale of common equity securities of an issuer pursuant to an effective registration statement under the Securities Act of 1933.

(d) EFFECTIVE DATE.—Notwithstanding section 2(a)(19) of the Securities Act of 1933 and section 3(a)(80) of the Securities Exchange Act of 1934, an issuer shall not be an emerging growth company for purposes of such Acts if the first sale of common equity securities of such issuer pursuant to an effective registration statement under the Securities Act of 1933 occurred on or before December 8, 2011.

SEC. 102. DISCLOSURE OBLIGATIONS.

(a) EXECUTIVE COMPENSATION.—

(1) EXEMPTION.—Section 14A(e) of the Securities Exchange Act of 1934 (15 U.S.C. 78n–1(e)) is amended—

(A) by striking "The Commission may" and inserting the following:

"(1) IN GENERAL.—The Commission may";

(B) by striking "an issuer" and inserting "any other issuer"; and

(C) by adding at the end the following:

"(2) TREATMENT OF EMERGING GROWTH COMPANIES.—

"(A) IN GENERAL.—An emerging growth company shall be exempt from the requirements of subsections (a) and (b).

"(B) COMPLIANCE AFTER TERMINATION OF EMERGING GROWTH COMPANY TREATMENT.—An issuer that was an emerging growth company but is no longer an emerging growth company shall include the first separate resolution described under subsection (a)(1) not later than the end of—

"(i) in the case of an issuer that was an emerging growth company for less than 2 years after the date of first sale of common equity securities of the issuer pursuant to an effective registration statement under the Securities Act of 1933, the 3-year period beginning on such date; and

"(ii) in the case of any other issuer, the 1-year period beginning on the date the issuer is no longer an emerging growth company.".

(2) PROXIES.—Section 14(i) of the Securities Exchange Act of 1934 (15 U.S.C. 78n(i)) is amended by inserting ", for any issuer other than an emerging growth company," after "including".

(3) COMPENSATION DISCLOSURES.—Section 953(b)(1) of the Investor Protection and Securities Reform Act of 2010 (Public Law 111–203; 124 Stat. 1904) is amended by inserting ", other than an emerging growth company, as that term is defined in section 3(a) of the Securities Exchange Act of 1934," after "require each issuer".

(b) FINANCIAL DISCLOSURES AND ACCOUNTING PRONOUNCEMENTS.—

(1) SECURITIES ACT OF 1933.—Section 7(a) of the Securities Act of 1933 (15 U.S.C. 77g(a)) is amended—

(A) by striking "(a) The registration" and inserting the following:

"(a) INFORMATION REQUIRED IN REGISTRATION STATEMENT.—

"(1) IN GENERAL.—The registration"; and

(B) by adding at the end the following:

"(2) TREATMENT OF EMERGING GROWTH COMPANIES.—An emerging growth company—

"(A) need not present more than 2 years of audited financial statements in order for the registration statement of such emerging growth company with respect to an initial public offering of its common equity securities to be effective, and in any other registration statement to be filed with the Commission, an emerging growth company need not present selected financial data in accordance with section 229.301 of title 17, Code of Federal Regulations, for any period prior to the earliest audited period presented in connection with its initial public offering; and

"(B) may not be required to comply with any new or revised financial accounting standard until such date that a company that is not an issuer (as defined under section 2(a) of the Sarbanes-Oxley Act of 2002 (15 U.S.C. 7201(a))) is required to comply with such new or revised accounting standard, if such standard applies to companies that are not issuers.".

(2) SECURITIES EXCHANGE ACT OF 1934.—Section 13(a) of the Securities Exchange Act of 1934 (15 U.S.C. 78m(a)) is amended by adding at the end the following: "In any registration statement, periodic report, or other reports to be filed with the Commission, an emerging growth company need not present selected financial data in accordance with section 229.301 of title 17, Code of Federal Regulations, for any period prior to the earliest audited period presented in connection with its first registration statement that became effective under this Act or the Securities Act of 1933 and, with respect to any such statement or reports, an emerging growth company may not be required to comply with any new or revised financial

accounting standard until such date that a company that is not an issuer (as defined under section 2(a) of the Sarbanes-Oxley Act of 2002 (15 U.S.C. 7201(a))) is required to comply with such new or revised accounting standard, if such standard applies to companies that are not issuers.".

(c) OTHER DISCLOSURES.—An emerging growth company may comply with section 229.303(a) of title 17, Code of Federal Regulations, or any successor thereto, by providing information required by such section with respect to the financial statements of the emerging growth company for each period presented pursuant to section 7(a) of the Securities Act of 1933 (15 U.S.C. 77g(a)). An emerging growth company may comply with section 229.402 of title 17, Code of Federal Regulations, or any successor thereto, by disclosing the same information as any issuer with a market value of outstanding voting and nonvoting common equity held by non-affiliates of less than $75,000,000.

SEC. 103. INTERNAL CONTROLS AUDIT.

Section 404(b) of the Sarbanes-Oxley Act of 2002 (15 U.S.C. 7262(b)) is amended by inserting ", other than an issuer that is an emerging growth company (as defined in section 3 of the Securities Exchange Act of 1934)," before "shall attest to".

SEC. 104. AUDITING STANDARDS.

Section 103(a)(3) of the Sarbanes-Oxley Act of 2002 (15 U.S.C. 7213(a)(3)) is amended by adding at the end the following:

"(C) TRANSITION PERIOD FOR EMERGING GROWTH COMPANIES.—Any rules of the Board requiring mandatory audit firm rotation or a supplement to the auditor's report in which the auditor would be required to provide additional information about the audit and the financial statements of the issuer (auditor discussion and analysis) shall not apply to an audit of an emerging growth company, as defined in section 3 of the Securities Exchange Act of 1934. Any additional rules adopted by the Board after the date of enactment of this subparagraph shall not apply to an audit of any emerging growth company, unless the Commission determines that the application of such additional requirements is necessary or appropriate in the public interest, after considering the protection of investors and whether the action will promote efficiency, competition, and capital formation.".

SEC. 105. AVAILABILITY OF INFORMATION ABOUT EMERGING GROWTH COMPANIES.

(a) PROVISION OF RESEARCH.—Section 2(a)(3) of the Securities Act of 1933 (15 U.S.C. 77b(a)(3)) is amended by adding at the end the following: "The publication or distribution by a broker or dealer of a research report about an emerging growth company that is the subject of a proposed public offering of the common equity securities of such emerging growth company pursuant to a registration statement that the issuer proposes to file, or has filed, or that is effective shall be deemed for purposes of paragraph (10) of this subsection and section 5(c) not to constitute an offer for sale or offer to sell a security, even if the broker or dealer is participating or will participate in the registered offering of the securities of the issuer. As used in this paragraph, the term 'research report' means a written, electronic, or oral communication that includes information, opinions, or recommendations with respect to securities of an issuer or an analysis of a security or an issuer, whether or not it provides information reasonably sufficient upon which to base an investment decision.".

(b) SECURITIES ANALYST COMMUNICATIONS.—Section 15D of the Securities Exchange Act of 1934 (15 U.S.C. 78o–6) is amended—

(1) by redesignating subsection (c) as subsection (d); and
(2) by inserting after subsection (b) the following:

"(c) LIMITATION.—Notwithstanding subsection (a) or any other provision of law, neither the Commission nor any national securities association registered under section 15A may adopt or maintain any rule or regulation in connection with an initial public offering of the common equity of an emerging growth company—

"(1) restricting, based on functional role, which associated persons of a broker, dealer, or member of a national securities association, may arrange for communications between a securities analyst and a potential investor; or

"(2) restricting a securities analyst from participating in any communications with the management of an emerging growth company that is also attended by any other associated person of a broker, dealer, or member of a national securities association whose functional role is other than as a securities analyst.".

(c) EXPANDING PERMISSIBLE COMMUNICATIONS.—Section 5 of the Securities Act of 1933 (15 U.S.C. 77e) is amended—

(1) by redesignating subsection (d) as subsection (e); and
(2) by inserting after subsection (c) the following:

"(d) LIMITATION.—Notwithstanding any other provision of this section, an emerging growth company or any person authorized to act on behalf of an emerging growth company may engage in oral or written communications with potential investors that are qualified institutional buyers or institutions that are accredited investors, as such terms are respectively defined in section 230.144A and section 230.501(a) of title 17, Code of Federal Regulations, or any successor thereto, to determine whether such investors might have an interest in a contemplated securities offering, either prior to or following the date of filing of a registration statement with respect to such securities with the Commission, subject to the requirement of subsection (b)(2).".

(d) POST OFFERING COMMUNICATIONS.—Neither the Commission nor any national securities association registered under section 15A of the Securities Exchange Act of 1934 may adopt or maintain any rule or regulation prohibiting any broker, dealer, or member of a national securities association from publishing or distributing any research report or making a public appearance, with respect to the securities of an emerging growth company, either—

(1) within any prescribed period of time following the initial public offering date of the emerging growth company; or

(2) within any prescribed period of time prior to the expiration date of any agreement between the broker, dealer, or member of a national securities association and the emerging growth company or its shareholders that restricts or prohibits the sale of securities held by the emerging growth company or its shareholders after the initial public offering date.

SEC. 106. OTHER MATTERS.

(a) DRAFT REGISTRATION STATEMENTS.—Section 6 of the Securities Act of 1933 (15 U.S.C. 77f) is amended by adding at the end the following:

"(e) EMERGING GROWTH COMPANIES.—

"(1) IN GENERAL.—Any emerging growth company, prior to its initial public offering date, may confidentially submit to the Commission a draft registration statement, for confidential nonpublic review by the staff of the Commission prior to public filing, provided that the initial confidential submission and all amendments thereto shall be publicly filed with the Commission not later than 21 days before the date on which the issuer conducts a road show, as such term is defined in section 230.433(h)(4) of title 17, Code of Federal Regulations, or any successor thereto.

"(2) CONFIDENTIALITY.—Notwithstanding any other provision of this title, the Commission shall not be compelled to disclose any information provided to or obtained by the Commission pursuant to this subsection. For purposes of section 552 of title 5, United States Code, this subsection shall be considered a statute described in subsection (b)(3)(B) of such section 552. Information described in or obtained pursuant to this subsection shall be deemed to constitute confidential information for purposes of section 24(b)(2) of the Securities Exchange Act of 1934.".

(b) TICK SIZE.—Section 11A(c) of the Securities Exchange Act of 1934 (15 U.S.C. 78k–1(c)) is amended by adding at the end the following new paragraph:

"(6) TICK SIZE.—

"(A) STUDY AND REPORT.—The Commission shall conduct a study examining the transition to trading and quoting securities in one penny increments, also known as decimalization. The study shall examine the impact that decimalization has had on the number of initial public offerings since its implementation relative to the period before its implementation. The study shall also examine the impact that this change has had on liquidity for small and middle capitalization company securities and whether there is sufficient economic incentive to support trading operations in these securities in penny increments. Not later than 90 days after the date of enactment of this paragraph, the Commission shall submit to Congress a report on the findings of the study.

"(B) DESIGNATION.—If the Commission determines that the securities of emerging growth companies should be quoted and traded using a minimum increment of greater than $0.01, the Commission may, by rule not later than 180 days after the date of enactment of this paragraph, designate a minimum increment for the securities of emerging growth companies that is greater than $0.01 but less than $0.10 for use in all quoting and trading of securities in any exchange or other execution venue.".

SEC. 107. OPT-IN RIGHT FOR EMERGING GROWTH COMPANIES.

(a) IN GENERAL.—With respect to an exemption provided to emerging growth companies under this title, or an amendment made by this title, an emerging growth company may choose to forgo such exemption and instead comply with the requirements that apply to an issuer that is not an emerging growth company.

(b) SPECIAL RULE.—Notwithstanding subsection (a), with respect to the extension of time to comply with new or revised financial accounting standards provided under section 7(a)(2)(B) of the Securities Act of 1933 and section 13(a) of the Securities Exchange Act of 1934, as added by section 102(b), if an emerging growth company chooses to comply with such standards to the same extent that a non-emerging growth company is required to comply with such standards, the emerging growth company—

(1) must make such choice at the time the company is first required to file a registration statement, periodic report, or other report with the Commission under section 13 of the Securities Exchange Act of 1934 and notify the Securities and Exchange Commission of such choice;

(2) may not select some standards to comply with in such manner and not others, but must comply with all such standards to the same extent that a non-emerging growth company is required to comply with such standards; and

(3) must continue to comply with such standards to the same extent that a non-emerging growth company is required to comply with such standards for as long as the company remains an emerging growth company.

SEC. 108. REVIEW OF REGULATION S-K.

(a) REVIEW.—The Securities and Exchange Commission shall conduct a review of its Regulation S-K (17 CFR 229.10 et seq.) to—

(1) comprehensively analyze the current registration requirements of such regulation; and

(2) determine how such requirements can be updated to modernize and simplify the registration process and reduce the costs and other burdens associated with these requirements for issuers who are emerging growth companies.

(b) REPORT.—Not later than 180 days after the date of enactment of this title, the Commission shall transmit to Congress a report of the review conducted under subsection (a). The report shall include the specific recommendations of the Commission on how to streamline the registration process in order to make it more efficient and less burdensome for the Commission and for prospective issuers who are emerging growth companies.

TITLE II—ACCESS TO CAPITAL FOR JOB CREATORS

SEC. 201. MODIFICATION OF EXEMPTION.

(a) MODIFICATION OF RULES.—

(1) Not later than 90 days after the date of the enactment of this Act, the Securities and Exchange Commission shall revise its rules issued in section 230.506 of title 17, Code of Federal Regulations, to provide that the prohibition against general solicitation or general advertising contained in section 230.502(c) of such title shall not apply to offers and sales of securities made pursuant to section 230.506, provided that all purchasers of the securities are accredited investors. Such rules shall require the issuer to take reasonable steps to verify

H. R. 3606—9

that purchasers of the securities are accredited investors, using such methods as determined by the Commission. Section 230.506 of title 17, Code of Federal Regulations, as revised pursuant to this section, shall continue to be treated as a regulation issued under section 4(2) of the Securities Act of 1933 (15 U.S.C. 77d(2)).

(2) Not later than 90 days after the date of enactment of this Act, the Securities and Exchange Commission shall revise subsection (d)(1) of section 230.144A of title 17, Code of Federal Regulations, to provide that securities sold under such revised exemption may be offered to persons other than qualified institutional buyers, including by means of general solicitation or general advertising, provided that securities are sold only to persons that the seller and any person acting on behalf of the seller reasonably believe is a qualified institutional buyer.

(b) CONSISTENCY IN INTERPRETATION.—Section 4 of the Securities Act of 1933 (15 U.S.C. 77d) is amended—

(1) by striking "The provisions of section 5" and inserting "(a) The provisions of section 5"; and

(2) by adding at the end the following:

"(b) Offers and sales exempt under section 230.506 of title 17, Code of Federal Regulations (as revised pursuant to section 201 of the Jumpstart Our Business Startups Act) shall not be deemed public offerings under the Federal securities laws as a result of general advertising or general solicitation.".

(c) EXPLANATION OF EXEMPTION.—Section 4 of the Securities Act of 1933 (15 U.S.C. 77d) is amended—

(1) by striking "The provisions of section 5" and inserting "(a) The provisions of section 5"; and

(2) by adding at the end the following:

"(b)(1) With respect to securities offered and sold in compliance with Rule 506 of Regulation D under this Act, no person who meets the conditions set forth in paragraph (2) shall be subject to registration as a broker or dealer pursuant to section 15(a)(1) of this title, solely because—

"(A) that person maintains a platform or mechanism that permits the offer, sale, purchase, or negotiation of or with respect to securities, or permits general solicitations, general advertisements, or similar or related activities by issuers of such securities, whether online, in person, or through any other means;

"(B) that person or any person associated with that person co-invests in such securities; or

"(C) that person or any person associated with that person provides ancillary services with respect to such securities.

"(2) The exemption provided in paragraph (1) shall apply to any person described in such paragraph if—

"(A) such person and each person associated with that person receives no compensation in connection with the purchase or sale of such security;

"(B) such person and each person associated with that person does not have possession of customer funds or securities in connection with the purchase or sale of such security; and

"(C) such person is not subject to a statutory disqualification as defined in section 3(a)(39) of this title and does not

H. R. 3606—10

have any person associated with that person subject to such a statutory disqualification.

"(3) For the purposes of this subsection, the term 'ancillary services' means—

"(A) the provision of due diligence services, in connection with the offer, sale, purchase, or negotiation of such security, so long as such services do not include, for separate compensation, investment advice or recommendations to issuers or investors; and

"(B) the provision of standardized documents to the issuers and investors, so long as such person or entity does not negotiate the terms of the issuance for and on behalf of third parties and issuers are not required to use the standardized documents as a condition of using the service.".

TITLE III—CROWDFUNDING

SEC. 301. SHORT TITLE.

This title may be cited as the "Capital Raising Online While Deterring Fraud and Unethical Non-Disclosure Act of 2012" or the "CROWDFUND Act".

SEC. 302. CROWDFUNDING EXEMPTION.

(a) SECURITIES ACT OF 1933.—Section 4 of the Securities Act of 1933 (15 U.S.C. 77d) is amended by adding at the end the following:

"(6) transactions involving the offer or sale of securities by an issuer (including all entities controlled by or under common control with the issuer), provided that—

"(A) the aggregate amount sold to all investors by the issuer, including any amount sold in reliance on the exemption provided under this paragraph during the 12-month period preceding the date of such transaction, is not more than $1,000,000;

"(B) the aggregate amount sold to any investor by an issuer, including any amount sold in reliance on the exemption provided under this paragraph during the 12-month period preceding the date of such transaction, does not exceed—

"(i) the greater of $2,000 or 5 percent of the annual income or net worth of such investor, as applicable, if either the annual income or the net worth of the investor is less than $100,000; and

"(ii) 10 percent of the annual income or net worth of such investor, as applicable, not to exceed a maximum aggregate amount sold of $100,000, if either the annual income or net worth of the investor is equal to or more than $100,000;

"(C) the transaction is conducted through a broker or funding portal that complies with the requirements of section 4A(a); and

"(D) the issuer complies with the requirements of section 4A(b).".

(b) REQUIREMENTS TO QUALIFY FOR CROWDFUNDING EXEMPTION.—The Securities Act of 1933 (15 U.S.C. 77a et seq.) is amended by inserting after section 4 the following:

"SEC. 4A. REQUIREMENTS WITH RESPECT TO CERTAIN SMALL TRANSACTIONS.

"(a) REQUIREMENTS ON INTERMEDIARIES.—A person acting as an intermediary in a transaction involving the offer or sale of securities for the account of others pursuant to section 4(6) shall—

"(1) register with the Commission as—
"(A) a broker; or
"(B) a funding portal (as defined in section 3(a)(80) of the Securities Exchange Act of 1934);

"(2) register with any applicable self-regulatory organization (as defined in section 3(a)(26) of the Securities Exchange Act of 1934);

"(3) provide such disclosures, including disclosures related to risks and other investor education materials, as the Commission shall, by rule, determine appropriate;

"(4) ensure that each investor—
"(A) reviews investor-education information, in accordance with standards established by the Commission, by rule;
"(B) positively affirms that the investor understands that the investor is risking the loss of the entire investment, and that the investor could bear such a loss; and
"(C) answers questions demonstrating—
"(i) an understanding of the level of risk generally applicable to investments in startups, emerging businesses, and small issuers;
"(ii) an understanding of the risk of illiquidity; and
"(iii) an understanding of such other matters as the Commission determines appropriate, by rule;

"(5) take such measures to reduce the risk of fraud with respect to such transactions, as established by the Commission, by rule, including obtaining a background and securities enforcement regulatory history check on each officer, director, and person holding more than 20 percent of the outstanding equity of every issuer whose securities are offered by such person;

"(6) not later than 21 days prior to the first day on which securities are sold to any investor (or such other period as the Commission may establish), make available to the Commission and to potential investors any information provided by the issuer pursuant to subsection (b);

"(7) ensure that all offering proceeds are only provided to the issuer when the aggregate capital raised from all investors is equal to or greater than a target offering amount, and allow all investors to cancel their commitments to invest, as the Commission shall, by rule, determine appropriate;

"(8) make such efforts as the Commission determines appropriate, by rule, to ensure that no investor in a 12-month period has purchased securities offered pursuant to section 4(6) that, in the aggregate, from all issuers, exceed the investment limits set forth in section 4(6)(B);

"(9) take such steps to protect the privacy of information collected from investors as the Commission shall, by rule, determine appropriate;

"(10) not compensate promoters, finders, or lead generators for providing the broker or funding portal with the personal identifying information of any potential investor;

"(11) prohibit its directors, officers, or partners (or any person occupying a similar status or performing a similar function) from having any financial interest in an issuer using its services; and

"(12) meet such other requirements as the Commission may, by rule, prescribe, for the protection of investors and in the public interest.

"(b) REQUIREMENTS FOR ISSUERS.—For purposes of section 4(6), an issuer who offers or sells securities shall—

"(1) file with the Commission and provide to investors and the relevant broker or funding portal, and make available to potential investors—
"(A) the name, legal status, physical address, and website address of the issuer;
"(B) the names of the directors and officers (and any persons occupying a similar status or performing a similar function), and each person holding more than 20 percent of the shares of the issuer;
"(C) a description of the business of the issuer and the anticipated business plan of the issuer;
"(D) a description of the financial condition of the issuer, including, for offerings that, together with all other offerings of the issuer under section 4(6) within the preceding 12-month period, have, in the aggregate, target offering amounts of—
"(i) $100,000 or less—
"(I) the income tax returns filed by the issuer for the most recently completed year (if any); and
"(II) financial statements of the issuer, which shall be certified by the principal executive officer of the issuer to be true and complete in all material respects;
"(ii) more than $100,000, but not more than $500,000, financial statements reviewed by a public accountant who is independent of the issuer, using professional standards and procedures for such review or standards and procedures established by the Commission, by rule, for such purpose; and
"(iii) more than $500,000 (or such other amount as the Commission may establish, by rule), audited financial statements;
"(E) a description of the stated purpose and intended use of the proceeds of the offering sought by the issuer with respect to the target offering amount;
"(F) the target offering amount, the deadline to reach the target offering amount, and regular updates regarding the progress of the issuer in meeting the target offering amount;
"(G) the price to the public of the securities or the method for determining the price, provided that, prior to sale, each investor shall be provided in writing the final price and all required disclosures, with a reasonable opportunity to rescind the commitment to purchase the securities;

H. R. 3606—13

"(H) a description of the ownership and capital structure of the issuer, including—

"(i) terms of the securities of the issuer being offered and each other class of security of the issuer, including how such terms may be modified, and a summary of the differences between such securities, including how the rights of the securities being offered may be materially limited, diluted, or qualified by the rights of any other class of security of the issuer;

"(ii) a description of how the exercise of the rights held by the principal shareholders of the issuer could negatively impact the purchasers of the securities being offered;

"(iii) the name and ownership level of each existing shareholder who owns more than 20 percent of any class of the securities of the issuer;

"(iv) how the securities being offered are being valued, and examples of methods for how such securities may be valued by the issuer in the future, including during subsequent corporate actions; and

"(v) the risks to purchasers of the securities relating to minority ownership in the issuer, the risks associated with corporate actions, including additional issuances of shares, a sale of the issuer or of assets of the issuer, or transactions with related parties; and

"(I) such other information as the Commission may, by rule, prescribe, for the protection of investors and in the public interest;

"(2) not advertise the terms of the offering, except for notices which direct investors to the funding portal or broker;

"(3) not compensate or commit to compensate, directly or indirectly, any person to promote its offerings through communication channels provided by a broker or funding portal, without taking such steps as the Commission shall, by rule, require to ensure that such person clearly discloses the receipt, past or prospective, of such compensation, upon each instance of such promotional communication;

"(4) not less than annually, file with the Commission and provide to investors reports of the results of operations and financial statements of the issuer, as the Commission shall, by rule, determine appropriate, subject to such exceptions and termination dates as the Commission may establish, by rule; and

"(5) comply with such other requirements as the Commission may, by rule, prescribe, for the protection of investors and in the public interest.

"(c) LIABILITY FOR MATERIAL MISSTATEMENTS AND OMISSIONS.—

"(1) ACTIONS AUTHORIZED.—

"(A) IN GENERAL.—Subject to paragraph (2), a person who purchases a security in a transaction exempted by the provisions of section 4(6) may bring an action against an issuer described in paragraph (2), either at law or in equity in any court of competent jurisdiction, to recover the consideration paid for such security with interest thereon, less the amount of any income received thereon, upon the tender of such security, or for damages if such person no longer owns the security.

H. R. 3606—14

"(B) LIABILITY.—An action brought under this paragraph shall be subject to the provisions of section 12(b) and section 13, as if the liability were created under section 12(a)(2).

"(2) APPLICABILITY.—An issuer shall be liable in an action under paragraph (1), if the issuer—

"(A) by the use of any means or instruments of transportation or communication in interstate commerce or of the mails, by any means of any written or oral communication, in the offering or sale of a security in a transaction exempted by the provisions of section 4(6), makes an untrue statement of a material fact or omits to state a material fact required to be stated or necessary in order to make the statements, in the light of the circumstances under which they were made, not misleading, provided that the purchaser did not know of such untruth or omission; and

"(B) does not sustain the burden of proof that such issuer did not know, and in the exercise of reasonable care could not have known, of such untruth or omission.

"(3) DEFINITION.—As used in this subsection, the term 'issuer' includes any person who is a director or partner of the issuer, and the principal executive officer or officers, principal financial officer, and controller or principal accounting officer of the issuer (and any person occupying a similar status or performing a similar function) that offers or sells a security in a transaction exempted by the provisions of section 4(6), and any person who offers or sells the security in such offering.

"(d) INFORMATION AVAILABLE TO STATES.—The Commission shall make, or shall cause to be made by the relevant broker or funding portal, the information described in subsection (b) and such other information as the Commission, by rule, determines appropriate, available to the securities commission (or any agency or office performing like functions) of each State and territory of the United States and the District of Columbia.

"(e) RESTRICTIONS ON SALES.—Securities issued pursuant to a transaction described in section 4(6)—

"(1) may not be transferred by the purchaser of such securities during the 1-year period beginning on the date of purchase, unless such securities are transferred—

"(A) to the issuer of the securities;

"(B) to an accredited investor;

"(C) as part of an offering registered with the Commission; or

"(D) to a member of the family of the purchaser or the equivalent, or in connection with the death or divorce of the purchaser or other similar circumstance, in the discretion of the Commission; and

"(2) shall be subject to such other limitations as the Commission shall, by rule, establish.

"(f) APPLICABILITY.—Section 4(6) shall not apply to transactions involving the offer or sale of securities by any issuer that—

"(1) is not organized under and subject to the laws of a State or territory of the United States or the District of Columbia;

H. R. 3606—15

"(2) is subject to the requirement to file reports pursuant to section 13 or section 15(d) of the Securities Exchange Act of 1934;

"(3) is an investment company, as defined in section 3 of the Investment Company Act of 1940, or is excluded from the definition of investment company by section 3(b) or section 3(c) of that Act; or

"(4) the Commission, by rule or regulation, determines appropriate.

"(g) RULE OF CONSTRUCTION.—Nothing in this section or section 4(6) shall be construed as preventing an issuer from raising capital through methods not described under section 4(6).

"(h) CERTAIN CALCULATIONS.—

"(1) DOLLAR AMOUNTS.—Dollar amounts in section 4(6) and subsection (b) of this section shall be adjusted by the Commission not less frequently than once every 5 years, by notice published in the Federal Register to reflect any change in the Consumer Price Index for All Urban Consumers published by the Bureau of Labor Statistics.

"(2) INCOME AND NET WORTH.—The income and net worth of a natural person under section 4(6)(B) shall be calculated in accordance with any rules of the Commission under this title regarding the calculation of the income and net worth, respectively, of an accredited investor.".

(c) RULEMAKING.—Not later than 270 days after the date of enactment of this Act, the Securities and Exchange Commission (in this title referred to as the "Commission") shall issue such rules as the Commission determines may be necessary or appropriate for the protection of investors to carry out sections 4(6) and section 4A of the Securities Act of 1933, as added by this title. In carrying out this section, the Commission shall consult with any securities commission (or any agency or office performing like functions) of the States, any territory of the United States, and the District of Columbia, which seeks to consult with the Commission, and with any applicable national securities association.

(d) DISQUALIFICATION.—

(1) IN GENERAL.—Not later than 270 days after the date of enactment of this Act, the Commission shall, by rule, establish disqualification provisions under which—

(A) an issuer shall not be eligible to offer securities pursuant to section 4(6) of the Securities Act of 1933, as added by this title; and

(B) a broker or funding portal shall not be eligible to effect or participate in transactions pursuant to that section 4(6).

(2) INCLUSIONS.—Disqualification provisions required by this subsection shall—

(A) be substantially similar to the provisions of section 230.262 of title 17, Code of Federal Regulations (or any successor thereto); and

(B) disqualify any offering or sale of securities by a person that—

(i) is subject to a final order of a State securities commission (or an agency or officer of a State performing like functions), a State authority that supervises or examines banks, savings associations, or credit unions, a State insurance commission (or an agency

H. R. 3606—16

or officer of a State performing like functions), an appropriate Federal banking agency, or the National Credit Union Administration, that—

(I) bars the person from—

(aa) association with an entity regulated by such commission, authority, agency, or officer;

(bb) engaging in the business of securities, insurance, or banking; or

(cc) engaging in savings association or credit union activities; or

(II) constitutes a final order based on a violation of any law or regulation that prohibits fraudulent, manipulative, or deceptive conduct within the 10-year period ending on the date of the filing of the offer or sale; or

(ii) has been convicted of any felony or misdemeanor in connection with the purchase or sale of any security or involving the making of any false filing with the Commission.

SEC. 303. EXCLUSION OF CROWDFUNDING INVESTORS FROM SHAREHOLDER CAP.

(a) EXEMPTION.—Section 12(g) of the Securities Exchange Act of 1934 (15 U.S.C. 78l(g)) is amended by adding at the end the following:

"(6) EXCLUSION FOR PERSONS HOLDING CERTAIN SECURITIES.—The Commission shall, by rule, exempt, conditionally or unconditionally, securities acquired pursuant to an offering made under section 4(6) of the Securities Act of 1933 from the provisions of this subsection.".

(b) RULEMAKING.—The Commission shall issue a rule to carry out section 12(g)(6) of the Securities Exchange Act of 1934 (15 U.S.C. 78c), as added by this section, not later than 270 days after the date of enactment of this Act.

SEC. 304. FUNDING PORTAL REGULATION.

(a) EXEMPTION.—

(1) IN GENERAL.—Section 3 of the Securities Exchange Act of 1934 (15 U.S.C. 78c) is amended by adding at the end the following:

"(h) LIMITED EXEMPTION FOR FUNDING PORTALS.—

"(1) IN GENERAL.—The Commission shall, by rule, exempt, conditionally or unconditionally, a registered funding portal from the requirement to register as a broker or dealer under section 15(a)(1), provided that such funding portal—

"(A) remains subject to the examination, enforcement, and other rulemaking authority of the Commission;

"(B) is a member of a national securities association registered under section 15A; and

"(C) is subject to such other requirements under this title as the Commission determines appropriate under such rule.

"(2) NATIONAL SECURITIES ASSOCIATION MEMBERSHIP.—For purposes of sections 15(b)(8) and 15A, the term 'broker or dealer' includes a funding portal and the term 'registered broker or dealer' includes a registered funding portal, except to the extent that the Commission, by rule, determines otherwise, provided that a national securities association shall only examine for and enforce against a registered funding portal rules of such national securities association written specifically for registered funding portals.".

(2) RULEMAKING.—The Commission shall issue a rule to carry out section 3(h) of the Securities Exchange Act of 1934 (15 U.S.C. 78c), as added by this subsection, not later than 270 days after the date of enactment of this Act.

(b) DEFINITION.—Section 3(a) of the Securities Exchange Act of 1934 (15 U.S.C. 78c(a)) is amended by adding at the end the following:

"(80) FUNDING PORTAL.—The term 'funding portal' means any person acting as an intermediary in a transaction involving the offer or sale of securities for the account of others, solely pursuant to section 4(6) of the Securities Act of 1933 (15 U.S.C. 77d(6)), that does not—

"(A) offer investment advice or recommendations;

"(B) solicit purchases, sales, or offers to buy the securities offered or displayed on its website or portal;

"(C) compensate employees, agents, or other persons for such solicitation or based on the sale of securities displayed or referenced on its website or portal;

"(D) hold, manage, possess, or otherwise handle investor funds or securities; or

"(E) engage in such other activities as the Commission, by rule, determines appropriate.".

SEC. 305. RELATIONSHIP WITH STATE LAW.

(a) IN GENERAL.—Section 18(b)(4) of the Securities Act of 1933 (15 U.S.C. 77r(b)(4)) is amended—

(1) by redesignating subparagraphs (C) and (D) as subparagraphs (D) and (E), respectively; and

(2) by inserting after subparagraph (B) the following:

"(C) section 4(6);".

(b) CLARIFICATION OF THE PRESERVATION OF STATE ENFORCEMENT AUTHORITY.—

(1) IN GENERAL.—The amendments made by subsection (a) relate solely to State registration, documentation, and offering requirements, as described under section 18(a) of Securities Act of 1933 (15 U.S.C. 77r(a)), and shall have no impact or limitation on other State authority to take enforcement action with regard to an issuer, funding portal, or any other person or entity using the exemption from registration provided by section 4(6) of that Act.

(2) CLARIFICATION OF STATE JURISDICTION OVER UNLAWFUL CONDUCT OF FUNDING PORTALS AND ISSUERS.—Section 18(c)(1) of the Securities Act of 1933 (15 U.S.C. 77r(c)(1)) is amended by striking "with respect to fraud or deceit, or unlawful conduct by a broker or dealer, in connection with securities or securities transactions." and inserting the following: ", in connection with securities or securities transactions

"(A) with respect to—

"(i) fraud or deceit; or

"(ii) unlawful conduct by a broker or dealer; and

"(B) in connection to a transaction described under section 4(6), with respect to—

"(i) fraud or deceit; or

"(ii) unlawful conduct by a broker, dealer, funding portal, or issuer.".

(c) NOTICE FILINGS PERMITTED.—Section 18(c)(2) of the Securities Act of 1933 (15 U.S.C. 77r(c)(2)) is amended by adding at the end the following:

"(F) FEES NOT PERMITTED ON CROWDFUNDED SECURITIES.—Notwithstanding subparagraphs (A), (B), and (C), no filing or fee may be required with respect to any security that is a covered security pursuant to subsection (b)(4)(B), or will be such a covered security upon completion of the transaction, except for the securities commission (or any agency or office performing like functions) of the State of the principal place of business of the issuer, or any State in which purchasers of 50 percent or greater of the aggregate amount of the issue are residents, provided that for purposes of this subparagraph, the term 'State' includes the District of Columbia and the territories of the United States.".

(d) FUNDING PORTALS.—

(1) STATE EXEMPTIONS AND OVERSIGHT.—Section 15(i) of the Securities Exchange Act of 1934 (15 U.S.C. 78o(i)) is amended—

(A) by redesignating paragraphs (2) and (3) as paragraphs (3) and (4), respectively; and

(B) by inserting after paragraph (1) the following:

"(2) FUNDING PORTALS.—

"(A) LIMITATION ON STATE LAWS.—Except as provided in subparagraph (B), no State or political subdivision thereof may enforce any law, rule, regulation, or other administrative action against a registered funding portal with respect to its business as such.

"(B) EXAMINATION AND ENFORCEMENT AUTHORITY.—Subparagraph (A) does not apply with respect to the examination and enforcement of any law, rule, regulation, or administrative action of a State or political subdivision thereof in which the principal place of business of a registered funding portal is located, provided that such law, rule, regulation, or administrative action is not in addition to or different from the requirements for registered funding portals established by the Commission.

"(C) DEFINITION.—For purposes of this paragraph, the term 'State' includes the District of Columbia and the territories of the United States.".

(2) STATE FRAUD AUTHORITY.—Section 18(c)(1) of the Securities Act of 1933 (15 U.S.C. 77r(c)(1)) is amended by striking "or dealer" and inserting ", dealer, or funding portal".

TITLE IV—SMALL COMPANY CAPITAL FORMATION

SEC. 401. AUTHORITY TO EXEMPT CERTAIN SECURITIES.

(a) IN GENERAL.—Section 3(b) of the Securities Act of 1933 (15 U.S.C. 77c(b)) is amended—

(1) by striking "(b) The Commission" and inserting the following:

"(b) ADDITIONAL EXEMPTIONS.—

"(1) SMALL ISSUES EXEMPTIVE AUTHORITY.—The Commission"; and
(2) by adding at the end the following:
"(2) ADDITIONAL ISSUES.—The Commission shall by rule or regulation add a class of securities to the securities exempted pursuant to this section in accordance with the following terms and conditions:
"(A) The aggregate offering amount of all securities offered and sold within the prior 12-month period in reliance on the exemption added in accordance with this paragraph shall not exceed $50,000,000.
"(B) The securities may be offered and sold publicly.
"(C) The securities shall not be restricted securities within the meaning of the Federal securities laws and the regulations promulgated thereunder.
"(D) The civil liability provision in section 12(a)(2) shall apply to any person offering or selling such securities.
"(E) The issuer may solicit interest in the offering prior to filing any offering statement, on such terms and conditions as the Commission may prescribe in the public interest or for the protection of investors.
"(F) The Commission shall require the issuer to file audited financial statements with the Commission annually.
"(G) Such other terms, conditions, or requirements as the Commission may determine necessary in the public interest and for the protection of investors, which may include—
"(i) a requirement that the issuer prepare and electronically file with the Commission and distribute to prospective investors an offering statement, and any related documents, in such form and with such content as prescribed by the Commission, including audited financial statements, a description of the issuer's business operations, its financial condition, its corporate governance principles, its use of investor funds, and other appropriate matters; and
"(ii) disqualification provisions under which the exemption shall not be available to the issuer or its predecessors, affiliates, officers, directors, underwriters, or other related persons, which shall be substantially similar to the disqualification provisions contained in the regulations adopted in accordance with section 926 of the Dodd-Frank Wall Street Reform and Consumer Protection Act (15 U.S.C. 77d note).
"(3) LIMITATION.—Only the following types of securities may be exempted under a rule or regulation adopted pursuant to paragraph (2): equity securities, debt securities, and debt securities convertible or exchangeable to equity interests, including any guarantees of such securities.
"(4) PERIODIC DISCLOSURES.—Upon such terms and conditions as the Commission determines necessary in the public interest and for the protection of investors, the Commission by rule or regulation may require an issuer of a class of securities exempted under paragraph (2) to make available to investors and file with the Commission periodic disclosures regarding the issuer, its business operations, its financial condition, its corporate governance principles, its use of investor funds, and other appropriate matters, and also may provide for the suspension and termination of such a requirement with respect to that issuer.
"(5) ADJUSTMENT.—Not later than 2 years after the date of enactment of the Small Company Capital Formation Act of 2011 and every 2 years thereafter, the Commission shall review the offering amount limitation described in paragraph (2)(A) and shall increase such amount as the Commission determines appropriate. If the Commission determines not to increase such amount, it shall report to the Committee on Financial Services of the House of Representatives and the Committee on Banking, Housing, and Urban Affairs of the Senate on its reasons for not increasing the amount.".
(b) TREATMENT AS COVERED SECURITIES FOR PURPOSES OF NSMIA.—Section 18(b)(4) of the Securities Act of 1933 (as amended by section 303) (15 U.S.C. 77r(b)(4)) is further amended by inserting after subparagraph (C) (as added by such section) the following:
"(D) a rule or regulation adopted pursuant to section 3(b)(2) and such security is—
"(i) offered or sold on a national securities exchange; or
"(ii) offered or sold to a qualified purchaser, as defined by the Commission pursuant to paragraph (3) with respect to that purchase or sale;".
(c) CONFORMING AMENDMENT.—Section 4(5) of the Securities Act of 1933 is amended by striking "section 3(b)" and inserting "section 3(b)(1)".

SEC. 402. STUDY ON THE IMPACT OF STATE BLUE SKY LAWS ON REGULATION A OFFERINGS.

The Comptroller General shall conduct a study on the impact of State laws regulating securities offerings, or "Blue Sky laws", on offerings made under Regulation A (17 CFR 230.251 et seq.). The Comptroller General shall transmit a report on the findings of the study to the Committee on Financial Services of the House of Representatives, and the Committee on Banking, Housing, and Urban Affairs of the Senate not later than 3 months after the date of enactment of this Act.

TITLE V—PRIVATE COMPANY FLEXIBILITY AND GROWTH

SEC. 501. THRESHOLD FOR REGISTRATION.

Section 12(g)(1)(A) of the Securities Exchange Act of 1934 (15 U.S.C. 78l(g)(1)(A)) is amended to read as follows:
"(A) within 120 days after the last day of its first fiscal year ended on which the issuer has total assets exceeding $10,000,000 and a class of equity security (other than an exempted security) held of record by either—
"(i) 2,000 persons, or
"(ii) 500 persons who are not accredited investors (as such term is defined by the Commission), and".

Appendix B: Bill H.R. 3606

H. R. 3606—21

SEC. 502. EMPLOYEES.

Section 12(g)(5) of the Securities Exchange Act of 1934 (15 U.S.C. 78l(g)(5)), as amended by section 302, is amended in subparagraph (A) by adding at the end the following: "For purposes of determining whether an issuer is required to register a security with the Commission pursuant to paragraph (1), the definition of 'held of record' shall not include securities held by persons who received the securities pursuant to an employee compensation plan in transactions exempted from the registration requirements of section 5 of the Securities Act of 1933.".

SEC. 503. COMMISSION RULEMAKING.

The Securities and Exchange Commission shall revise the definition of "held of record" pursuant to section 12(g)(5) of the Securities Exchange Act of 1934 (15 U.S.C. 78l(g)(5)) to implement the amendment made by section 502. The Commission shall also adopt safe harbor provisions that issuers can follow when determining whether holders of their securities received the securities pursuant to an employee compensation plan in transactions that were exempt from the registration requirements of section 5 of the Securities Act of 1933.

SEC. 504. COMMISSION STUDY OF ENFORCEMENT AUTHORITY UNDER RULE 12G5–1.

The Securities and Exchange Commission shall examine its authority to enforce Rule 12g5–1 to determine if new enforcement tools are needed to enforce the anti-evasion provision contained in subsection (b)(3) of the rule, and shall, not later than 120 days after the date of enactment of this Act transmit its recommendations to Congress.

TITLE VI—CAPITAL EXPANSION

SEC. 601. SHAREHOLDER THRESHOLD FOR REGISTRATION.

(a) AMENDMENTS TO SECTION 12 OF THE SECURITIES EXCHANGE ACT OF 1934.—Section 12(g) of the Securities Exchange Act of 1934 (15 U.S.C. 78l(g)) is further amended—

(1) in paragraph (1), by amending subparagraph (B) to read as follows:

"(B) in the case of an issuer that is a bank or a bank holding company, as such term is defined in section 2 of the Bank Holding Company Act of 1956 (12 U.S.C. 1841), not later than 120 days after the last day of its first fiscal year ended after the effective date of this subsection, on which the issuer has total assets exceeding $10,000,000 and a class of equity security (other than an exempted security) held of record by 2,000 or more persons,"; and

(2) in paragraph (4), by striking "three hundred" and inserting "300 persons, or, in the case of a bank or a bank holding company, as such term is defined in section 2 of the Bank Holding Company Act of 1956 (12 U.S.C. 1841), 1,200 persons".

(b) AMENDMENTS TO SECTION 15 OF THE SECURITIES EXCHANGE ACT OF 1934.—Section 15(d) of the Securities Exchange Act of 1934 (15 U.S.C. 78o(d)) is amended, in the third sentence, by striking "three hundred" and inserting "300 persons, or, in the case of bank or a bank holding company, as such term is defined

H. R. 3606—22

in section 2 of the Bank Holding Company Act of 1956 (12 U.S.C. 1841), 1,200 persons".

SEC. 602. RULEMAKING.

Not later than 1 year after the date of enactment of this Act, the Securities and Exchange Commission shall issue final regulations to implement this title and the amendments made by this title.

TITLE VII—OUTREACH ON CHANGES TO THE LAW

SEC. 701. OUTREACH BY THE COMMISSION.

The Securities and Exchange Commission shall provide online information and conduct outreach to inform small and medium sized businesses, women owned businesses, veteran owned businesses, and minority owned businesses of the changes made by this Act.

Speaker of the House of Representatives.

Vice President of the United States and President of the Senate.

Index

ABestWeb, 117
Accredited investors, 55
Advantages, of crowdfunding, 14, 15–17
Affiliate marketing, 116–17
Appbackr, 93
ArtistShare, 56

Big-picture view, 94–95
Blogs, 109–10
Brand evangelists, 17

Campaigns
    completion of. *See* End of campaign
    excitement level, 22
    keeping records, 204
    platform example. *See* Kickstarter
    rerunning after failure, 18
    successful. *See* Success
    typical, 56–59
Capital Act (H.R. 2930). *See* H.R. 2930
Cash mobs, 225
Causes (website), 45
Channeling, YouTube, 166–67
Cofolio, 93, 224
Community crowdfunding ventures, 226–27. *See also* Local investing
Concept, appeal of, 21
Control, maintaining, 17
Copyrights, 194–95
Cortese, Amy, 222
Crowdfunding
    advantages, 14, 15–17
    campaigns. *See* Campaigns
    debt-based, 52–54
    definition and description, 13, 14–15, 49
    disadvantages, 17–20
    donation-based, 51
    equity-based. *See* Equity-based crowdfunding
    JOBs act supporting. *See* JOBs act (H.R. 3606)
    minimal financial risk, 16
    origins on Internet, 55–56
    reward-based, 51–52
    Statue of Liberty, 50
    success factors, 21–22
    types of, 51–55
CrowdFund Local initiative, 227–28
Crowdpurchasing, 27
Crowds
    ability to improve thinking of, 31–33
    not thinking well, 30–31
    thinking ability of, 30–33
Crowdsourcing, 23–35
    crowdcasting and, 28
    crowdpurchasing and, 27
    crowds not thinking well and, 30–31
    crowdvoting and, 26–27
    definition and description, 23, 24, 26
    exemplary companies, 33–35
    group thinking ability and, 30–33
    historical perspective, 24–25
    lack of context and, 30
    leadership void and, 31
    limited demographics and, 31
    microwork and, 27
    poor decision-making and, 30
    today, 26
    websites, 28–30
CrowdSPRING, 35
Crowdvoting, 26–27

Dawkins, Tom, 101, 239, 242
Debt-based crowdfunding, 52–54
Demand, testing, 16
Design patents, 191
Digital media, comfort with, 21. *See also* Facebook; Internet; Social media; Twitter; *Website references*; YouTube
Disadvantages, of crowdfunding, 17–20
Disruptive innovations, 24, 33, 211
Docracy, 28–29
Domain name, registering, 106
Donation-based crowdfunding, 51
DonorsChoose, 46
Druskat, Vanessa Urch, 32
Duration of campaign, 102

E-commerce, 108–9
Editing software, for video, 179–82
End of campaign, 199–207
    about: overview of, 199, 200
    day after, 201–2
    first update after, 201
    getting your money, 205
    keeping records, 204

Index

next steps, 200–202
surveys at, 203–4
Equity-based crowdfunding, 245–53
   about: overview of, 54–55, 245
   equity defined, 246
   historical perspective, 246–51
   H.R. 2930 and, 54–55, 251–52, 253
   legislation on, 54–55, 245. *See also* JOBs act (H.R. 3606)
   leverage and, 248
   rise of, 251
   "Roaring Twenties" and, 246–48
   Securities Act of 1933 and, 249–50
   state security laws and, 250–51
   stock market crash of 1929 and, 247, 248–49
   waiting for, 264–65
Excitement level, 22

Facebook, 149–62
   about: overview of, 110, 149
   ads, using, 158–59
   analyzing your presence, 160–62
   business best practices, 159–60
   business pages, 155–58
   creating ads on, 111
   demographics of users, 150–51
   enlisting existing customers, 157
   fan pages, 110–11
   history of, 150
   "Like" button, 111
   newsfeed, 111, 112, 155, 158
   optimizing page, 160–61
   outreach plan including, 101–2
   pages vs. profiles, 155–56
   profiles, 155–56
   promoting your page, 157–58

searchability of page, 157–58
setting up business page, 156–57
"Subscribe" button, 112
terminology, 154–55
uses of, 151–52
why your business needs to be on, 152–54
Failure, 18, 20
Financial risk, 16
Flint and Tinder campaign, 216–17
Following up with donors, 42, 44, 207, 240
Fundraising, 37–47
   amount to ask for, 43–44
   common organizations, 38–40
   creating urgency for, 41–42, 94
   defined, 38
   donor importance, 43
   following up with donors, 42, 44, 207
   getting your money, 205
   grassroots, 39
   incentives and premiums, 41
   Internet as tool for, 44–45
   making payment easy, 43
   message, 40–41
   political campaigns, 39
   professionals, 40
   public broadcasting, 39–40
   religious organizations, 38–39
   setting goal, 21–22, 69, 96–98
   storytelling for, 240–42
   telling donors purpose of donation, 41
   things to always do, 40–42
   things to never do, 42–44
   tithing and, 39
   websites, 45–47
   word-of-mouth advertising, 44
Fund St. Louis, 227

Gengo, 28
Givezooks!, 46
Glossary, 266–70
Goals, setting
   guidelines, 21–22, 96–98, 239
   Kickstarter example, 69
   reasonableness check, 98
   setting properly, 98
   setting too high, 97–98
   setting too low, 96–97
   social change campaigns, 239
Google+, 114–16
Google AdWords campaign
   ad copy, 125, 130–32
   ad groups, 125
   cost and budget, 125
   Google ad rankings and, 123–24
   keywords, 125, 126–30
   monitoring and modifying, 126
   setting up, 124–26
   split testing, 132–33
Google search engine
   ad rankings, 123–24
   organic and sponsored searches, 122
   relevancy and, 122
   what it does, 121
Grassroots fundraising, 39
Guidance, lack of, 18

H.R. 2930, 54–55, 251–52, 253
H.R. 3606. *See* JOBs act (H.R. 3606)

Indiegogo, 78–80
   about: overview of, 78–79, 92
   Features section, 80
   Pricing and Fees section, 80
   Why Indiegogo section, 79–80
InnoCentive, 34

Intellectual property. *See* Protecting ideas
Internet. *See also* Facebook; Social media; Twitter; *Website references*
　crowdfunding origins on, 55–56
　fundraising using, 44–45
　platform example. *See* Kickstarter
　videos on. *See* Video; Video production; YouTube
Investing. *See also* Equity-based crowdfunding
　accredited vs. nonaccredited investors, 55
　defined, 220
　local. *See* Local investing
iStockphoto, 33
It's a Wonderful Life, local investing in, 220–21

Jantsch, John, 118
JOBs act (H.R. 3606)
　about: overview of, 245, 255, 256–59
　alternative liability standards, 263–64
　crowdfunding intermediary requirements, 262–63
　implementation timeline, 264
　other issues, 263–64
　overview of titles, 257–59
　passage and signing, 54, 253, 255, 256–57
　S. 1791 proposed, 252
　state security law pre-emption, 263
　text of, 271–81
　Title III "Crowdfunding", 260–61
　waiting for equity crowdfunding, 264–65

Jumo, 47
JustGive, 46–47

Keywords
　broad matches, 128
　exact matches, 128–29
　matching guidelines, 127–30
　negative matches, 129
　phrase matches, 128
　researching, 125
　selecting best, 126–27
　YouTube tags, 171
Kickstarter, 61–76
　about: as platform example, 61
　About You section, 75
　Account section, 75–76
　Backers section, 66
　Basics sections, 65–66, 74
　bio (yours), 71, 75
　Blog tab, 64–65
　building project (title, image, short description), 70–71
　campaign format overview, 62
　company overview, 62
　crafting, submitting proposal to, 72–76
　creating rewards, 68–69
　Creators section, 66
　defining project, 68
　Discover tab, 63–64
　Guidelines sections, 66–68, 73
　Help tab, 65–68
　introductory page, 63
　project parameters and prohibitions, 66–68
　project updates, 71–72
　promoting project, 71
　reviewing and submitting campaign, 76
　reward fulfillment, 72

　Rewards section, 74
　School, 68–72
　setting goal, 69
　starting project, 72–76
　Story section, 74–75
　video production importance, 69–70
Kickstarter campaign example, 56–59
　about: website overview, 56–57
　results and rewards, 58–59
　text, 58
　video, 57–58
Kyes, Korean, 221

LEGO Mindstorms NXT, 34
LinkedIn, 114
Loans. *See also* Equity-based crowdfunding
　debt-based crowdfunding, 52–54
　direct vs. indirect, 53
　P2P lending, 52–53
　secured vs. unsecured, 54
Local investing, 219–29
　advantages, 228–29
　attitudes toward, 221–22
　cash mobs and, 225
　community crowdfunding ventures, 226–27
　crowdfunding websites, 223–26
　CrowdFund Local initiative, 227–28
　investing defined, 220
　It's a Wonderful Life example, 220–21
　Korean Kye example, 221
　opportunity of, 228–29
Lucky Ant, 93, 223–24

Index

Marillion, 55–56
Marketing. *See also* Facebook; Fundraising; Google AdWords campaign; Pay-per-click (PPC) advertising; Social media; Twitter; YouTube
  affiliate, 116–17
  brand vs. direct, 120
  outreach (promotional) plan, 101–2, 147
  promoting project (Kickstarter), 71
Microwork, 27
Mosquita y Mari, 211–13

National Crowdfunding Association (NLCFA), 227–28
Natural Resources campaign, 213–14
Network for Good, 46
Nonaccredited investors, 55
Nonprofits, 332–33. *See also* Social enterprises

Outreach (promotional) plan, 101–2, 147, 239
Ownership, keeping, 17

Packaging, shipping products, 206–7
Patents, 189–93
  definition and description, 189–90
  design, 191
  determining if idea already patented, 196–97
  obtaining, 192–93, 195–97
  patentability guidelines, 191–92, 196–97
  plant, 191
  provisional applications, 192–93
  search organizations, 197
  types of, 190–91
  utility, 190–91
Pay-per-click (PPC) advertising, 119–33. *See also* Google AdWords campaign
  brand vs. direct marketing and, 120
  how search engines work and, 121
  organic, sponsored searches and, 122
  outreach plan including, 101–2
  popularity rankings and, 121
  relevancy and, 122
  split testing, 132–33
Peerbackers, 85–86, 92
Peer-to-peer lending (P2P), 52–53
Pitch, crafting, 93–95
Plant patents, 191
Political campaigns, 39
Press releases, 101–2
Pricing Prophets, 29
Professionalism, crowdfunding and, 20
Project example. *See* Kickstarter
Promotional plan. *See* Outreach (promotional) plan
Protecting ideas, 187–97
  copyrights for, 194–95
  documenting everything, 189
  intellectual property concept, 188–89
  obtaining patents and trademarks, 195–97
  patents for, 189–93, 195–97
  trademarks for, 193–94, 195–97
Public broadcasting, 39–40

Quirky, 86–89
  about: overview of, 86–87
  Blog tab, 89
  Learn tab, 89
  Participate tab, 88
  Shop tab, 87–88
  Upcoming tab, 88

Records, keeping, 204
Reddit, 101, 117–18
Relevancy, 122
Religious organizations, 38–39
Rerunning campaigns, 18
Reward-based crowdfunding
  about: overview of, 14–15, 51–52
  appropriateness of rewards, 22
  effective reward structure, 98–100
  platform example. *See* Kickstarter
  retail model vs., 52
  reward fulfillment, 72
  shipping products, 205–7
  tiered structure, 99–100
  types of rewards, 14–15, 68–69
  typical campaign example. *See* Kickstarter campaign example
RocketHub, 81–85
  about: overview of, 81–82, 92
  Blog link, 85
  Explore tab, 83
  Learn tab, 83–84
  main page, 82
  Partner tab, 84
  services offered, 81–82
  Success tab, 84
RSS feeds, 71

Search engines. *See also* Google AdWords campaign

ad rankings, 123–24
organic and sponsored searches, 122
popularity rankings, 121
relevancy and, 122
what they do, how they work, 121
Securities Act of 1933, 249–50
She and the Sun campaign, 215–16
Shipping products, 205–7
Smallknot, 225–26
Social change campaigns. *See also* Social enterprises
communicating with pledgers, 240
crowdfunding, 237–38
deadlines for, 243
lessons for success, 242–43
outreach plan, 239
persisting in asking, 243
preparing for, 238–40
priming pump, 243
rewarding pledgers, 240
social entrepreneurs and, 236–37
storytelling for fundraising, 240–42
Social enterprises
about: overview of, 232
categories of, 234–35
functions of, 234–35
government failure and, 236
historical precedents, 236
market failure and, 235–36
necessity of, 235–36
nonprofits and, 332–33
Social entrepreneurs, 236–37
Social media, 103–18. *See also* Facebook; Twitter; YouTube
affiliate marketing, 116–17

benefits and uses, 104–5
blogs and, 109–10
defined, 104
firms helping outreach efforts, 20
Google+, 114–16
importance of understanding, 19, 21
LinkedIn, 114
managing, 118
outreach plan including, 101–2
power of, 104
Reddit, 101, 117–18
strategy for using, 105–6
websites to send people from. *See* Website, creating
Social news services, 101. *See also* Reddit
Sparked, 47
Split testing, 132–33
StartSomeGood, 93
Statue of Liberty, 50
Story (pitch), crafting, 93–95
Storytelling for fundraising, 240–42
Success, 91–102
additional keys to, 102
big-picture view and, 94–95
completion of campaign. *See* End of campaign
creating sense of urgency, 94
duration of campaign and, 102
examples of. *See* Successful campaign examples
goal setting for, 96–98
key factors overview, 21–22
lacking, crowdfunding not working, 18, 20
outreach (promotional) plan for, 101–2, 147
passionate pitch for, 93–95

rerunning campaign after failure, 18
reward structure for, 98–100. *See also* Reward-based crowdfunding
site selection for, 92–93
social change campaign lessons, 242–43
video for, 69–70, 95–96
Successful campaign examples, 209–17
Flint and Tinder, 216–17
Mosquita y Mari, 211–13
Natural Resources, 213–14
She and the Sun, 215–16
TikTok+LunaTik watch campaigns, 210–11
Surveys, 203–4

Text, for campaign site, 58
Threadless, 35
Three Revolutions, 225
TikTok+LunaTik watch campaigns, 210–11
Tithing, 39
Trademarks, 193–94, 195–97
Trendwatching, 29–30
Twitter, 135–47
about: overview of, 112, 136–37
anatomy of tweets, 138–39
business best practices, 144–47
business page, 113
communities, 113, 136–37, 146
connecting websites to, 143
educating followers, 147
establishing voice, 144
finding people on, 142–43
gathering information on, 136
getting on, 141–42

Index

hashtags and @mentions, 138, 145
length of tweets, 145
outreach (promotional) plan including, 101–2, 147
promotional plan and, 147
reasons for using, 137–38
replies, 139
responding quickly, 145–46
retweeting, 139, 146
shortened URL links, 139
spreading out tweets, 146
statistics, 136
third-party applications, 139–41
tweeting on, 112

Updates. *See* Following up with donors
Urgency, creating sense of, 41–42, 94
Utility patents, 190–91

Video
crafting, 95–96. *See also* Video production
embedding in webpages, 169–70
function and value, 69–70
importance of, 69–70, 95, 174
Kickstarter example, 57–58
linking to YouTube, 169. *See also* YouTube
search optimization, 170–72
Video equipment, 177–78
Video production, 173–86
developing pitch, 175–76
editing software, 179–82
equipment for, 177–78
final checklist, 184–85

master shots and cutaways, 182–83
nonlinear editing (NLE), 179–80, 181, 184
pitch checklist, 176–77
posting final video, 185–86. *See also* YouTube
quality of, 95–96
recording audio, 179
recording video, 177–78
researching other videos, 174–75
storyboarding, 183
Visibility, 19

Watch campaigns (TikTok+LunaTik), 210–11
Web host selection, 107
Website, creating, 106–9
designing site, 107–8
domain name registration, 106
e-commerce and, 108–9
testing site, 108
web host selection, 107
Websites
connecting to Twitter, 143
creating. *See* Website, creating
crowdfunding. *See* Websites, crowdfunding
crowdsourcing, 28–30
fundraising, 45–47
Websites, crowdfunding. *See also* Kickstarter; RocketHub
Appbackr, 93
Cofolio, 93, 224
Indiegogo, 78–80, 92
local websites, 223–26
Lucky Ant, 93, 223–24
NewJelly, 93
Peerbackers, 85–86, 92

Quirky, 86–89
Wefunder, 93
Wefunder, 93
Wolff, Stephen B., 32
Work, of crowdfunding, 18, 22

YouTube, 163–72
about: overview of, 163
channeling, 166–67
comments, 167–68
communities, 165–66
embedding videos in webpages, 169–70
history of, 164
hosting video content, 169–70
linking to, 169
outreach plan including, 101–2
response videos, 168
search optimization, 170–72
tags, 171
titles, 171
today, 164–65
tracking statistics, 172
video descriptions, 171–72

We Have EVERYTHING® on Anything!

With more than 19 million copies sold, the Everything® series has become one of America's favorite resources for solving problems, learning new skills, and organizing lives. Our brand is not only recognizable—it's also welcomed.

The series is a hand-in-hand partner for people who are ready to tackle new subjects—like you!

For more information on the Everything® series, please visit *www.adamsmedia.com*

The Everything® list spans a wide range of subjects, with more than 500 titles covering 25 different categories:

Business	History	Reference
Careers	Home Improvement	Religion
Children's Storybooks	Everything Kids	Self-Help
Computers	Languages	Sports & Fitness
Cooking	Music	Travel
Crafts and Hobbies	New Age	Wedding
Education/Schools	Parenting	Writing
Games and Puzzles	Personal Finance	
Health	Pets	